Music Speaks

Eastman Studies in Music

Ralph P. Locke, Senior Editor
Eastman School of Music

Additional Titles on Song Opera, and Dance

The Ballet Collaborations of Richard Strauss
Wayne Heisler Jr.

Beethoven's Century:
Essays on Composers and Themes
Hugh Macdonald

Berlioz: Scenes from the Life and Work
Edited by Peter Bloom

Berlioz's Semi-Operas: Roméo et Juliette *and* La damnation de Faust
Daniel Albright

French Music, Culture, and National Identity, 1870–1939
Edited by Barbara L. Kelly

György Kurtág:
Three Interviews and Ligeti Homages
Bálint András Varga

Irony and Sound: The Music of Maurice Ravel
Stephen Zank

Music in German Immigrant Theater:
New York City, 1840–1940
(Includes CD)
John Koegel

The Music of Luigi Dallapiccola
Raymond Fearn

Musicking Shakespeare:
A Conflict of Theatres
Daniel Albright

Opera and Ideology in Prague:
Polemics and Practice at the National Theater, 1900–1938
Brian S. Locke

Othmar Schoeck: Life and Works
Chris Walton

The Poetic Debussy: A Collection of His Song Texts and Selected Letters
(Revised Second Edition)
Edited by Margaret G. Cobb

Schubert in the European Imagination,
Volume 1: The Romantic and Victorian Eras
Scott Messing

Schubert in the European Imagination,
Volume 2: Fin-de-Siècle Vienna
Scott Messing

The Substance of Things Heard:
Writings about Music
Paul Griffiths

Wagner and Venice
John W. Barker

Wagner and Wagnerism in Nineteenth-Century Sweden, Finland, and the Baltic Provinces: Reception, Enthusiasm, Cult
Hannu Salmi

A complete list of titles in the Eastman Studies in Music Series, in order of publication, may be found at the end of this book.

Music Speaks

On the Language of Opera, Dance, and Song

Daniel Albright

UNIVERSITY OF ROCHESTER PRESS

Copyright © 2009 Daniel Albright

All rights reserved. Except as permitted under current legislation, no part of this work may be photocopied, stored in a retrieval system, published, performed in public, adapted, broadcast, transmitted, recorded, or reproduced in any form or by any means, without the prior permission of the copyright owner.

First published 2009
University of Rochester Press
668 Mt. Hope Avenue, Rochester, NY 14620, USA
www.urpress.com
and Boydell & Brewer Limited
PO Box 9, Woodbridge, Suffolk IP12 3DF, UK
www.boydellandbrewer.com

ISBN-13: 978-1-58046-324-9
ISBN-10: 1-58046-324-X
ISSN: 1071-9989

Library of Congress Cataloging-in-Publication Data

Albright, Daniel, 1945–
   Music speaks : on the language of opera, dance, and song / Daniel Albright.
      p. cm.—(Eastman studies in music, ISSN 1071–9989 ; v. 69)
   Includes bibliographical references and index.
   ISBN-13: 978–1–58046–324–9 (hardcover : alk. paper)
   ISBN-10: 1–58046–324–X
   1. Opera. 2. Songs—History and criticism. 3. Music and literature. 4. Dance—History. I. Title.
   ML1700.A42 2009
   781.'1—dc22
                                                                                      2009033160

A catalogue record for this title is available from the British Library.
This publication is printed on acid-free paper.
Printed in the United States of America.

"Syringa" from HOUSEBOAT DAYS by John Ashbery. Originally appeared in *Poetry*. Copyright © 1975, 1977 by John Ashbery. Reprinted by permission of Georges Borchardt, Inc., on behalf of the author.

Reprinted by permission of Farrar, Straus and Giroux, LLC: 12 lines from "Sandpiper," 17 lines from "The View of the Capitol from the Library of Congress," and 8 lines from "O Breath" from THE COMPLETE POEMS 1927–1979 by Elizabeth Bishop. Copyright © 1979, 1983 by Alice Helen Methfessel. 6 lines from "Across the Yard: La Ignota" from COLLECTED POEMS by Robert Lowell. Copyright © 2003 by Harriet Lowell and Sheridan Lowell.

"Prologue: The Birth of Architecture," © 1976 by Edward Mendelson, William Meredith, and Monroe K. Spears, Executors of the Estate of W. H. Auden, from COLLECTED POEMS by W. H. Auden. Used by permission of Random House, Inc.

Contents

	List of Illustrations	vii
	Note on the Text	xi
	Preface	xiii
	Part One: Music	
1	Music's Pentecost, Music's Stupidity	3
2	Heine and the Composers	15
3	The Diabolical Senta	39
4	*Les Troyens:* The Undoing of Opera	58
5	Far Sounds in Zemlinsky and Schreker	72
6	Butchering Moses	94
7	Elliott Carter and Poetry: Listening to, Listening Through	105
8	Sophoclean Opera	122
9	Belletristic Music in the Twentieth Century	145
	Part Two: Dance	
10	Golden Calves: The Role of Dance in Opera	163
11	Elephant Swan Space Grace	178
	Notes	197
	Selected Bibliography	209
	Index	213

Illustrations

1.1	Rimsky-Korsakov: *Sheherazade*, Sultan	4
1.2	Rimsky-Korsakov: *Sheherazade*, Sinbad	5
1.3	Strauss: *Ein Heldenleben*, wife	7
1.4	Britten: *Six Metamorphoses after Ovid*, Bacchus	8
1.5	Britten: *Six Metamorphoses after Ovid*, Pan	9
1.6	Strauss: *Till Eulenspiegel*, beginning	10
1.7	Strauss: *Till Eulenspiegel*, big toe	11
2.1	Schubert: *Der Doppelgänger*, beginning	17
2.2	Schubert: *Der Doppelgänger*, climax	18
2.3	Schubert: *Der Atlas*, beginning	19
2.4	Schubert: *Der Atlas*, climax	20
2.5	Schubert: *Die Stadt*	21
2.6	Schumann: *Der arme Peter II*	25
2.7	Schumann: *Ich grolle nicht*	27
2.8	Schumann: *Die alten, bösen Lieder*	34
3.1	Weill: *Die Dreigroschenoper*, "Und das Schiff mit acht Segeln"	39
3.2	Wagner: *The Flying Dutchman*, "Trafft ihr das Schiff im Meere an"	39
3.3	Marschner: *Der Vampyr*, Emmy's romance	43
3.4	Wagner: *The Flying Dutchman*, "Doch kann dem bleichen Manne Erlösung"	44
3.5	Wagner: *The Flying Dutchman*, "Johoe! Hui! Wie ein Pfeil fliegt er hin, ohne Ziel"	45
3.6	Wagner: *Parsifal*, "Hilfe! Herbei!"	45
3.7	Wagner: *The Flying Dutchman*, Overture, storm	48
3.8	Wagner: *The Flying Dutchman*, spinning song figure	49

3.9	Wagner: *The Flying Dutchman*, Steuermann chorus figure	49
3.10	Schumann: *Des Sängers Fluch*, Curse	53
3.11	Strauss: *Feuersnot*, Meister Reichhart	55
3.12	Tippett: *Songs for Dov*, "The Flying Dutchman"	57
4.1	Berlioz: *Les Troyens*, Cassandre	63
4.2	Berlioz: *Les Troyens*, "Ah! . . . fuis"	63
4.3	Berlioz: *Les Troyens*, "Adieu, beau ciel d'Afrique, astres que j'admirai"	65
4.4	Berlioz: *Les Troyens*, satyrs' dance	68
4.5	Berlioz: *Les Troyens*, Andromaque	69
4.6	Berlioz: *Les Troyens*, "Stat Roma"	71
5.1	Schreker: *Der ferne Klang*, prelude	77
5.2	Schreker: *Der ferne Klang*, Nachtmusik	78
5.3	Schreker: *Der ferne Klang*, "Mir ist so seltsam zumut!"	79
5.4	Holst: *The Planets*, "Neptune"	80
5.5	Zemlinsky: *Der Traumgörge*, "Sie kam"	82
5.6	Zemlinsky: *Der Traumgörge*, "Ein Hauch"	82
5.7	Wagner: *Siegfried*, the name Siegfried	83
5.8	Zemlinsky: *Der Traumgörge*, rustling	83
5.9	Zemlinsky: *Der Traumgörge*, valkyrie	85
5.10	Zemlinsky: *Der Zwerg*, abominable beauty	86
5.11	Zemlinsky: *Der Zwerg*, freak of nature	87
5.12	Zemlinsky: *Der Zwerg*, warm grass	87
5.13	Zemlinsky: *Der König Kandaules*, recent thought	89
6.1	Schoenberg: *Moses und Aron*, xylophone	98
6.2	Schoenberg: *Moses und Aron*, trumpet	98
6.3	Schoenberg: *Moses und Aron*, triads	99
6.4	Schoenberg: *Moses und Aron*, pseudo-retrograde	100
6.5	Schoenberg: *Moses und Aron*, end of Act 2	103

7.1	Carter: *A Mirror on which to Dwell*, "Sandpiper"	107
7.2	Carter: *A Mirror on which to Dwell*, unheard band	109
7.3	Carter: *In Sleep, in Thunder*, Brünnhilde	113
7.4	Wagner: *Die Walküre*, "Hojotoho"	114
7.5	Wagner: *Die Walküre*, Valkyrie motive	114
7.6	Carter: *Syringa*, Eros	117
8.1	Mendelssohn: *Antigone*, Hades abducts	127
8.2	Honegger: *Antigone*, icon of disorder	130
8.3	Orff: *Antigone*, war	131
8.4	Stravinsky: *Oedipus Rex*, beginning	134
8.5	Stravinsky: *Oedipus Rex*, choral prayer	135
8.6	Strauss: *Elektra*, truth and lies	136
8.7	Strauss: *Elektra*, Agamemnon's ghost	136
8.8	Stravinsky: *Oedipus Rex*, god's truth	137
8.9	Stravinsky: *Oedipus Rex*, parentage revealed	137
8.10	Stravinsky: *Oedipus Rex*, I will save you	138
8.11	Stravinsky: *Oedipus Rex*, Jocasta	139
8.12	Stravinsky: *Oedipus Rex*, dawning light	140
8.13	Stravinsky: *Oedipus Rex*, telegram	141
8.14	de Chirico: *The Disturbing Muses*	142
9.1	Wolff: *Edges*	158
11.1	Beethoven: Piano Variations, Op. 35, beginning	179
11.2	Balla: set design for *Fireworks*	184
11.3	Boccioni: *Unique Forms of Continuity in Space*	186
11.4	Schlemmer: Figurines for *Das triadische Ballett*	187
11.5	Moser: *The Dancer Loïe Fuller*	188
11.6	Toulouse-Lautrec: *Miss Loïe Fuller*	189
11.7	Flötner: anthropomorphic alphabet	194
11.8	Naxi Happy Birthday	195

Note on the Text

Reasonable efforts have been made to obtain permission to reprint material under copyright. Where it has been possible to identify rights holders, credit has been given in the usual manner; elsewhere, I have tried to establish a clear system of citation in the endnotes. I would welcome any updated information on rights and would reflect this in future editions.

For familiar, universally available material not under copyright, I have thought it better not to clutter the text with notes. As for the translations, they are all by me, unless otherwise credited.

Preface

The volume you have in your hand is a sort of rehearsal-piano reduction of a number of multimedia lectures I've given in the past few years.

I might argue that there's a hidden unity behind this book's miscellaneous character by pointing to some of the features that bind these essays together. My continuing preoccupations are these:

1. How to deal with the problems of articulating the meaning or meanings of music.
2. How to deal with the larger question of how music and language interact, whether music is "like" spoken/literary language, whether it transcends language, and whether our musical apperceptions are of a different sort from those we engage in regard to words or visual images.
3. How, especially in the world of Lieder, text settings highlight certain areas of meter or theme or ironic undertone and leave others in darkness.
4. How a musical composition can behave as a critique of a previous composition: how it can be an homage or an act of affectionate mockery or a full-scale repudiation.
5. How music interacts with bodily gesture (and again, how both become "legible"). Sometimes dance seems to spell out words with an alphabet of the whole body; sometimes it refuses to constitute itself as a language.
6. How one might rehabilitate certain underappreciated or much-scorned figures, such as Meyerbeer, by showing that the very terms of invective used against them can be seen, from another angle, as an indication of what is exciting in their work.

I mean to show how music history has an aesthetic of its own, and how music history interacts with intellectual history (from Rousseau and the *encyclopédistes* to Paul de Man). The method of these essays is juxtapositive: by abutting music against literature and painting and by abutting the musics of different centuries, I try to frame a particular work, to isolate what is arresting and important in it.

Some readers are likely to object to my preference for a contrapuntal rather than a linear mode of argument. Almost all of the chapters take detours forward or back in time, sometimes of a few decades, sometimes of centuries. But I hope that the lack of chronological boundaries, or genre boundaries, or language-region boundaries, might be seen as a natural extension of the freedom that the individual chapters allow themselves—to make one genre comment on another, to make one era comment on another, to make one artistic medium comment on another.

I might also note that this book can be understood as a tribute to mechanical and electronic reproduction—the LP record, the compact disc, the mp3 file—formats that have integrated music into our daily lives in a way once scarcely available even to kings, and that not only have gratified an appetite for music but also have created one.

All these pieces (except one) were written in a span of four years (2004–8), and mostly concern the music of the last two centuries. During much of this period I was working on Jacobean and Restoration music for a project on Shakespeare, and I found it most pleasant to turn from Robert Johnson and Nicholas Lanier and Henry Purcell—delightful though they are—to the composers treated here, my oldest loves. As for the two essays on dance that conclude this volume, they were called forth by my friend Simon Morrison of Princeton University, who, on the Day of Judgment, may have to answer for them.

Daniel Albright
Cambridge, Massachusetts

Part One

Music

Chapter One

Music's Pentecost, Music's Stupidity

> Musik ist sprachähnlich. . . . Aber Musik ist nicht Sprache. Ihre Sprachähnlichkeit weist den Weg ins Innere, doch auch ins *Vage*.
>
> Music is speechlike. . . . But music is not speech. Its speechlikeness points the way into the interior, but also into the *vague*.
>
> Theodor Adorno, "Fragment über die Sprache," *Quasi una Fantasia*

We often think of music as a translation of emotional states. You know that a violin playing droopy phrases means you're supposed to weep; you know that Sousa marches mean you're supposed to feel exhilarated. But these conventional mood settings seem pretty vague. Can music aspire to more precise kinds of translation? Can sentences, stories, dramas be translated into music? If so, does the resulting music have any of the properties of spoken or written language? I want to discuss the ways in which music—instrumental music—has a linguistic character, as if it translated texts (real or imaginary) into wordless sound, and then to discuss the ways in which music resists any linguistic character, even proposes itself as an antilanguage incapable of translating anything. We'll start with the first case.

Music as a Language

According to this model, music is the one universal language, a sort of pentecostal tongue of fire, in that it behaves as a language not learned systematically but understood intuitively by everyone. This model is in some ways obviously untenable: how could one say, "The persimmons are mottled but unripe" without recourse to spoken words? But it provides a powerful dream for activating certain potentialities of musical expression, even though it is most pervasive as a trope of comedy, as (for example) when Harpo Marx (in *Duck Soup*) carries on one end of a telephone conversation strictly by means of a bicycle horn. Still, a respectable case can be made for the thesis that music

---

First published as "Stances toward Music as a Language," in *Phrase and Subject: Studies in Literature and Music*, ed. Delia da Sousa Correa (London: Legenda, 2006), 12–20.

can operate as a complete language, since every formal property of speech—formal in the sense of nondenotative—can, I believe, be understood as a formal property of music.

Among the schemes for classifying the formal properties of speech are those based on small units, such as inflection and phoneme construction; those based on middle-sized units, such as syntax; and those based on large units, such as the structures of rational persuasion that we call rhetoric, or the structures of seduction that we call narrative and drama. There isn't space to offer a comprehensive review, but I can suggest how profoundly we understand music as a language—or, to put it better, how profoundly language understands music as a language, since language tends to understand everything as a language.

The vocabulary of music analysis is amazingly dependent on terms from linguistics, as the words *phrase* and *theme* quickly show, and I suspect that the history of music has been strongly shaped by the conscious or unconscious tendency of composers to literalize the vocabulary of music analysis. Consider the term *subject:* the instant that I denote the main melodic entity in a composition as a subject, I have thereby promoted that thing into a little person, or at least into a crucial matter with as-yet-unexplained properties, and I compel a tacit grammatical search for a way of explaining the rest of the composition as a predicate to that subject. The rest of the composition becomes a way of learning about the subject; of teasing out its attributes; of defining its contours, its submissions to new harmonic contexts, its recalcitrances against ill treatment. The term *subject* imparts a prestige, a centrality that the sequence of notes might not otherwise possess. Indeed, the term *subject* has an implicit push toward narrative in that the vicissitudes of the subject during the course of the composition start to become heard as adventures. This process is sometimes quite explicit, as in Rimsky-Korsakov's *Sheherazade* (1888), in which the composer used the same theme to represent (in the opening bars) the sultan listening to his new wife's stories (figure 1.1) and Sindbad navigating his boat through seasickening orchestral swells (figure 1.2):

Figure 1.1. Rimsky-Korsakov: *Sheherazade,* Sultan, from Nikolai Rimsky-Korsakov, *Scheherazade,* symphonic suite for orchestra, Op. 35, piano two-hands, transcription by P. Gilson (New York: G. Schirmer, ca.1918), 3.

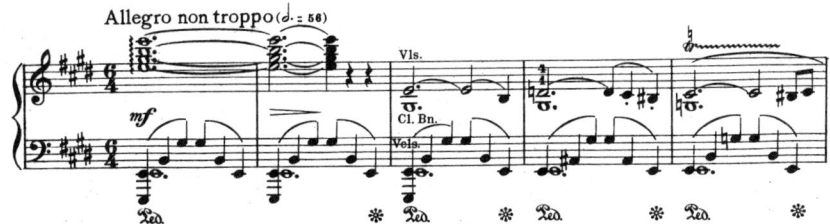

Figure 1.2. Rimsky-Korsakov: *Sheherazade,* Sinbad, from Nikolai Rimsky-Korsakov, *Scheherazade,* symphonic suite for orchestra, Op. 35, piano two-hands, transcription by P. Gilson (New York: G. Schirmer, ca.1918), 3.

In a nice psychological touch, the sultan imagines himself as the hero of his wife's story, just like a boy reading a Superman comic book and imagining Superman with his own face.

Large musical structures can recall other sorts of large speech structures. The opening of the slow movement of Beethoven's Fourth Piano Concerto (1807)—in which the piano and the orchestral don't speak at the same time but are confined to separate acoustic and emotional domains—impresses most listeners not as a narrative, not as a piece of rhetoric, but as a drama. What is the story here? I once heard a radio broadcast that reported that the pianist Krystian Zimerman thought that the movement represented Christ before Pontius Pilate. In his 1859 biography of Beethoven, A. B. Marx sketched out an Orpheus scenario in the fourth concerto.[1]

The novelist E. M. Forster also heard Orpheus:

> This famous little movement consists of a dialogue between orchestra and piano, the orchestra rough, the piano plaintive, the orchestra gradually calmer. It is very easy music; it strikes or strokes immediately, and elderly gentlemen before myself have called it "Beauty and the Beast." What about Orpheus and the Furies, though? That is the idea that has slipped into my mind to the detriment of the actual musical sounds, and when the movement begins I always repair to the entrance of Hell and descend under the guidance of Gluck [in the second act of *Orfeo ed Euridice* (1762)] through diminishing opposition to the Elysian Fields. There has been no word-making, to be sure, but there has been a big operatic import. . . . The piano turns into Orpheus and *via* him into Miss Marie Brema, whom I best remember in that rôle, and the strings and wind, waving less and less their snaky locks, sink at last into acquiescence with true love. Then the third movement starts. The parallel breaks, and I am back in a world which seems four-square and self-contained, the world of the opening.[2]

Forster felt sad when the concerto lost its linguistic character and disenchanted itself back into "mere" music—as if Beethoven's imagination had failed him at the instant that the music failed to approximate some sort of speech act. It is slightly disquieting, perhaps contrary to experience, to think that music is less potent, in a sense less music, if it fails to support clear story outlines.

Sometimes music addresses itself not to the imagination but to the discerning intellect, and attempts to ape the language of oratory. In his 1739 treatise *Der vollkommene Capellmeister* Johann Mattheson understands the art of musical composition as classical rhetoric transposed into a language of tones, cleanly organized into *inventio* (invention), *dispositio* (articulation of the invented idea into parts), *decoration* (decoration), and *pronuntiato* (delivery). Mattheson even plays with forensic models of musical rhetoric, in which a composition is divided into *exordium* (introduction), *narratio* (statement of facts), *divisio* (forecast of main points in the speaker's favor), *confirmation* (confirmation), *confutatio* (rebuttal), and *peroratio* (peroration). Mattheson and other musical rhetoricians also provided tables of figures of speech complete with examples, so that the reader could ponder the musical equivalent of (say) exclamation, ellipsis, and pleonasm. Many of the tropes in the tables pertain to insistence, and it is clear that music is quite handy at repeating, ornamenting, developing, augmenting, or otherwise waxing large on an idea. In that sense music is much like spoken oratory.

Let us look at an example of an easy translation of a figure of speech from the domain of language to the domain of music. If you begin every sentence with the same few words, you're using the trope called anaphora: "We shall fight in France, we shall fight on the seas and oceans, we shall fight them in the air, we shall fight them on the beaches," in Churchill's splendid anaphora from 1940. The old musical theorists discovered anaphora in musical compositions; one of them (Athanasius Kircher) defined it as a repetition of the same theme on different notes in different parts. Kircher's example of anaphora is taken from an old motet by Heinrich Schütz, *Freuet euch des Herren*, SWV 367, from *Symphoniarum sacrarum secunda pars*, Op. 10 (1647), where the words "Singet dem" keep staggering from one voice to another. It is the rhetoric of "We shall fight . . . we shall fight" translated into music. If the singers were replaced by violins, you'd still have anaphora, even though utterly without a text.

On the other hand, a table of figures of speech in spoken discourse looks very different. In speech and writing, most tropes pertain not to insistence but to transposition: here the basic figures are metaphor and simile, which, alas, seem not to exist in the world of music, or to exist only tangentially. How can one sequence of notes take the place of, or allude to, or hover along side of, an absent sequence of notes? Furthermore, a central oratorical device is contradiction: not only am I right, but you are wrong. But music, although it may have many parts of speech, seems to lack a privative, an intelligible *not*. A musical event can't easily be annulled or vitiated or dismissed by another musical event. To some extent, a strong contrast or a bar or two of silence may act as a negation, but the listener may well regard the subsequent material as a supplement to the previous material instead of a denial of it. There are a few effective acts of musical negation: the opening of the fourth movement of Beethoven's Ninth (1824), with its huge discord that proceeds to annihilate the themes of the preceding movements one by one; the great shriek in the Adagio of Mahler's Tenth; and a number of moments in Schnittke's work. But these can be seen as special stunts, and their methods would be hard to promote into a general model of contradiction via music.

So to evaluate music as a reasonable discourse becomes a frustrating matter. A musical composition may have many discursive aspects: like Ives's Second Quartet (1907–13), it may even represent a bunch of guys screaming at each other about topics concerning the American Civil War, but finally seems able to go only so far in mapping itself according to oratorical form. In the second movement, the second violinist, whom Ives called a "Rollo"—that is, a sissy—tries to calm the argument. Ives marks this passage *andante emasculata*. This is perhaps the only piece of homophobic chamber music in the whole repertoire.

Perhaps the most successful of all strategies for discursifying (if that's a permissible word) music lies on the level of inflection. Here we have not only such stunts as Harpo's bicycle horn, but also the hero's wife in Strauss's *Ein Heldenleben* (1899), who "speaks" so intelligibly through a violin that it tempts the listener to imagine actual verbal dialogue, wheedling, cajoling, pouting, vituperating, or as Strauss indicates in one particularly challenging instruction to the violinist, "hypocritically languishing" (figure 1.3).

Figure 1.3. Strauss: *Ein Heldenleben*, wife, from Richard Strauss, *Tone Poems: Series II: Till Eulenspiegels lustige Streiche, "Also sprach Zarathustra," Ein Heldenleben* (Mineola: Dover Publications, 1979), 210.

Another example is "Bacchus at whose orgies is heard the noise of gaggling women's tattling tongues and shouting out of boys," the fourth of Britten's *Six Metamorphoses after Ovid* (1951), in which a solo oboe tattles and shouts a language that the listener has never been taught and yet understands quite clearly (figure 1.4).

Figure 1.4. Britten: *Six Metamorphoses after Ovid,* Bacchus, from Benjamin Britten, *Six Metamorphoses after Ovid* (London: Hawkes and Son, n.d.), 4.

By choosing Bacchus as the god of speech music, Britten stresses the Dionysiac character of this art: music seems to be nothing more than speech grown so excited that only the excitement is intelligible, not the words. Britten seems to appeal to old fantasies of an all-compulsive archaic language of sound gestures. Rousseau, for example, imagined that a modern European, only faintly acquainted with Arabic, would prostrate himself, abandon his Christian beliefs, and march in the armies of Islam if he had heard Muhammad preach, burning with the enthusiasm of his prophecy.[3]

And yet even in these examples, where music seems ready to assert itself as a language, as a modality of word inflection in the absence of the word, certain counterpressures threaten to destroy music's linguistic character. The first of Britten's *Six Metamorphoses after Ovid* is "Pan who played upon the reed pipe which was Syrinx, his beloved." This nobly poised cantilena (figure 1.5) makes the Bacchus movement seem by contrast almost submusical, a kind of woodwind gargling.

Figure 1.5. Britten: *Six Metamorphoses after Ovid*, Pan, from Benjamin Britten, *Six Metamorphoses after Ovid* (London: Hawkes and Son Ltd, n.d.), 1.

To introduce musical speechifying into a composition usually means that the composer thereby specifies other areas of a composition with higher melodic contour and clearer harmonic articulation—in short, more like music because less like speech. An old but effective example of this tendency can be found in Charpentier's miniature opera *Les Plaisirs de Versailles* (early 1680s), in which La Musique and La Conversation debate whether Louis XIV would be more delighted to hear music or to engage in a lively chat. La Conversation argues in favor of talk by singing her lines in a *langue frétillante* (frisky language), a garrulous gabble above a hectoring bass viol. In contrast, La Musique, preening in *accords charmants* (charming chords), sings her lines in a long, slow, ravishing legato. Though Charpentier characterizes La Conversation by musical means, music itself seems the exact opposite of talkiness.

Furthermore, there is a notable lack of coordination among the various linguistic models possible to music. Britten's "Bacchus" movement is extremely talkative on the level of inflection, but not at all talkative on the level of rhetoric or narrative. There's scarcely even the ghost of a story or an argument, just as series of speech gestures. Similarly, the examples of rhetoric that Mattheson cites don't tend to have any inflectional force behind them. In Strauss's tone poems, one can find several examples of inflectional imitation, but often oddly detached from the story, indeed slowing down the momentum of the story. From the point of view of the narrative, Strauss's hero's wife is a tedious digression, inhibiting the hero from getting on with his business. Strauss's chatterboxes—the monks in *Don Quixote* (1898), for example—provide comic relief, as if discursivity were a sort of local color or amusement pasted onto the music, instead of the crucial matter of music. Even the narrative aspect of tone poems can seem dangerously extrinsic—which is why composers have often been so uneasy about publishing such narratives. Strauss is famous for narrative specificity, but the program of *Till Eulenspiegels lustige Streiche* (Till Eulenspiegel's Merry Pranks, or Lusty Strokes, 1895) remains unpublished. It is known only through a table of twenty-three motives that exists in the manuscript score, and to some help Strauss gave to Wilhelm Mauke when Mauke was writing a guide to the work. The tone poem begins with a "once upon a time" gesture, and soon we hear the "subject"—Till himself—in a famous horn theme poised for a moment on a minor third before completing itself on the major third (G♯ to A, in the key of F) (figure 1.6).

Figure 1.6. Strauss: *Till Eulenspiegel*, beginning, from Richard Strauss, *Tone Poems: Series II: Till Eulenspiegels lustige Streiche, "Also sprach Zarathustra," Ein Heldenleben* (Mineola: Dover Publications, 1979), 3.

At the end of the horn theme, we hear a bit of the endless sequence of orchestral titters, giggles, and razzes that Strauss has at his command. At last, after many rascally tricks, Till is caught and hanged—and in this famous passage, figures on the clarinet and other solo instruments suggest, above the drum roll, that Till keeps joking on the gallows. You hear that drop of a major seventh—"der Tod"—just as Till falls and breaks his neck.

But let me return to an earlier episode, where Strauss offers some amazingly precise notations of complicated events. At one point Till disguises himself, as Strauss said, "Dressed as a priest he oozes unction and morality." At the end of this passage a clarinet plays a figure glossed by Strauss as follows: "But the rogue's big toe protrudes beneath the cassock." (In the published score this moment is marked *schelmisch*, that is, roguish) (figure 1.7).

Strauss felt that he had reached such a pitch of mastery of representation that the sudden emerging of a toe could be depicted by purely orchestral means; whether it's Till's right big toe or his left big toe, Strauss doesn't say. On the other hand, there are also episodes of utter vagueness ("On to new pranks"). Every tone poem I know has episodes where a program is not only superfluous but also impossible to construct. Strauss in particular always inserts blurs, patches of inenarrable confusion, like the gray blob that disturbs the center of Manet's painting *Music in the Tuileries Garden*.

The more closely we examine the hypothesis that music is a language, whether in theory or in practice, the less tenable it appears. After exhaustive study of Mattheson's tables of tropes and of many other old treatises, the musicologist George J. Buelow—to whom I'm much indebted—concludes, "Many of

Figure 1.7. Strauss: *Till Eulenspiegel*, big toe, from Richard Strauss, *Tone Poems: Series II: Till Eulenspiegels lustige Streiche, "Also sprach Zarathustra," Ein Heldenleben* (Mineola: Dover Publications, 1979), 19.

the musical figures . . . originated in attempts to explain or justify irregular, if not incorrect, contrapuntal writing."[4] In other words, the rhetorical aspects of music seem to be concentrated in various areas of deviance from accepted musical practice, so we are left with the uncomfortable dilemma that (1) music is a kind of rhetoric; and (2) music is more rhetorical when it breaks the rules than when it obeys them. I believe that similar paradoxes result from any attempt to impose a linguistic character on music. Perhaps the finest of all recent students of musical narrative, Carolyn Abbate, has announced, in effect, that the more she studies musical narrative, the less she finds: "In my own interpretations . . . I will interpret music as *narrating* only rarely. It is not narrative, but it possesses moments of narration, moments that can be identified by their bizarre and disruptive effect."[5] Jean-Jacques Nattiez offered a still bleaker view, seeming to deny even those rare moments of narration that Abbate found:

> "Music has no past tense," as Carolyn Abbate rightly observes. It can evoke the past by means of citations or stylistic borrowings, but it cannot narrate, cannot speak what *took place* in time past. . . . Literary narrative is an invention, a lie. Music cannot lie. The responsibility for joining character-phantoms with action-shadows lies with me, the listener, since it does not lie within *music's* capacities to join subject and predicate.[6]

A musical narrative, then, is a confabulation by the listener or by the composer, who is evidently merely another listener with no special interpretive credentials. It seems that music behaves linguistically only in a spasmodic, haphazard, and irregular manner. The search for music's tongue seems to render music completely mute.

Furthermore, from the beginning of theoretical discourse about music, there are strong hints that something is desperately wrong about the attempt to understand music as a language. For example, in his curious manual of advice for writing a bad opera, *Il teatro alla moda* (ca. 1720), Benedetto Marcello informs the apprentice hack how to organize his arias:

> Let [the composer] see to it that the arias, to the very end of the opera, are alternatively a lively one and a pathetic one, without regard to the words, the modes, or the proprieties of the scene. If substantive nouns, e.g., *padre, impero* [empire], *amore, arena, beltà* [beauty], *lena* [vigor], *core* [heart], etc. . . . should occur in the arias, the modern composer should base upon them a long passage; e.g., *pa . . . impeeee . . . amoooo . . . areeee . . . reeee . . . beltàaaaa . . . lenaaaaa. . . .* The object is to get away from the ancient style, which did not use passages on substantive nouns or on adverbs, but only on words signifying some passion or movement; e.g., *tormento, affanno* [breathlessness], *canto, volar* [to fly], *cader* [to fall], etc.[7]

Marcello is profoundly suspicious of nouns; he would like to banish solid objects from serious attention by musicians. This makes sense, in that the denotative functions of language have always seemed the least translatable into music. On the other hand, what hope is there for creating a language without nouns? Jorge Luis Borges once imagined a language (in "Tlön, Uqbar, Orbis Tertius," 1947) consisting entirely of impersonal verbs: "there is no word corresponding to the word 'moon,' but there is a verb which in English would be 'to moon' or 'to moonate.' 'The moon rose above the river' is *hlör u fang axaxaxas mlö,* or literally: 'upward behind the on-streaming it mooned.'"[8] Understanding the behavior of the ocean in Debussy's *La Mer* (1905) in similar terms has a certain attraction. "Onward beneath the up-diamonding it surged," one might say of certain passages. And yet, to accept music as a defective language is merely to call increasing attention to its defectiveness, rather than to its power.

Music as a Nonlanguage

If music slips through our grasp if we try to understand it as a language, the next step is to try to put together a nonlinguistic theory of music. On this side of the divide there are distinguished historical precedents: Pythagoras, who heard music as a sort of celestial arithmetic, a sound map of the starry sky, and Eduard

Hanslick, the Viennese music critic and champion of Brahms, who defined music as *tönend bewegte Form*—a term that might be translated literally as "soundingly moved form," or less literally as "dynamic sound-form" or "form set into motion through sound" or (perhaps best) "motion-form perceptible through the ear." It is no wonder that Hanslick and Wagner detested one another—Wagner even toyed with the idea of using the name Hanslick for the ignorant carping critic in *Die Meistersinger*—for Hanslick's asemantic theory of music is exactly opposed to Wagner's semantic, overcharged notions of music. For Hanslick, music is to the ear what Alexander Calder's mobiles, in the next century, would be to the eye: a shifting series of acoustic cross sections. To listen to a musical composition isn't to hear a displacement of speech but to attend to shapes opening through modulatory space and then closing up at cadences.

In the twentieth century, such nonlinguistic models would continue to attract certain composers. Erik Satie wrote a piece of *musique d'ameublement*—furniture music—which he entitled "Tapestry in Forged Iron." George Antheil considered his works to be paintings on a time canvas. Stravinsky audibly pieced together such works as *Renard* by the method of collage, pasting together short snippets into repetitive chains: the scissors and the gluepot have replaced the rhetoric book as means of organization. Stravinsky's famous distaste for expression—"I consider that music is, by its very nature, essentially powerless to *express* anything at all, whether a feeling, an attitude of mind, a psychological mood, a phenomenon of nature, etc."—has of course strong antilinguistic tendencies.[9] What Pythagoras, Hanslick, Satie, Antheil, and Stravinsky have in common is this: by refusing the idea that music is a language, they embrace the idea that music is a species of visual art realized in sound. When discourse seems to evaporate, pictures fly in to occupy the empty space, for theory, like nature, abhors a vacuum.

And yet, it's clear that the opposition between discourse and the visual arts can be sustained. From Apelles to Jackson Pollock and beyond, pictures have seemed pregnant with stories and have been understood through rhetorical models. It is possible that music's attempt to flee from language through reliance on pictorial methods will lead back to language only by means of an oblique route: we are all so thickly imprisoned in verbal constructions of reality that every escape tunnel we dig will turn out to lead us back to the same jail.

Of course, there are some composers whose methods seem to exclude any possibility of contamination by language: John Cage, for example, whose post-1951 reliance on various sorts of aleatory construction and indeterminate performance vitiates any normal notion of the semantic, or the rhetorical, or the grammatical, or the speech inflective. If Cage's compositions are music, then music would seem not only to be nonlinguistic, but the antidote to language. But it is just here, where music and speech seem to diverge utterly, that they start to swerve together, for Cage treats speech simply as a form of nonsung mouth music by constructing discourse according to the same aleatory procedures that he used to govern his music. In one well-known example, he wrote out a series of random statements and then, during the question-and-answer session following a lecture, simply read the statements one after another, without regard to the actual questions. A more thorough deconstruction can be found in *Solo for Voice 2* (1960), in which Cage instructs the performer to write vowels and consonants on a transparent sheet, and then, through certain manipulations of this sheet over a piece of paper inscribed with lines, to devise an array of phonemes that will be the text to be performed.

This sort of antilanguage can be dismissed as a special stunt with no relevance to speech as we usually speak it. But the tendency of linguistics from Saussure to Derrida has been to remove physical objects from the domain of language; to understand language as chains of endlessly deferred signifiers, never terminating in any actual thing. Every attempt to dereferentialize language tends to turn what the TV weather reporter says into an occult version of *Solo for Voice 2,* in which the phonic aspects grow increasingly opaque, increasingly an occasion for aesthetic delight in their heard immediacy. Ludwig Wittgenstein's later philosophy repeatedly stresses the musical aspects of normal speech; as he says in *Philosophical Investigations,* "Understanding a sentence is much more akin to understanding a theme in music than one may think. What I mean is that understanding a sentence lies nearer than one thinks to what is ordinarily called understanding a musical theme."[10] It fascinates me that these two sentences are, in effect, musical variations of the same sentence, as if Wittgenstein were proving his point in the act of making it. For Wittgenstein, music isn't like speech; instead, speech is a special case of music. Some of the things you say to me I understand in the way I understand Mozart; some of them in the way I understand Cage; and some of them in the way I understand Britney Spears. But in all cases, speech is a game with sounds, just as music is a game with sounds. Neither strictly possesses meaning or conviction, but meaning and conviction may glide around either.

Recent rhetoricians, such as Andrzeij Warminsky and Paul de Man, also describe a rhetoric that looks musical rather than discursive. According to de Man, "every text generates a referent that subverts the grammatical principles to which it owed its constitution. . . . [There is] a fundamental incompatibility between grammar and referential meaning."[11] But if the language is beset by the same problems of jarring and incommensurable, un-unifiable models that beset music, then music and language are in exactly the same uncomfortable situation. Yes, Strauss's tone poem *Till Eulenspiegel* lurches wildly from narrative to speech inflection to exasperating tangles of unconstruables, but a written chronicle of Till's adventures would behave identically. So we are left in paradox: the more we try to understand music as language, the more strongly it resists that understanding. The more we try to understand music as the opposite of language, the more sweetly, strongly, plainly it speaks to the ear. We understand the siren's song only at the moment when we stop trying to understand it.

Chapter Two

Heine and the Composers

Self-Scrutiny 1

We are in a cozy salon, which we see in soft focus, lit with warm red, full of upholstered leather furniture in the best modern taste. The soprano, sober in a fur-collared jacket, gazes at us as the pianist plays the gentle prelude. There is something odd about the windows, though. The left window shows a somewhat jittery scene, as if there were a minor earthquake that no one was noticing; the right window shows the right eye and part of the mouth of the soprano's huge face.

Self-Scrutiny 2

Heinrich Heine and Franz Schubert were born in the same year, 1797. If Heine had died when Schubert died, in 1828, it would have been an enormous loss to German letters and German music alike. For one thing, Wagner might never have written *The Flying Dutchman*, which he based on a brief satirical episode in one of Heine's novels. But the history of the German Lied might not have been drastically changed, because most of Heine's lyric poems—which inflamed the imaginations of countless composers, not just in Germany—had already been published, many of them in the *Lyrisches Intermezzo* section (first published 1823) of the *Buch der Lieder* (1827).

Schubert had only a little time to take note of Heine's work, but six of the fourteen songs in *Schwanengesang* (a song cycle compiled, not without skill, by a publisher, in collaboration with Schubert's brother, after Schubert's death) are settings of texts by Heine. One of these songs is "Der Doppelgänger":

Still ist die Nacht, es ruhen die Gassen,	The night is quiet, the small streets still,
In diesem Hause wohnte mein Schatz;	Here, in this house, a girl lived once.
Sie hat schon längst die Stadt verlassen,	She left the city long ago,
Doch steht noch das Haus auf demselben Platz.	But the house still stands, just as it was.

First published in *Parnassus* 31, nos. 1–2 (Spring 2009).

Da steht auch ein Mensch und starrt in die Höhe	And a man stands there, and cranes his neck,
Und ringt die Hände vor Schmerzensgewalt;	His knuckles white, mouth agape,
Mir graust es, wenn ich sein Antlitz sehe—	I shudder as I come to look:
Der Mond zeigt mir meine eigne Gestalt.	The moon shows me my own shape.
Du Doppelgänger, du bleicher Geselle!	My double—pale companion-ghost!
Was äffst du nach mein Liebesleid,	Why do you ape my inner pain,
Das mich gequält auf dieser Stelle	The torture of the love I lost,
So manche Nacht, in alter Zeit?[1]	The hurt I need to feel again?

This poem succinctly states Heine's whole lyric agon. The poet is drawn to revisit some scene of havoc and desolation, to relive rejection, loss, pain, vain yearning. But he stands aloof from his own feeling, takes a restrained delight in cultivating a persona of ruin. Yeats once said that the traditional masks of the lyric poet are lover or saint, sage or sensualist, or mere mocker of all life. Heine evolved a new and compelling mask, the lover as ironist, at once rendered immune by his ironic distance and yet intimately self-excoriated by his inability to take full part in his own feeling. (Heine's own description of his art was "malicious-sentimental.") In "Der Doppelgänger," it is far from clear which is the ghost and which is the real man. The poet himself may be the revenant haunting the place where he once felt authentic emotion, where some fragment of an authentic being still lingers to feel it.

Schubert's setting is based on a four-note figure: scale degrees $\hat{1}$–$\sharp\hat{7}$–$\hat{3}$–$\hat{2}$ in B minor, in slow, steady dotted half notes: B–A♯–D–C♯ (figure 2.1). This is the sort of figure more common in instrumental music than in songs: it might be the head of a fugue subject or the basis of a passacaglia. In fact, Leopold Godowsky wrote a passacaglia on a striking, somewhat similar figure from Schubert's Unfinished Symphony (speaking of B minor!). Beethoven's Piano Sonata, Op. 110, isolates a four-note figure only slightly different in shape from that of "Der Doppelgänger." Not far away is the famous B–A–C–H figure (in English note spelling, B♭–A–C–B♮), which haunts instrumental compositions by Schumann, Liszt, and Rimsky-Korsakov, not to mention works by many other composers, including Bach himself. In the song, the figure is an obsessive presence: first, in that the piano keeps repeating it in a simple harmonization (i–V–III–V, sometimes deforming to i–v–III–V^7, with a corresponding drop of the figure's ♯7 to ♮7); second, in that almost every chord in the song contains an F♯, a dominant pedal, until the great *fff* chord on the second syllable of "Gestalt" ("The moon shows me my own *shape*") (figure 2.2).

The song's vocal line also begins on a monotone F♯ and shows a strong tendency to return to that note—again, until the word "Gestalt," when it rises a

Figure 2.1. Schubert: *Der Doppelgänger*, beginning, from Franz Schubert, *Complete Song Cycles: Die schöne Müllerin, Die Winterreise, Schwanengesang*, ed. Eusebius Mandyczewski (New York: Dover Publications, 1970), 180.

semitone to G. The Doppelgänger and the poet are right next to one another, only a semitone apart, and yet they belong to different harmonic universes: the *fff* chord is, in effect, a simple C^7, but Schubert pushes it to an extremity of pallid horror.

This is the pattern for some of his other Heine settings. They tend not to have tuneful vocal lines. Of course Schubert could write catchy melodies, such as "Heidenröslein," which is almost a folk song by now, but a surprising number of his finest songs don't inspire humming in the shower. For Schubert, Heine's texts invite a special kind of declamatory gesture that hovers anxiously in the forbidden spaces near the tonic: a minor or major second below and above. "Der

Figure 2.2. Schubert: *Der Doppelgänger*, climax, from Franz Schubert, *Complete Song Cycles: Die schöne Müllerin, Die Winterreise, Schwanengesang*, ed. Eusebius Mandyczewski (New York: Dover Publications, 1970), 181.

Atlas," for example, a far more desperate and urgent song, sounds nothing like "Der Doppelgänger," but it's confected to the same recipe:

Ich unglücksel'ger Atlas! Eine Welt,	I am the luckless Atlas! A world,
Die ganze Welt der Schmerzen muß ich tragen,	I have to bear the whole world of sorrows,
Ich trage Unerträgliches, und brechen	I bear the unbearable, and the heart
Will mir das Herz im Leibe.	In my body wants to break.
Du stolzes Herz, du hast es ja gewollt!	Arrogant heart, you, you wanted this!
Du wolltest glücklich sein, unendlich glücklich,	You wanted to be happy, forever happy,
Oder unendlich elend, stolzes Herz,	Or forever wretched, arrogant heart.
Und jetzo bist du elend.	It happened: you are wretched.

Here Heine uses an unrhymed verse form, derived from Horace, suitable for this classical theme; but unlike Hölderlin or (at times) Goethe, he doesn't try to make German sound like Latin by using dispersed syntax held together only by the case endings of the nouns and adjectives. Instead, all is tidy, regular, chaste in Heine's normal chastened manner. This Atlas of pain can't escape from his burden, and the poem can't escape from its tight-lipped, grim formality, although the loss of rhyme may provide the poem with a small solace.

Schubert, in finding a tone equivalent, once again constructed the song from a four-note figure: scale degrees $\hat{1}$–$\hat{3}$–$\sharp\hat{7}$–$\hat{1}$ in G minor, harmonized i–i–V–i (figure 2.3).

This is the most ordinary harmonization possible, just a regular tonic-dominant movement. Schubert's early songs can be amazingly adventurous across the harmonic field. For example, "Gretchen am Spinnrade" (1814) weaves its *distrait* way through any number of keys, but some of his late songs are harmonically austere, for the sake of maximizing dissonance, not suppressing it. In "Der Atlas," Schubert puts extraordinary stress on the F♯ in the dominant chord, heightening

Figure 2.3. Schubert: *Der Atlas,* beginning, from Franz Schubert, *Complete Song Cycles: Die schöne Müllerin, Die Winterreise, Schwanengesang,* ed. Eusebius Mandyczewski (New York: Dover Publications, 1970), 167.

its dissonance with G, the tonic note: it's as if Atlas sags a semitone under pitch under the overwhelming weight, then with a weight lifter's grunt heaves the world back to its original position. Indeed, in the vocal line, the singer sings only the first three notes of the figure: he needs to take a breath before resuming the tonic note. The song proceeds just as "Der Doppelgänger" proceeds: at "brechen Will das Herz," there's an episode based on rising chromatics (the comparable moment in "Der Doppelgänger" occurs at "Du Doppelgänger, du bleicher Geselle!"), and a climactic wail that takes the singer a semitone too high. He repeats the line "Die ganze Welt der Schmerzen muß ich tragen" in an emphatic tonic arpeggio, rising through an octave, but then pushes past the G to A♭,

Figure 2.4. Schubert: *Der Atlas,* climax, from Franz Schubert, *Complete Song Cycles: Die schöne Müllerin, Die Winterreise, Schwanengesang,* ed. Eusebius Mandyczewski (New York: Dover Publications, 1970), 169.

harmonized to a *fff* B♭^{7} chord—nothing particularly strange in itself (just a seventh chord in the relative major), but Schubert wrings the maximum dissonance out of that A♭ abutted brutally against the preceding G (figure 2.4).

As at the climax of "Der Doppelgänger," the startling glare of a major chord represents a spasm of pain after the habitual minor of the rest of the song: in a gasp of strength, Atlas lifts the world a little higher than it's supposed to be, then sinks back into his usual dejection. But "Der Atlas" differs from "Der Doppelgänger" in one important way: "Der Atlas" is a highly rhythmic song, almost a sort of dance of sheer misery—Atlas juggles. Both the rhythm and the melodic contour of the four-note figure have a certain resemblance to the old tune *La folia,* or *Les folies d'Espagne,* popularized long ago by Corelli, C. P. E. Bach, and others. It sometimes operates (as the title might suggest) as a badge of madness: for example, in Vivaldi's opera *Orlando furioso* (1727) the crazed Orlando sings "La, la, la" to the tune of *La folia.* I don't know if Schubert was conscious of the similarity, but the music may hint that the world's weight has driven Atlas mad. Susan Youens has argued, in *Heine and the Lied,* that the song is "a resonant prison for all eternity," but maybe the hopeless madness of the situation, like the loss of rhyme fetters, offers an escape—even if only the escape of psychosis.[2]

Perhaps the most sophisticated of the six Heine settings in *Schwanengesang* is "Die Stadt." The poem is quite similar to "Der Doppelgänger," depicting a visit to a significant extinct place. But in this case it's not the poet, but the city itself that is its own phantom double:

Am fernen Horizonte	On the far horizon
Erscheint, wie ein Nebelbild,	Appears, like shapes in a cloud,
Die Stadt mit ihren Türmen,	The city with its towers;
In Abenddämmrung gehüllt.	The twilight's like a shroud.
Ein feuchter Windzug kräuselt	A damp gust makes ripples
Die graue Wasserbahn;	In the gray canal;
Mit traurigem Takte rudert	The oarsman rows my skiff
Der Schiffer in meinem Kahn.	With *tempo mesto* pull.

Die Sonne hebt sich noch einmal	From the world's edge rises
Leuchtend vom Boden empor	Once again the sun
Und zeigt mir jene Stelle,	And shines upon the place
Wo ich das Liebste verlor.	Where I lost someone.

The song begins in a state of sheer rhythmlessness. The piano shivers with faint arpeggios of a diminished chord—and the score adds the marking *diminuendo*, as if harmony and volume alike were an exercise in diminishing (figure 2.5).

Figure 2.5. Schubert: *Die Stadt*, from Franz Schubert, *Complete Song Cycles: Die schöne Müllerin, Die Winterreise, Schwanengesang*, ed. Eusebius Mandyczewski (New York: Dover Publications, 1970), 175.

As the voice enters, the rhythm suddenly becomes quite pronounced, with double-dotted chords in the tonic, C minor; the vocal line begins as little more than a monotone on G, occasionally rising a semitone to A♭. The song offers little in the way of melody, little in the way of figuration—only the light finger ripples of the diminished chord and a declamatory voice, singing mostly on the tonic or the dominant note and lifting itself a half step when stabbed by insight. Keats writes in a famous line, "My heart aches, and a drowsy numbness pains." "Die Stadt" is about drowsy numbness interspersed with small tightenings, clenches. The paralysis is almost complete: the singer, having taken a boat into nonexistence, illustrates his limbo with nonmelodies, forms of talking to oneself carried out by other means.

Of course it's only an accident that Schubert happened to die soon after writing his Heine settings, but they can appear to be at once a climax of his song art and a repudiation of singing itself. If a song were to be much sparer than "Die Stadt," it would be little more than reciting the poem aloud; perhaps only Othmar Schoeck, in "Lebendig begraben" (1927), advanced the art of the Lied into a condition even closer to speech. In "Die Stadt," song is little more than speech's Doppelgänger.

Clowns

In many of Heine's poems, the extreme evenness of the meter cloaks a massive disruption of the time scheme. Atlas is stuck in a bad place, where no Hercules will ever come to relieve him of the world's weight; his lyric cry is strictly eternal. Similarly, in "Der Doppelgänger" and "Die Stadt," the poet is like that character in Yeats's "Purgatory" (1938) who helplessly watches, over and over again, the ghosts of his parents in the act of begetting him, his drunken father raping his mother, lit up in a ruined house, a catastrophe that happened once and for all and yet never ends. The poet keeps approaching an emotional fact he can neither bear nor dispense with.

But there is another side to this Heinesque condition of bombed-out stasis. In some of his poems, time, far from standing still, moves way too fast. In one of his poems Heine managed to convey both lethargy and acceleration at the same time:

Es treibt mich hin, es treibt mich her!	It drives me here, it drives me there!
Noch wenige Stunden, dann soll ich sie schauen,	A few hours more, and I'll see my fill
sie selber, die schönste der schönen Jungfrauen;—	Of her, beautifulest of the beautiful.
du treues Herz, was pochst du so schwer!	Why are you pounding so, my heart?

Die Stunden sind aber ein faules Volk!	The hours are a lazy folk!
Schleppen sich behaglich träge,	Thick complacent-schlepping slugs,
schleichen gähnend ihre Wege;—	Gross and gaping, clumpish clogs—
tummle dich, du faules Volk!	Hurry up, you lazy folk!
Tobende Eile mich treibend erfaßt!	Impatience has me in her grasp!
Aber wohl niemals liebten die Horen;—	The hours hate the wretch lovelorn,
heimlich im grausamen Bunde verschworen,	They titter with a secret scorn
spotten sie tückisch der Liebenden Hast.	And, evil, mock the lover's haste.

This poem, too, was set to memorable music, not by Schubert but by Robert Schumann, as the second in his *Liederkreis*, Op. 24 (1840). The song begins *Sehr rasch*, very impetuously, but its headlong velocity soon starts slowing, until it diminishes, at a fermata, to zero; then suddenly it resumes at full gallop. Schumann provides many other imaginative solutions to the riddles of Heine's poems.

Schumann, more than Schubert, attended to the note of self-derision in Heine's poems. Schumann creates highly articulate musical personae that not only scrutinize themselves but mock themselves (though, as with Heine himself, there's a certain safety in this subject position: the fragment of your being that does the laughing has abstracted itself from your ridiculous lower self). A good example of a clown poem is "Der arme Peter" (Schumann, *Romanzen und Balladen* iii, Op. 53, no. 3, 1840):

1.

Der Hans und die Grete tanzen herum,	They twirl and whirl, this Jack and Jill,
Und jauchzen vor lauter Freude.	From sheer joy they shout;
Der Peter steht so still und so stumm,	But Peter's silent and stock-still,
Und ist so blaß wie Kreide.	His face as pale as chalk.
Der Hans und die Grete sind Bräut'gam und Braut,	Jack kisses his bride right on the lips,
Und blitzen im Hochzeitsgeschmeide.	Got up in splendid fashion;
Der arme Peter die Nägel kaut	Peter chews his fingertips,
Und geht im Werkeltagkleide.	Not dressed for the occasion.
Der Peter spricht leise vor sich her,	Peter mutters, inaudible,
Und schauet betrübet auf beide:	Gazing with some alarm;
Ach! wenn ich nicht gar zu vernünftig wär,'	If I weren't so sensible,
Ich täte mir was zuleide.	I'd do myself some harm.

2.

"In meiner Brust, da sitzt ein Weh,
Das will die Brust zersprengen;
Und wo ich steh' und wo ich geh,'
Will's mich von hinnen drängen.

"Es treibt mich nach der Liebsten Näh,'
Als könnt die Grete heilen;
Doch wenn ich der ins Auge seh,'
Muß ich von hinnen eilen.

"Ich steig' hinauf des Berges Höh,'
Dort ist man doch alleine;
Und wenn ich still dort oben steh,'
Dann steh' ich still und weine."

"In my breast there sits a woe,
I think it might explode;
And where I stay and where I go,
I follow it, my goad.

"I hope for comfort at Jill's side,
I don't know what to say;
And when I look into her eyes,
I must go far away.

"It drives me to climb, up and up,
Until I'm all alone,
And when I'm on the mountain top,
I weep, still as a stone."

3.

Der arme Peter wankt vorbei,
Gar langsam, leichenblaß und scheu.
Es bleiben fast, wie sie ihn sehn,
Die Leute auf den Straßen stehn.

Die Mädchen flüstern sich ins Ohr:
"Der stieg wohl aus dem Grab hervor."
Ach nein, ihr lieben Jungfräulein,
Der steigt erst in das Grab hinein.

Er hat verloren seinen Schatz,
Drum ist das Grab der beste Platz,
Wo er am besten liegen mag
Und schlafen bis zum Jüngsten Tag.

Poor Peter totters down the road,
Pale as a corpse, shy and slow;
The passersby, they have to stop
And stare, and stare, and staring gape.

Girls whisper in each other's ear,
"He's stumbled from a grave, I fear."
Oh no, my pretty little one,
Into the grave he's stumbling on.

For him who's lost whom he'd embrace,
The grave's the best and surest place;
There he'll rest and safely stay
And sleep until the Judgment Day.

This is an unusual poem in that the situation ascribed elsewhere to the poet himself (mourning at the true love's wedding; leading a hopelessly blighted life in consequence) is ascribed instead to a third party, poor Peter. Schumann's treatment of Part 2 is of particular interest (figure 2.6). It begins frantically, with Peter seeming to be a sort of Petrushka puppet with his strings jerked every which way. But as at the beginning of "Es treibt mich hin," the impetus gets slower and slower until Peter stops dead, paralyzed on the top of the mountain—though at the very end there's a brief relapse into frenzy. The frenzy figure can be heard as stylized laughing. The world is pointing a derisive figure at Peter; or Peter is pointing a derisive finger at himself.

Schumann's most searching engagement with Heine can be found in his incomparable cycle *Dichterliebe,* Op. 48 (1840—the same year in which every Schumann song here discussed was written!). We might start with (maybe) the most celebrated of its songs, "Ich grolle nicht" (no. 7):

Figure 2.6. Schumann: *Der arme Peter II*, from Robert Schumann, *Selected Songs for Solo Voice and Piano*, ed. Clara Schumann (New York: Dover Publications, 1981), 205.

Ich grolle nicht, und wenn das Herz auch bricht,	I don't complain, though my heart breaks from pain,
Ewig verlor'nes Lieb! Ich grolle nicht.	Love forever lost! I don't complain.
Wie du auch strahlst in Diamantenpracht,	However you shine with adamantine light,
Es fällt kein Strahl in deines Herzens Nacht.	There falls no ray into your heart's night.
Das weiß ich längst.	I've known that long.
Ich grolle nicht, und wenn das Herz auch bricht,	I don't complain, though my heart breaks from pain,
Ich sah dich ja im Traum,	In a dream I saw your face,
Und sah die Nacht in deines Herzens Raum,	And saw the night in your heart's space,
Und sah die Schlang,' die dir am Herzen frißt,	And saw the coiling snake that eats your heart,
Ich sah, mein Lieb, wie sehr du elend bist.	Dear one, I saw how wretched you are.

There is a rhetorical device called *praeteritio:* you mention something by announcing that you're not going to mention it. It's a strange kind of device in that it keeps swallowing its own tail, somewhat in the manner of the Cretan liar, who announces that everything he says is a lie—a statement that is true if and only if it is not true. A poem that begins, "I don't complain" and continues not to complain in an articulate and detailed manner is obviously a complaint. This sort of internal instability, self-contradiction, invites musical treatment, since the vertical structure of music (harmony, counterpoint) provides opportunities for presenting conflicting voices.

(I might note in passing that composers like irony better than metaphor. One of the reasons for Heine's popularity among composers is his comparative lack of interest in metaphor. There is a metaphor in "Ich grolle nicht"—the snake that devours the woman's heart—but Schumann pays no attention to it: the music refuses all invitation to slither. Music is extraordinarily adept at rhetorical figures involving emphasis, but not at all adept in rhetorical figures in involving transposition. The old rhetoricians of music, such as Kircher and Mattheson, had no trouble finding illustrations of anaphora but had a lot of trouble finding illustrations of metaphor.)

The German verb *grollen* means "grumble," "rumble," "begrudge," "resent," "be angry with"; and the piano part of "Ich grolle nicht" consists of a continuous rumble of chords in even eighth notes (figure 2.7). The meter is common time, the key is C major—not only do I not complain, I'm not complaining in the most candid of keys and the most usual meter. But things start to go wrong from the beginning. In the first line, when the singer sings "und wenn mein Herz doch bricht," Schumann plays the Schubertesque game of raising the vocal line (at the word

Figure 2.7. Schumann: *Ich grolle nicht,* from Robert Schumann, *Selected Songs for Solo Voice and Piano,* ed. Clara Schumann (New York: Dover Publications, 1981), 156.

"Herz") to a "wrong" note, A♭, supported by an F-minor chord. The uncomplained complaint starts to twist the harmony as it gropes for expression beneath the singer's aplomb, his airy dismissal of his grudge. More serious distortions follow: as we hear of the beloved's diamond splendor, the utter darkness of her heart—"Es fällt kein Strahl"—the piano plays an F♯ major chord, 180 degrees away from C major, harmonically speaking. The augmented fourth (as from C to F♯) is, according to Western music theory, a forbidden interval, the devil's own dissonance ("*si–fa,* diabolus in musica," as the old rhyme goes). The singer may refuse to complain, but the devil is leering from the piano part. When we hear of the snake that eats the woman's heart, we may think of her as half-victim, half-temptress: she seems to be Satan and Eve in one. In Oliver Herrmann's film *Dichterliebe* (2000), Christine Schäfer (the soprano whose monstrous countenance stares at herself in the manner I described at the beginning of this essay) sings "Ich grolle nicht" in a Berlin nightclub: as the song proceeds, she slowly writes on a blackboard, "It is easier to scratch your ass than to scratch your heart." It is as if the woman described in "Ich grolle nicht" had usurped the male singer's subject position; it is as if the snake were writing a little message to those who might regard the song as more sentimental than malicious.

It is hard to take a clear stance toward the poem's speaker: he may be canny, fully aware of the irony of his own rhetorical maneuver, or he may be another of Heine's clowns, trying to rise above his own abjection but spilling out unconscious bile on all sides.

There is an odd sequel to "Ich grolle nicht" in the world of late-twentieth-century opera, a moving clown show by Michael Nyman, *The Man Who Mistook His Wife for a Hat* (1986). Christopher Rawlence's libretto to this opera, based on an actual case study by Dr. Oliver Sacks, depicts a celebrated musician who suffers from a neurological deficit called prosopagnosia—the inability to match perceived objects with mental categories. Not only does Dr. P mistake his wife for a hat, but he also continually chats with pieces of furniture and claps a friendly arm around mailboxes. So epistemologically damned is he that he even confuses his shoe with his foot: his own body is an alien presence to his confounded mind. At one moment in the opera, Dr. S[acks] shows Dr. P a glove and asks him what it is. Dr. P thinks, correctly, that it might be a container—but a container for what?

> Coins of five different sizes.
> It's a purse, a special purse. . . .
> The pigskin case
> Of some precious device
> For the probing
> Of my brain?[3]

It is as if Dr. P lives in a dangerous realm, a world of scalpels, for every innocent object is a blade that cuts his innermost tissue, painfully reveals his inadequacy at matching concept with object. Dr. P's daily life is one long psychological test, one long semantic game in which meaning always recedes before his blunt gaze.

Dr. P's salvation is his music. Although he can no longer read musical notation, he remembers songs and is still a brilliant baritone. Indeed he organizes his daily routine around song cues, melodic sequences that inform his shaving, his eating, his bathing, his social relations, and so forth. Since his system of visual recognition is almost extinct, he depends on a system of acoustic recognition instead. In other words, Dr. P lives in a kind of ongoing opera, in which Schumann, Britten, and other composers "tell" him where to go and what to do through an intricate file of arbitrary musical signs. Nyman has, in effect, only given a public musical expression to the private Singspiel of Dr. P's ordinary existence. Nyman decided to make certain Schumann songs the root material for his exploration of Dr. P's inner sound world. One of the high points of the opera comes when (at Dr. S's encouragement) Dr. P gives a splendid performance of Schumann's "Ich grolle nicht." This scene illustrates a kind of triumph of musicality over the encroaching chaos of the rest of Dr. P's life. It is the psychological equivalent of the old myth, dear to musicians, that the firmament is established, the universe harmonized, by some divine act of creation through song, the music of the spheres.

But why did Nyman choose "Ich grolle nicht"? Sacks made no mention of a particular organizing song. Just as Heine's text mentions a snake that devours the heart of the speaker's beloved, there is a kind of snake in Dr. P's brain, eating away the foundations of his life. But when accounting for his choice of this song, Nyman stressed the importance not of Heine's words but of Schumann's music:

> I chose "Ich grolle nicht" partly for the appropriateness of its text but largely for its musical resources: unbroken sequences of repeated quavers [eighth notes] are meat and drink to me.... Thus, in the sequence following "Ich grolle nicht" ... the harmony of the first four bars of the song is rhythmically re-articulated. But subsequently ... bars five through eight undergo a gradual perceptual shift as the strong melodic line and its supporting functional harmony degenerate into figuration and mere pattern-making, losing its "representational" quality by a process of simultaneously speeding up the melody while slowing down the rate of harmonic change.[4]

When Nyman explains how he abstracted, isolated, and brought into the foreground certain submerged elements of Schumann's song in order to provide the continuation of the scene, he offers the key to his opera. He abstracts Schumann's song, at once denuding it of all emotional content and seeking in its harmonic skeleton some source of physiological authority. In the fascinating duet immediately following the performance of "Ich grolle nicht," Dr. S shows Dr. P a number of geometrical figures, testing his power of recognition of abstract shapes ("te-te-te-te-te-te-tetrahedron"). Nyman's music is a sort of refaceting of the first four bars of Schumann's song, emphasizing the vacillation between the notes E and F in the top line of the piano accompaniment and spinning off little chord circuits that whirligig around Schumann's chord progressions. As Dr. S displays his tetrahedrons, Schumann's song is tetrahedralized, so to speak.

Much of the opera concerns the aesthetic value of abstractionism. At one point, Mrs. P shows Dr. S a series of paintings by Dr. P, some of which are representational scenes with a strong emotional content: "Displaced Europeans... The grief of survivors / The weeping and sobbing...." But as Dr. P's mental decline takes effect, the paintings turn increasingly cubistic, abstract. Dr. S describes these later paintings as worthless except as neurological relevations:

> Painted gesture
> Has degenerated in mere marks,
> Lines without meaning,
> Empty shapes....
> I see the advancing pathology
> Making no sense
> Of the world out here[5]

But Mrs. P is deeply insulted by these characterizations:

> You're an arrogant, ignorant man.
> He progressed to the abstract....
> Pure painful,
> Painted emotion...
> Feeling embodied in
> Measured brushstrokes.[6]

Now, Mrs. P has generally been an unreliable observer through the opera, eager to find excuses for her husband's bizarre behavior. What are we to make of her opinion of his recent painting? One clue is found in Nyman's musical settings, some of the most distinguished in the score. When Dr. S sings of the senselessness of Dr. P's paintings, the music is repetitive, deliberately unmeaning, like an orchestra of country fiddles making preparatory gestures toward a square dance. But when Mrs. P denounces Dr. S and defends her husband's art, the music instantly, unmistakably, changes into stylized chromatic lamentation—one of the oldest code gestures in Western music. Nyman evidently means that the painting varies in its meaninglessness or meaningfulness according to the observer. A neurologist will find it tellingly absurd (and therefore a confirmation of his diagnostic powers), a doting wife will find it a calculated expression of all the world's suffering (and therefore a confirmation of her husband's genius). The painting itself is little or nothing, only a blank surface on which contradictory interpretations proliferate, none better or worse than another.

This same observation might be made of the music of Schumann—or of Nyman. When Nyman deconstructed Schumann's nobly emotive melody into monotonous bass figures, he was searching, in a sense, for the song's deepest level, where its meaning, however shrunken and impoverished, was most unassailable: the level where the song retained its Orphic power to organize reality for Dr. P. "Ich grolle nicht," so to speak, was capable of thinking for Dr. P, of providing a pattern to govern his feeling and action; the song performed for Dr. P the same service that music performed for Wordsworth's idiot boy:

> As Conscience, to the centre
> Of being, smites with irresistible pain,
> So shall a solemn cadence, if it enter
> The mouldy vaults of the dull idiot's brain,
> Transmute him to a wretch from quiet hurled—
> Convulsed as by a jarring din;
> And then aghast, as at the world
> Of reason partially let in
> By concords winding with a sway
> Terrible for sense and soul![7]

By essentializing and reducing Schumann's song, Nyman seeks the ultimate source of music's power to inform human intelligence—the minimum cadence, the basic code through which music operates on our nervous systems. He abstracts "Ich grolle nicht" until it has lost all complaint, all noncomplaining, all emotional content whatsoever, until it has become a mere acoustic stimulus to motor and perceptual neurons. As Oliver Sacks himself noted,

> In *Awakenings* I describe a patient, Edith T., a former music teacher with severe Parkinsonism, who constantly finds herself brought to a complete halt, unable to move unless or until she imagines a tune. She herself talks of being "unmusicked" by Parkinsonism, and having to be "remusicked" back into motion. Neurologists speak of "kinetic melody" here. But there is a "perceptual melody" as well, and it is this which is lost (among other things) in Dr. P, who sees the world as abstract, meaningless shapes, and can only make sense of it, proceed, when he is "remusicked." . . . The real hero in "The Hat" is surely music—the power of music to organize and integrate, to knit or reknit a shattered world into sense.[8]

It is as if, to Nyman, music becomes more physiologically potent as it become more stripped down, more minimal; he tries to uncover the controlling, corporeal root language. Nyman quoted with approval a comment by Roland Barthes:

> In Schumann's *Kreisleriana* (1838), I actually hear no note, no theme, no grammar, no meaning, nothing that would permit me to reconstruct an intelligible structure of the work. No, what I hear are blows, I hear what beats in the body, or better: I hear this body that beats.[9]

But of course (as Barthes knew well) *Kreisleriana* is full of memorable themes that are quite obedient to certain principles of musical grammar and (to some extent) assigned a specific meaning by the composer. To hear in the music only pulse throbs and biceps contractions (what Barthes called "somathemes" elsewhere in this essay) is to neglect a great deal of the far from negligible. What Nyman has done (in effect) is to recompose Schumann's "Ich grolle nicht" according to the recipe of Barthes's experience of *Kreisleriana*: to remove from it all that is not directly pertinent to the body. Barthes evidently conceived Schumann as a kind of Scarpia, beating, beating, beating on the body of his auditor. It is interesting that Nyman congruently conceived the ideally sensitive listener of Schumann as someone who had undergone much physical and mental degradation. It is as if Heine's Poor Peter, stumbling into the grave, punched senseless by the blows of fate, has become the prototype of the operatic hero in a state of extreme postmodernist decline.

The Self-Canceling-Out of Art

In a notebook, Franz Kafka jotted the cryptic phrase "the self-canceling-out of art"—a procedure that Heine, a century before, had understood well. "Ich grolle nicht" is a self-canceling song in that it's a complaining noncomplaint; but other Heine poems extend the principle of self-excoriation to an excoriation of one's own poetry.

Both of Schumann's song cycles based on Heine's poetry—*Liederkreis*, Op. 24, and *Dichterliebe*, Op. 48—conclude with poems in which the poet builds a sarcophagus for his own songs. This is the first one—though Schumann, a great lover of myrtles, used a version of the poem with a myrtle in the first line:

Mit Rosen, Zypressen und Flittergold	Make my book a black wood box,
Möcht ich verzieren, lieblich und hold,	Adorn with rose and golden flecks,
Dies Buch wie einen Totenschrein,	It shall be coffin large enough
Und sargen meine Lieder hinein.	For the songs inspired by my love.
O könnt' ich die Liebe sargen hinzu!	I want to bury Love in that chest!
Auf dem Grabe der Liebe wächst Blümlein der Ruh,'	For on Love's grave there blossoms Rest,
da blüht es hervor, da pflückt man es ab,—	A flower I would gladly have—
doch mir blüht's nur, wenn ich selber im Grab.	But it blooms, I know, on my own grave.
Hier sind nun die Lieder, die einst so wild,	Here are the songs I once belched up
wie ein Lavastrom, der dem Ätna entquillt,	Like lava spewed from Etna's top,

Hervorgestürtzt aus dem tiefsten Gemüt,	With blinding sparks and rumbles vast
und rings viel blitzende Funken versprüht!	From my heart's own pyroclast.
Nun liegen sie stumm und totengleich,	On these pages lie corpse-cold,
nun starren sie kalt und nebelbleich,	Dumb, cloud-pale, the words I told;
doch aufs neu die alte Glut sie belebt,	But they might kindle once again
wenn der Liebe Geist einst über sie schwebt.	If Love herself would enter in.
Und es wird mir im Herzen viel Ahnung laut:	I feel my songs will soon renew
der Liebe Geist einst über sie taut;	When Love upon them sheds her dew—
einst kommt dies Buch in deine Hand,	This book once opened by your hand,
du süßes Lieb im fernen Land.	My darling in a distant land.
Dann löst sich des Liedes Zauberbann,	If Love will chant her magic there
die blaßen Buchstaben schaun dich an,	The letters of the text will stare
sie schauen dir flehend ins schöne Aug,'	Imploringly on your fair face
und flüstern mit Wehmut und Liebeshauch.	And breathe a whisper of Love's grace.

This gentle poem is a model of reader-response theory: the song moulders in the book until the reader, the One Right Reader, ensorcels it, ensouls it. Its sequel, at the end of *Dichterliebe,* is far more ambiguous:

Die alten, bösen Lieder,	The putrid, evil songs,
Die Träume schlimm und arg,	Bad dreams that will not stop,
Die laßt uns jetzt begraben,	It's time to dig a hole,
Holt einen großen Sarg.	Time to coffin them up.
Hinein leg' ich gar manches,	I won't say what they are,
Doch sag' ich noch nicht, was;	But lots are going in;
Der Sarg muß sein noch größer,	The coffin must be larger
Wie's Heidelberger Faß.	Than the Heidelberg Tun.
Und holt eine Totenbahre,	And for this coffin, fetch
Von Brettern fest und dick;	Planks of the stoutest kinds;
Auch muß sie sein noch länger,	It has to be as long,
Als wie zu Mainz die Brück.'	Long as the bridge at Mainz.
Und holt mir auch zwölf Riesen,	And fetch twelve giants, oh,
Die müssen noch stärker sein	Strong to lift huge stones,
Als wie der heil'ge Christoph	Strong as that Christopher
Im Dom zu Köln am Rhein.	Cathedraled at Cologne.

Figure 2.8. Schumann: *Die alten, bösen Lieder,* from Robert Schumann, *Selected Songs for Solo Voice and Piano,* ed. Clara Schumann (New York: Dover Publications, 1981), 178.

Die sollen den Sarg forttragen,	The giants heave the coffin,
Und senken ins Meer hinab;	Toss it into the deep,
Denn solchem großen Sarge	For such an enormous thing
Gebührt ein großes Grab.	Only the sea can keep.
Wißt ihr, warum der Sarg wohl	It had to be heavy, huge—
So groß und schwer mag sein?	Shall I tell you why?
Ich legt' auch meine Liebe	My pains had all to fit,
Und meinen Schmerz hinein.	In it my love must lie.

Not so gentle. Schumann's setting (in the key of C♯ minor) begins with a huge gesture, a thrusting down the whole diapason by means of a figure prominent in both the piano and the vocal line: C♯–G♯–C♯ (figure 2.8).

When the singer mentions the Heidelberg Tun, the great bridge at Mainz, and Köln Cathedral, the piano utters a little figure of glee, similar to the figure that Wagner would use, ten years later in *Das Rheingold,* to represent the arrogance of the dwarf king Alberich, when he exercises the power of the Ring. It is a laughing figure, but as elsewhere in Schumann's Heine settings, the laughter may redound to mock the poet, at once burying his vile poems and subliminally congratulating himself at his stature—you need a really big box if it's to contain all *my* poems! The mood of the song softens toward the end: the emphatic gestures peter out into hesitant syncopations, as if the singer were regretting his hasty decision, in this loud palinode, to unsing his songs. (When Dante Gabriel Rossetti, a few years later, buried the manuscripts of his poems in his wife's coffin, he was forced to exhume her body in order to publish them.) The song terminates in a long postlude for the piano in the tonic major, *Andante espressivo,* which might be regarded as (1) a sample of the defunct sad-sentimental lyric stuff that will trouble the world no longer; (2) a warm requiem hymn over the poems' grave (rest in peace, my songs); or (3) as a strange moment of triumph, the song's quietly insistent refusal to remain buried, its assertion of its merit against the poet's own wishes—the song wriggles out of its marine casket and floats to the surface. Myself, I incline to the last interpretation: great art has often been made out of art's confessions of impotence, inadequacy.

Bells

Heine spent most of his adult life in Paris, at first a voluntary exile from Germany, then (because of his liberal politics) an involuntary one. And Heine has always been a poet popular in France. Indeed, he may have influenced the course of French poetry to some degree. If we listen to the radical ironists of late-nineteenth-century France, such as Jules Laforgue, we sometimes a certain Heinesque note:

Non, je resterai seul, ici-bas,	Devoted, alone, I'll stay here, ach!,
Tout à la chère morte phtisique,	With my dear consumptive dead,
Berçant mon coeur trop hypertrophique	Cradling my hypertrophied head
Aux éternelles fugues de Bach.	In the eternal fugues of Bach.
Et tous les ans, à l'anniversaire,	On her birthday I'll unfurl
Pour nous, sans qu'on se doute de rien,	At my organ with squelched heart,
Je déchaînerai ce *Requiem*	Just for us, with my best art,
Que j'ai fait pour la mort de la Terre![10]	This requiem made for the end of the world!

This is more grotesque and brittle, more technical, than any of Heine's poems. Yet the blasted lover who dramatizes his own ruin and the appeal to Judgment Day, both recall "Der arme Peter." Laforgue's various Pierrots can be considered as wispier, more artificial, more metaphysical versions of the Heine clown.

French composers, as well as German ones, were attracted to Heine. There's an excellent but little-known cycle by the Breton composer Joseph Guy Ropartz, *Quatre poèmes d'après l'Intermezzo de Henri Heine* (1899). One of the most striking features of this composition is a bell that keeps tolling through the piano part.[11]

Heine's poems seem to invite bells. Neither Schubert nor Schumann, in setting Heine, was particularly sensitive to such sonorities, though the four-note figure in Schubert's "Doppelgänger" might be considered a sort of knell. (And in the *Dichterliebe* film, as Schäfer sings Schumann's "Hör' ich das Liedchen klingen," Hermann's camera observes a metronome ticking in the foreground, as if to remind us that the songs are all about tempo, time.) But Robert Franz's magnificent setting of "Ja, bist du elend" is based on a figure that's unmistakably an urgent chiming:

Ja, bist du elend, und ich grolle nicht;	Yes, you are wretched, and I don't complain;
Mein Lieb, wir sollen beide elend sein!	O let's be unhappy together, my love,
Bis uns der Tod das kranke Herz bricht,	Until death ends our sickly hearts' moan,
Mein Lieb, wir sollen beide elend sein!	O let's be unhappy together, my love.
Wohl seh ich Spott, der deinen Mund umschwebt,	I see the mock that hovers round your mouth,
Und seh dein Auge blitzen trotziglich,	And see your eyes flash spitefully,
Und seh den Stolz, der deinen Busen hebt,	And see the arrogance that lifts your breast,
Und elend bist du doch, elend wie ich.	And yet you are wretched, wretched as I.
Unsichtbar zuckt auch Schmerz um deinen Mund,	Pain twitches your mouth, imperceptible,

Verborgne Träne trübt des Auges Schein,	Hidden tears make your eyes muddy, grave,
Der stolze Busen hegt geheime Wund,	The proud breast a secret wound conceals,
Mein Lieb, wir sollen beide elend sein!	O let's be unhappy together, my love!

This reads like a revisiting of the psychic material of "Ich grolle nicht," reconstituted in slightly different form. In fact, "Ich grolle nicht" is Heine's *Lyrisches Intermezzo* 18, and "Ja, bist du elend" is *Lyrisches Intermezzo* 19. Franz's setting is daringly monotonous, consisting of the chime phrase and not much else. Each of the twelve lines is sung to roughly the same music, with a little sequential development. But Franz makes the monotony into a convincing image of harassed stasis, a misery that will never change, a misery in some sense treasured because it is the only form of intimacy that the poet and his beloved can hope to know.

In Ropartz's Heine cycle, the bell is intermittent, but when it tolls its four notes it makes its presence felt, because it turns the bell motive from Wagner's *Parsifal* into a kind of *Dies irae*:

Depuis que nul rayon de tes yeux bien-aimés
N'arrive plus aux miens obstinément fermés,
Je suis enveloppé de ténèbres morales.
L'étoile de l'amour s'est éteinte pour moi
Plus de douce clarté, rien que l'ombre et l'effroi!
Un gouffre large ouvert me veut dans ses spirales
Nuit éternelle engloutis-moi![12]

Wo ich bin, mich rings umdunkelt
Finsterniß so dumpf und dicht,
Seit mir nicht mehr leuchtend funkelt,
Liebste, Deiner Augen Licht.

Mir erloschen ist der süßen
Liebessterne goldne Pracht.
Abgrund gähnt zu meinen Füßen.
Nimm mich auf, uralte Nacht.

Where I am is ringed with dark,
Dark so hollow, close, drear,
Since I lost the last spark
Of your eye's light, my dear.

Quenched forever is the sweet
Splendor of that gold starlight.
Abyss gapes beneath my feet,
Take me now, O primal night.

It is remarkable how often composers setting Heine, even composers not using a German text, default to a figure of four notes. It is time's chime, iterated into a kind of eternity; it is also Heine's normal tetrameter beat, liberated from the poem, turned autonomous. When he first published the *Lyrisches Intermezzo*, Heine himself predicted that its poems would attract composers, but his poems have had an odd way of making composers respect the purely poetic aspects of Heine's craft, those aspects of his craft that resist melody. A Heine song is often simply a kind of declamation superimposed on a bell-like beat, as if the melody of the words themselves were so compelling that it resisted the sorts of tunes that composers normally invent.

To my mind, the most ravishing of all Schumann's settings of Heine is "Belsatzar," Op. 57 (1840). The poem belongs to a peculiar class, a specialty of Heine's, the dehydrated narrative—a long story compressed into a few lines (another example is "Die heil'gen drei Kön'ge aus Morgenland," set by Richard Strauss, Op. 56, no. 6). To set Heine's couplet version of the story of Belshazzar, Schumann used a recitation figure, the sort of music to which a bard might chant an epic—a figure without any expressive character of its own, but pithy, lilting, full of a certain momentum. (The music for one of the old epic recitation figures still exists, that for Wolfram von Eschenbach's *Titurel*.) But remarkably enough, when we come to the climax of the song—the moving finger that writes on the wall, You have been weighed in the balance and found wanting—the melodic motion contracts almost to zero: the singer does little more than read Heine's lines aloud. I imagine that having written scores of masterpieces to Heine's texts during his *annus mirabilis* of 1840, Schumann grinned, sat back, and said to himself, Heinrich, why do I have to do anything at all? See, your poems compose their own music.

Chapter Three

The Diabolical Senta

Bored with her life of repetitive chores, a girl dreams of a dark ship full of death and annihilation, an escape from the mundane into some fantastic passion (figure 3.1):

Figure 3.1. Weill: *Die Dreigroschenoper*, "Und das Schiff mit acht Segeln," from Kurt Weill, *Die Dreigroschenoper*, Ein Stück mit Musik ein einem Vorspiel und acht bildern nach dem Englischen des John Gay, übersetzt von Elisabeth Hauptmann, Deutsche Bearbeitung von Bert Brecht, Klavierauszug Norbert Gingold (Vienna: Universal Edition No. 8851, 1956), 17. © 1928 by European American Music Corporation. © Renewed. All rights reserved. Used by permission of European American Music Corporation.

Bored with her life of repetitive chores, a girl dreams of a dark ship full of death and annihilation, an escape from the mundane into some fantastic passion (figure 3.2):

Figure 3.2. Wagner: *The Flying Dutchman*, "Trafft ihr das Schiff im Meere an," from Richard Wagner, *The Flying Dutchman (Der fliegende Holländer)*, A Romantic Opera in Three Acts (New York: G. Schirmer, 1925), 99.

First published in *Opera Quarterly* 21, no. 3 (2005): 465–85.

But I repeat myself; and in a sense Kurt Weill, in the famous refrain of "Pirate Jenny" from *The Threepenny Opera* (1928) repeated Wagner from eighty-five years before. Weill's refrain has a similar profile to that of Senta's phrase, from her ballad in *The Flying Dutchman* (1843): each melody falls from D to F♯ while traversing a progression that can be construed as a i–V cadence, though Wagner gets to the dominant via the supertonic, and Weill via the subdominant. Critics have sometimes read "Pirate Jenny," with its proletarian barmaid daydreaming of mass murder, as a parody of Wagner's romantical ballad about a girl whose imagination is captured by a sailor cursed to roam the seas forever. But in this chapter I'm going to try to argue that Weill's Pirate Jenny isn't a parody but a reprise of Senta, for Senta herself is a dark character caught up in a black comedy.

The greatest mystery about the composition of *The Flying Dutchman* is its relation to its acknowledged source, Heine's *Aus den Memoiren des Herrn von Schnabelewopski* (1833).[1] In chapters 6 and 7, Heine's hero goes to an Amsterdam theater and sees a play about the Flying Dutchman. He's not particularly excited by what he sees and makes snarky comments on the plot: "Poor Dutchman! He's often happy enough to be redeemed from marriage itself, happy to be released from his redeemer, and then he sets out again on his ship."[2] In fact the Polish nobleman is far less interested in the play than in a seductive blonde spectator who drops an orange peel on his head, whether accidentally or by design. At last he stops pursuing his elective affinities with the blonde long enough to notice what's happening on stage:

> When I returned to the theater, I came upon the play's last scene, where on a high sea cliff the wife of the Flying Dutchman, Mrs. Flying Dutchman, wrings her hands in despair, while on the sea, on the deck of his uncanny ship, her unlucky husband can be seen. He loves her and wants to abandon her, to save her from perishing, and he confesses to her his grisly fate and the terrible curse fallen on him. But she calls with a loud voice, "I have been true to you until this very hour, and I know a sure way of keeping myself true until death!"
>
> At these words the loyal wife plunges into the sea, and now the curse on the Flying Dutchman ends, he is redeemed, and we see the ghostly ship sink into the depths of the sea.
>
> The moral of the play is that women should take care not to marry any Flying Dutchmen; and we men observe from this play how we ruin ourselves through women, even in the most favorable case.[3]

The puzzle is this: Why did Wagner write an opera that seems designed specifically for the sake of being parodied by Heine? Every overblown gesture, farfetched motive, ridiculous piece of behavior that Heine derides, Wagner commits. Furthermore, Wagner's comments on his opera, in *Eine Mittheilung an meine Freunde* (1851), are full of the long-winded, tortuous, superserious rhetoric that invites mockery. Wagner speaks of the story of the Flying Dutchman as "a mythic-poetic creation of the folk: a primeval trait of human nature" and claims that its theme is "the longing for peace in the wake of life's storms."[4] It blends the tales of Odysseus and the Wandering Jew:

> Just as Ahasuerus, he yearns for an end of his sorrows though death. But this redemption, withheld from the Wandering Jew, is put within reach of the Dutchman in the form of—a woman who will sacrifice herself for love. The longing for death drives him to seek out such a woman. But that woman is no longer the domestic paragon, Penelope, as courted in ancient times by Odysseus; it is now the epitome of woman [*das Weib überhaupt*], woman as yet unmanifest, only longed-for, dimly intuited, an infinitely feminine being—let me just say it outright: the *woman of the future*.[5]

Senta, then, isn't a homebody, but instead the "infinitely feminine" woman—the "woman of the future." Wagner seems to dream of a future in which spunky women try to conjure up some fine, damned soul worth dying for. As you can see, it's hard to read this passage without laughing at it.

And yet, it's possible that Wagner's opera has resources of irony not usually ascribed to it. I think that it's a strange combination of the wretched melodrama that Heine imagined, plus the critique that Heine's protagonist made of that melodrama. And it's possible that Senta is not quite the same as those other sleek, muscular virgins who populate Wagner's later operas. When we think of Elisabeth's music in *Tannhäuser* (1845), the first thing that comes to mind is probably her aria of delight in her hall; when we think of Elsa's music in *Lohengrin* (1848), probably her dream of a knight in shining armor; and so on. Wagner's heroines get a lot of excited music in bright, major keys—even Brünnhilde with her *Hojotohos*. But when we think of Senta's music, we think of her ballad, a spooky piece in G minor. The woman of the future stares out at a future that comprises a man she's never met, a man she knows only from a picture and a song. She has assimilated, incorporated the Flying Dutchman into herself; perhaps the woman of the future is the woman who has the farthest psychic reach, the greatest power of empathic imagination. Elsa too is a woman of the future in that she has Lohengrin's music inside her before she meets him. But Lohengrin, except for the taboo concerning his name, isn't a very dangerous character—whereas Senta, by possessing an internal Flying Dutchman, is in a perilous state indeed.

Wagner composed Senta's ballad first, and felt that the rest of the opera was a sort of gigantic expansion of the ballad, which "contained the condensed image of the entire drama."[6] In that sense Senta's sensibility is the matrix in which the whole opera takes place. The Flying Dutchman can be conceived as a demon that projects an aspect of Senta's being, something monstrous, pallid, phallic, intolerable within her.

Much of this strategy comes from the obvious prototype of Senta's ballad, Emmy's romance in Heinrich Marschner's opera *Der Vampyr* (1828), which Wagner had prepared for performance a few years before beginning work on *The Flying Dutchman*:

Sieh, Mutter, dort den bleichen Mann
Mit seelenlosem Blick.
Kind, sieh den bleichen Mann nicht an,
Sonst ist es bald um dich getan,
Weich' schnell von ihm zurück!
Schon manches Mägdlein, jung und schön,
Tat ihm zu tief ins Auge sehn,
Musst' es mit bittern Qualen
Und seinem Blut bezahlen!
Denn still und heimlich sag' ich's dir:
Der bleiche Mann ist ein Vampyr!
Bewahr' uns Gott auf Erden,
Ihm jemals gleich zu werden![7]

See, mother, there, the pale man who seems to have no soul. Child, don't look at him, or you'll be done for—get away from him—now! Many beautiful young girls have stared too deeply into his eyes, and paid for it with their blood! I whisper this secret: the pale man is a vampire! May God keep us from ever becoming like him!

Note that the phrase *Der bleiche Mann* chimes through Wagner's descriptions of the Flying Dutchman; and note that the strophic pairing of ghastly shudder and consoling prayer is identical to that of Senta's ballad. Emmy is a somewhat marginal character, but she gives by far the most melodically intense projection of the vampire that is heard in the opera (figure 3.3). In contrast, the vampire himself is attended by all sort of orchestral twitches and tremors and hoohaas and mournful blats, but his arias tend to be flaccid or shapeless and recitativelike. In Wagner's opera, the Flying Dutchman's own music is impressive and memorable, especially his big aria "Die Frist ist um," but is often not easily parsed into simple, repetitive, melodic units; something of the ocean's uncircumscribability passes into his music. It is as if the tightly constrained, leashed energy in Emmy's romance or Senta's ballad escapes into the free-form rhetoric of the vampire or the Dutchman.

At the end of her romance, Emmy offers a prayer, for she fears that she will herself become a vampire if she's bitten. *The Flying Dutchman* has nothing specifically to do with vampires, but I think that the terror of contagion lurks in the background. Erik doesn't want Senta to fall in love with the Flying Dutchman because he loves her himself. Mary and the spinner girls don't want Senta to become preoccupied with the Flying Dutchman, because it interferes with her work. But behind all of this is a deeper anxiety—that Senta will become, in

Figure 3.3. Marschner: *Der Vampyr*, Emmy's romance, from Heinrich Marschner, *Der Vampyr*, Romantische Oper in zwei Aketen, Dichtung von Wilhelm August Wohlbrück, neu eingerichtet von Hans Pfitzner, Klavierauszug (Berlin: Adolph Fürstner, 1925), 175.

Heine's words, Mrs. Flying Dutchman, a zombie with the rest of the zombie mariners, a damned thing. But she's in a sense prebitten, already turned: when she sings her ballad, with its *Johohoes*, its quotations of the Flying Dutchman's hollow-fifth fanfare, the blood has already drained from her cheeks and her canine teeth have lengthened. She speaks in the Flying Dutchman's voice as she cries out his oath; she hears what Satan hears, she knows what Satan does. Of course she also sings the gentle music of redemption, in the relative major (figure 3.4):

Figure 3.4. Wagner: *The Flying Dutchman,* "Doch kann dem bleichen Manne Erlösung," from Richard Wagner, *The Flying Dutchman (Der fliegende Holländer),* A Romantic Opera in Three Acts (New York: G. Schirmer, 1925), 101.

But such a phrase only balances, and does not cancel out, the diabolical phrase that precedes it (figure 3.5):

Figure 3.5. Wagner: *The Flying Dutchman,* "Johoe! Hui! Wie ein Pfeil fliegt er hin, ohne Ziel," from Richard Wagner, *The Flying Dutchman (Der fliegende Holländer),* A Romantic Opera in Three Acts (New York: G. Schirmer, 1925), 100.

Figure 3.5. *(concluded)*

The extreme chromaticism here foreshadows certain features of late Wagner. Again, Senta really is a woman of the future:

Figure 3.6. Wagner: *Parsifal*, "Hilfe! Herbei!," from Richard Wagner, *Parsifal*, A Stage-Consecrating Festival-Play, Complete Vocal Score by Karl Klindworth (New York: G. Schirmer, n.d.), 209.

One of Senta's futures can be heard in the role of Kundry at the end of Act 2 of *Parsifal* (1882), Wagner's last opera (figure 3.6). Kundry is a temptress, compelled by magic against her will to seduce the pure Parsifal in order to ruin the Knights of the Grail. Like the Dutchman, Kundry is an avatar of Ahasuerus, cursed and immortalized for insulting Christ on the cross.[8] Kundry makes explicit the Dutchman who lurks inside Senta. It is perhaps odd to think of Senta as a forerunner of Kundry, but they are a matched pair. Indeed, *Parsifal* completes an arch begun forty years before with Wagner's first canonical opera, *The Flying Dutchman*. Wagner started thinking about a Parsifal opera only four years after he completed *The Flying Dutchman*—and the kinship shows.

There are a number of occult resemblances between the two operas. To take a small example, the bell music from *Parsifal* is the retrograde of the theme that accompanies the Flying Dutchman's vision of the Last Judgment, in his aria "Die Frist ist um." A pattern of fourths connected by a second—the old romanesca ground bass—is a remarkably frequent musical symbol of apocalyptic transcendence, as in the finale of Mahler's First Symphony (1888) or Philip Glass's *Satyagraha* (1983).

Kundry, like Senta, comprises the full round of salvation and damnation: each works for good and for evil. The sexually experienced Kundry can sing music of the greatest innocence and tenderness, as when she reminds Parsifal of his mother's love for him. The virginal Senta suffers from a sort of libidinous demonic possession when she sings her ballad. This may be another aspect of the woman of the future: she has the whole human repertoire of possible identities within her. Wagner didn't discover Schopenhauer until 1854, when he read the whole of *The World as Will and Idea* (1819) four times; but he felt that his own compositional practice had unconsciously followed the theory even before he knew it. Wagner grew up in an intellectual world shaped to some degree by the German idealist philosophers of the 1790s, such as Fichte, who postulated the existence of an "absolutes Ich," an absolute ego, a single great subject of which every finite subject is a part—any human mind is a fragmentary manifestation of the intelligence that thought the universe into being. Schopenhauer considered that every desiring agent—from a sunflower to a flatworm to Alexander the Great to you yourself, gentle desirer—was an organ or tentacle of the one desiring agent, the one hunger, what he called the Will. Senta and Kundry manifest such a tangle of conflicting desires and possibilities that each is more like the whole Will, the universal subject, than like any particular individual. Perhaps the woman of the future is, simply, everybody at once. Working along Adornian lines, Carolyn Abbate speaks of Kundry as a "metempsychotic" character—that is, an indelible character outside of time or space.[9] I think that it might be argued that Wagner is so given to metempsychosis that all his women are a single woman who mutates endlessly through the whole gamut of the human.

What Madness Sounds Like

With a central character like Senta, ungainly and excessive, erratic, not to say mad, the danger of unintentional comedy is great. Senta's ballad features exactly the same tropes that Purcell uses in "Bess of Bedlam," or that Strauss uses in his Opus 67 Ophelia songs, to indicate insanity—a rapid oscillation, without transition, between contradictory states of affect. Imagine the sort of contemporary opera that could be written about a girl who becomes so enamored of a dragon in a game of Dungeons and Dragons that she thinks the dragon really exists. Then her father shows up at the door with the dragon—swinging the scaly horror of its folded tail but wearing a Spanish hat with a jaunty feather—and urges her to marry it. The only plausible treatment I can imagine is a psychotic farce. To resist this possibility, Wagner keeps the division between salvation and damnation as clear as he can, and he tries to relegate all the comic elements to Daland, the father who tries to arrange the marriage between the unwed and the undead. But the opera has to participate in Senta's fantasy in order to render her a credible and serious character, and every motion toward validating Senta's weird obsession tends to fringe the opera with a certain frivolity. Wagner half-rejects, half-courts, the ridicule of Heine's Herr von Schnabelewopski, or the ridicule of Nietzsche, who puns on "Senta" and "sentimental" in *The Case of Wagner*.[10] Nietzsche also claims that Wagner's heroines are modern hysterics along the lines of Madame Bovary.[11] My guess is that Wagner on some level agreed with this interpretation and tried in a deliberately half-hearted way to avoid it.

Wagner's comments on Senta are peculiar. On one hand he insists that she is heathy, solid, naïve, and Nordic: "Don't construe her dreamy character in terms of a modern, sickly sentimentality!" On the other hand, he says that she suffers from "a powerful delusion [*Wahnsinn*]. . . . It has been observed how Norwegian girls have on occasion succumbed to feeling of such overwhelming strength that a sudden seizure of the heart causes their death."[12] So she suffers from a delusion of such intensity that it causes heart failure, but it is a naïve madness, a folk madness, not a modern, sentimental madness. I feel that Wagner's argument doesn't make sense: Senta's expertise in chromaticism and her participation in an opera of unprecedented motivic sophistication, tend to place her in the modern world. It is true that she is ruined by a folk ballad, or rather a pseudofolk ballad, a cunning fake, whereas Madame Bovary is ruined by slick romance novels, both sentimental and *sentimentalisch* in Schiller's sense. Nevertheless, Senta and Madame Bovary and Francesca da Rimini are all victims of literature, of second-hand experience. Senta is indeed a woman of the past, caught up in archaic fantasy; but she's also a woman of the future and of the present, and of the mental diseases of the present. She is less healthy in herself than sickness's dream of health. Neither in the opera nor in his comments on the opera can Wagner quite dispel the ironic perspective, the inner Heine that see the potential for kitsch, bad faith, general wrongness in Senta's postures of noble self-sacrifice. In theory I disapprove of Harry Kupfer's 1978 Bayreuth production, which makes the opera the delirium of a lunatic Senta, because Kupfer destroys the delicate balance between the ideal and the ironic on which the opera depends; but better Kupfer's production, or a production in which Senta is costumed in a wig with a floor-length blonde braid, and outfitted with eyelashes à la Tammy Faye Bakker and Raggedy Ann splotches of red on her cheeks, than a production that presents Senta without the faintest acknowledgment that one might smile at her behavior.

Opera as Ballad

The Flying Dutchman was one of Wagner's first important experiments with the construction of an elaborate system of musical semantics based on binaries, though the chastity-licentiousness patterns of *Das Liebesverbot* are also fairly well developed. On one hand, eerie chromatics, hollow chords, and dark minor keys are associated with the Flying Dutchman and his mariners; on the other hand, we have the redemptive major tune associated with Senta's self-sacrifice, as well as cheerful sea shanties and spinning songs. On one hand are stiff tenorisms for Erik; on the other hand is jolly buffoonish music for Daland. Comedy and tragedy are kept apart, so that the opera doesn't degenerate into the fatuity that menaces it from every direction. But Wagner—the Heine-esque, ironic Wagner—has interesting ways of subverting his binaries even as he establishes them. The repeated flick of a major second is associated in the overture and the first scene with the storm that brings the Flying Dutchman to land (figure 3.7):

Figure 3.7. Wagner: *The Flying Dutchman*, Overture, storm, from Richard Wagner, *The Flying Dutchman (Der fliegende Holländer)*, A Romantic Opera in Three Acts (New York: G. Schirmer, 1925), 6.

But in the second act, the same figure is an integral part (as Thomas Grey has noticed)[13] of the spinning song (figure 3.8):

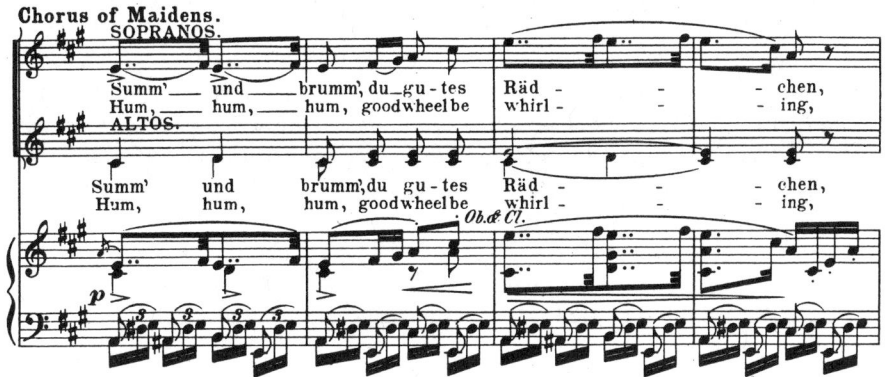

Figure 3.8. Wagner: *The Flying Dutchman,* spinning song figure, from Richard Wagner, *The Flying Dutchman (Der fliegende Holländer),* A Romantic Opera in Three Acts (New York: G. Schirmer, 1925), 79.

And in the third act, we find it again in the great sailors' chorus "Steuermann! Lass die Wacht!" (figure 3.9):

Figure 3.9. Wagner: *The Flying Dutchman,* Steuermann chorus figure, from Richard Wagner, *The Flying Dutchman (Der fliegende Holländer),* A Romantic Opera in Three Acts (New York: G. Schirmer, 1925), 182.

So one single figure can take the form of a buoyant sailors' yell, good for hauling rope or for expressing high spirits; and it can generate the motive force of the spinning wheel, in what Senta herself calls a "dummes Lied," a stupid song; and it can whip up the winds of a ocean storm. (And in a sad lullaby Wagner wrote around 1840, *Dors mon enfant,* the figure lulls a baby to sleep.) It spans the whole gamut of the sacred and profane, the silly and the significant; it's black enough and funny enough to be appropriate to the whole dark comedy. It helps to prepare us for a happy end in which the protagonists drown and a ship sinks with all hands aboard.

And yet there's a sense in which comedy and tragedy are irrelevant categories, because *The Flying Dutchman* is a less a drama per se than a drama yanked out of a narrative, or spliced into a narrative—for so I interpret Wagner's suggestion that the work might be called a "dramatic ballad."[14] This term implies that the personages in the opera are typal and absolute, remote, not warm, immediate, lovable. I've been speaking as if Senta's ballad were Senta's own property, but of course that's partly false: Senta only quotes it as a favorite old song, a song that she doesn't even want to sing herself but has to, since Mary refuses to sing it. Ballads are impersonal, a cold treatment of the hottest emotions, always at a certain aesthetic distance from the singer. Similarly, "Pirate Jenny" doesn't belong to any of the singers in *The Threepenny Opera:* in the first performances it was sung by Polly as a divertissement at her wedding and was only later transferred to the character of the prostitute Jenny, played by Weill's charismatic wife, Lotte Lenya.

When Wagner magnified Senta's ballad into an evening's entertainment, he preserved a balladlike quality in many passages. The first half of Act 3 in particular, with its large rhythm of call and response—first between the Norwegian maidens and the Norwegian sailors, then between the Norwegian sailors and the Flying Dutchman's crew—has the intensifying formality of an old ballad. This section of the opera, like Senta's ballad, was among the first parts that Wagner composed, when his project of writing an opera-poem was fresh in his mind.[15] As he said, he wanted to "relate the legend in a single breath, just as a good poem should be."[16]

One old ballad that illustrates this antiphonal call-and-response technique is the Scottish ballad "Edward," so memorably set by Carl Loewe in 1818, with its colloquy between a mother and a son who has just killed his father. Note the groans of "O!" that mark the shift of speakers:

Und was soll werden dein Hof und Hall?	And what wul ye doe wi' your towirs and your ha,'
Edward, Edward!	Edward, Edward?
und was soll werden dein Hof und Hall?	And what wul ye doe wi' your towirs and your ha,'
so herrlich sonst, so schön, O!	That were sae fair to see, O?
Ach, immer steh's und sink' und fall'!	Ile let thame stand tul they doun fa,'
Mutter, Mutter!	Mither, mither,

Ach, immer steh's und sink' und fall,'	Ile let thame stand tul they doun fa,'
ich werd' es nimmer seh'n! O!	For here nevir mair maun I bee, O.[17]

This dialogue culminates in the son's great curse on his mother. The exclamatory "O!"s might be compared with the cries of *Johohoe* that punctuate Senta's ballad. Wagner was so fond of Loewe's "O!"s that when a singer left them out, he demanded that the singer sing the ballad again, with the "O!"s restored. Wagner scolded him by saying, "Few people can feel how much I live inside this ballad.... Why do you omit this cry of 'O!'?—that is precisely what matters to me."[18] If Wagner lived inside the *Edward* ballad in 1875, he fully stated what it feels like to live inside a ballad—Senta's ballad—in 1843.

Another call-and-response ballad is Goethe's "Erlkönig," with its back-and-forth of a father and his dying son:

Wer reitet so spät durch Nacht und Wind?	Who's riding so late through night and wind?
Es ist der Vater mit seinem Kind;	It is a father, with his son;
er hat den Knaben wohl in dem Arm,	he shelters the child safe in his arm,
Es faßt ihn sicher, er hält ihn warm.	he holds him tight, he keeps him warm.
Mein Sohn, was birgst du so bang dein Gesicht?	My son, why hide your face in fear?
Siehst Vater du den Erlkönig nicht?	Father, see the erl-king there?
Den Erlenkönig mit Kron' und Schweif?	The erl-king, with his cape and crown?
Mein Sohn, es ist ein Nebelstreif.[19]	My son, just a streak of mist on the ground.

If I recall correctly, Wagner preferred Loewe's 1818 setting to Schubert's. I hear in Loewe's setting something of the *tinta* of *The Flying Dutchman*, especially in the phrase "Es ist der Vater mit seinem Kind," not unlike the peremptory motive of the Flying Dutchman himself. *The Flying Dutchman* can be conceived as an enormous ballad for chorus, soloists, and orchestra, into which operatic scenes involving Erik, Daland, and others are inserted, not always with an expert hand.

It is useful to compare *The Flying Dutchman* with the great choral ballads that Schumann wrote at the end of his career, particularly *Des Sängers Fluch* (The Singer's Curse, 1852), to a text by Uhland. Here two singers, an old harper and a young man, come to the king's court and perform some quite disturbing songs. First the young man sings a song from Provence, then the harper sings a ballad (figure 3.10):

In der hohen Hall' saß König Sifried:
"Ihr Harfner, wer weiß mir das schönste Lied?"
Und ein Jüngling trat aus der Schar behende,
Die Harf' in der Hand, das Schwert an der Lende:
"Drei Lieder weiß ich; den ersten Sang,
Den hast du ja wohl vergessen schon lang:
Meinen Bruder hast du meuchlings erstochen,

> Und aber: hast ihn meuchlings erstochen!
> Das andre Lied, das hab' ich erdacht
> In einer finstren, stürmischen Nacht:
> Mußt mit mir fechten auf Leben und Sterben!
> Und aber: mußt fechten auf Leben und Sterben!"
> Da lehnt' er die Harfe an den Tisch,
> Und sie zogen beide die Schwerter frisch,
> Und sie fochten lange mit wildem Schalle,
> Bis der König sank in der hohen Halle.
> "Nun sing' ich das dritte, das schönste Lied,
> Das werd' ich nimmer zu singen müd:
> König Sifried liegt in seinem roten Blut,
> Und aber: liegt in seinem roten Blut!"[20]

In his high hall there sat King Sifried: "Harpers, who among you knows the loveliest song?" And a youth stepped quickly out of the throng, his harp in his hand, his sword at his loins: "I know three songs; the first you've long forgotten: you coward, you stabbed my brother to death, and again: you coward, you stabbed my brother to death! I thought up the next song on a dark stormy night: you must fight with me till one of us dies! and again: you must fight with me till one of us dies!" Then he rested his harp on the table, and they both briskly drew their swords, and with wild noise they fought long, until the king sank in the high hall. "Now I'll sing the third song, the loveliest of all, that I will never grow tired of singing: King Sifried lies in a red pool of blood, and again: King Sifried lies in a red pool of blood."

The king smells a rat when he hear this song—no fool, he. This ballad is the kernel of the whole work, which is a strange conglomeration of narration and drama, though the plot eventually reverses the outcome of the ballad: the king kills the young man. But the singer has his revenge after all, for the king is forgotten by history, and his palace falls into ruin. Schumann was not altogether delighted by *The Flying Dutchman*, which he considered excessively somber.[21] In effect Schumann showed Wagner how the material of *The Flying Dutchman* could have be reconstructed as a choral ballad, even briefer than the one-act curtain-raiser that Wagner originally intended.[22] Schumann's work is only about a half-hour long but covers a wide range of feeling and event with remarkable intensity. The line between German romantic opera and choral ballad is thin. I suspect that the striking difference in nineteenth-century opera between German and Italian musical methods of characterization is partly caused by the debt of German opera to the ballad. Manrico and Leonora and the conte di Luna are distinct autonomous personages whose clashing desires generate the plot. Senta and the Flying Dutchman tend to melt together, sing one another's music, and rise together into the sky ringed with a single transfiguring halo, for they are only provisional avatars of an absolute desire that transcends them. It is not that the characters seek adequate expression through music: the music is primary, and it frames the characters, generates the characters. *Prima la musica, dopo i ruoli.*

Figure 3.10. Schumann: *Des Sängers Fluch*, Curse, from Robert Schumann, *Des Sängers Fluch*, Ballade nach Ludwig Uhland bearbeitet von Richard Pohl, für Solostimmen, Chor und Orchester, Op. 139, Klavierauszug (Wiesbaden: Breitkopf & Härtel, n.d.), 17.

When Wagner in 1851 spoke of the Flying Dutchman as "a mythic-poetic creation of the folk: a primeval trait of human nature," he was in the process of refiguring his opera according to his mature aesthetic. In his later music dramas Wagner sometimes sought some archaic musical truth as a sort of irrefutable foundation for his tonal architecture; the music of the future could exist only if established on some firm ground of the distant past. In *Tannhäuser* this *Urlaut* is represented by the *Minnesang* of Wolfram von Eschenbach and Walter von der

Vogelweide; in *Die Meistersinger* (1868) by the *Meistergesang* of the historical Hans Sachs and his comrades; in *The Ring of the Nibelung* by the simple device of the fundamental note of a triad, the great low E♭ at the beginning of *The Rhinegold*, the cosmic diapason. In the case of *Minnesang* and *Meistergesang* Wagner offered only specious substitutes, sometimes because little good information about the originals was available to him. But the primal musical entity of *The Flying Dutchman* is the ballad, and Wagner knew ballads. In some ways the continuity of the music of the past and the music of the future can be better illustrated by *The Flying Dutchman* than by the works, often quite superior works, which followed it.

The Dutchman's Afterlife

This essay began with some thoughts about the woman of the future. I'll conclude by glancing at some of the uses that the composers of the twentieth century made of Wagner's opera—that is, the music of *The Flying Dutchman*'s own future. One of the odd aspects of *The Flying Dutchman*'s voyage through music history is that the comic aspects have been prominent, not the *Schauerromantik;* it is as if the spirit of Heine kept peeking through the sober Wagnerian mask. At the end of Richard Strauss's second opera *Feuersnot* (Fire Famine, 1901), the magician hero Kunrad sings the praises of his illustrious predecessor magician, Meister Reichhart (that is, Richard Wagner), driven away by the townsmen of Munich. Kunrad tells the locals that Meister Reichhart tried to improve their lives by giving them wheels, but they preferred to crawl on all fours (figure 3.11). *Wagner* is German for wheelwright, and *Strauss* can mean *strife*, in addition to its more usual meanings of *bouquet* or *ostrich:*

> damit den Pfäfflein und alten Weiben
> nit etwa der Schnaufer möcht' ausbleiben.
> Sein Wagen kam allzu gewagt Euch vor,
> da triebt Ihr den Wagner aus dem Thor—
> den bösen Feind, den triebt Ihr nit aus—
> der stellt sich Euch immer auf's Neue zum Strauss.[23]

> [You wanted to keep up your slow trot,] so that not even the fellow panting heavily would get left behind with the old women and the little priests. His wagon happened by all too boldly for you, so you drove the wagoner from the gate— but you didn't drive the evil fiend away, for he puts himself anew to battle.

Here the Flying Dutchman theme becomes a smiling symbol for Wagner himself, considered as a force for progress, for mobility, as relentless a voyager through the mysteries of music as the Flying Dutchman was across the world's oceans.

Our next stop on the Flying Dutchman tour will be Walter Braunfels's charming opera *Die Vögel* (The Birds, 1920), based on Aristophanes. Here the Wren wakes up the Hoopoe to the tune of Wagner's spinning song. The Hoopoe is the king of the birds, once a human being, but now demoted; and in a sense the spinning song has suffered a demotion too, to the status of ornithological alarm clock.

Figure 3.11. Strauss: *Feuersnot*, Meister Reichhart, from Richard Strauss, *Feuersnot*, Op. 50, Ein Singgedicht in einem Akt von Ernst von Wolzogen, Klavierauszug von Otto Singer (Berlin: Adolph Fürstner, n.d.), 156.

 The most explicitly amusing use of *The Flying Dutchman* in twentieth-century music is Hindemith's string quartet called *Ouvertüre zum "Fliegenden Holländer" für Streichquartett, wie sie eine schlechte Kurkapelle morgens um 7 am Brunnen vom Blatt spielt* (Overture to The Flying Dutchman, as Sight-read by a poor Concert Orchestra at the Village Well at 7 o'clock in the Morning, ca. 1925). It is possible that Hindemith meant to satirize not Wagner but the hung-over musicians. Or it is possible that Hindemith wished to provide an acoustic image for the twisted way in which Nazi Wagnerites hear Wagner's music. (Hindemith was writing antimilitaristic satires, such as *Minimax*, during these years.) Or it is possible, given Hindemith's ready exasperation with certain trends in twentieth-century music, that his ridicule fell on certain ostentatiously dissonant composers, equated here with incompetent performers. A little later in the piece, the performers seem to get their sheet music mixed up, and start to play something that sounds like crackpot Johann Strauss. Perhaps the musicians would really prefer to be performing a little waltz, or perhaps Hindemith has an eye on composers who introduce popular music into serious pieces of music. In this sense Wagner's overture stands for "serious" music—and yet serious music that's oddly vulnerable to comic reconstitution. Heine, so to speak, laughed at Wagner's opera before it was even written; Hindemith is continuing a century-long tradition.

The Penelope or Senta at the end of the Flying Dutchman's sail through the century turned out to be Michael Tippett. In 1970 Tippett finished an opera called *The Knot Garden,* partly based on Shakespeare's *The Tempest,* but updated: Prospero is a psychoanalyst, Ariel is a Jewish composer named Dov, and Caliban is a black writer named Mel. Dov and Mel are homosexual lovers. As Tippett was completing the opera, he found that he had more to say about the character Dov than would fit into the drama, so he composed a sort of parergon for tenor and orchestra called *Songs for Dov.* Dov, it turns out, is not only a Jew but a Wandering Jew, always traveling, looking for a refuge that he will never find. At the beginning of the second song, Dov remembers Mignon's song from Goethe's *Wilhelm Meister,* "Know you the land where lemon bushes flower?" and he remembers other things as well (figure 3.12):

"Know you the land where lemon bushes flower?"
That's what the boy-girl sang
while the Ancient twanged his harp.
Sound, sound my harp!
"Mignon, Mignon" I cry.
"Shall I hurry to that land of flowering lemon?
Shall I, shall I?
The live horse
The iron horse,
Pegasus, the flying horse
(Or that Flying Dutchman)
It's all one.
"Smokes like lightning, shines like gold"
Ride off into the sunset
I'm on my way.[24]

"Smokes like lightning, shines like gold" is the first line of a blues song by Lightnin' Hopkins, concerning his dead baby. "I'm on my way" is Porgy's line at the end of *Porgy and Bess:* "O Lawd, I'm on my way I'm on my way to the Heavenly lan'." Dov is traveling not only over the surface of the earth but through the history of music, from primitive yelps and barks to pop songs to classical melisma. The rootless, ironic cosmopolitan seem to hanker after the simple directness of the blues. Perhaps that explains why he first fell in love with a black man, Mel-Caliban. I take it that this song, like "Pirate Jenny," isn't a parody of *The Flying Dutchman* but a revisiting of Wagner's own themes. The Flying Dutchman too is a modern man, full of advanced harmony and up-to-the-minute styles of declamation, lost on the infinite seas of modern art and eager to find some more limited and agreeable mode of life, mode of music. But he can't simply revert to his former life stuck inside a ballad; he's spilled out, diffused into chromaticism and irony and dark jokes, and no pressure will be enough to get him inside the bottle once again. Just as Tippett says he is, the Flying Dutchman is Ariel, the genius of imagination.

Figure 3.12. Tippett: *Songs for Dov,* "The Flying Dutchman," from Michael Tippett, *Songs for Dov,* for Tenor and Orchestra, music and text by Michael Tippett (London: Schott, 1970), 33. © 1972 by Schott Music. © Renewed. All rights reserved. Used by permission of European American Music Distributors LLC, sole U.S. and Canadian agent for Schott Music.

Chapter Four

Les Troyens

The Undoing of Opera

Berlioz found it easier to make money as a critic than as a composer, and much of his music is essentially critical in character. *Les Troyens,* for example, can be understood as a critique of opera and a critique of epic.

In the French imagination, opera and epic were only hazily separated. In the Diderot-d'Alembert *Encyclopédie,* the author of the entry on opera (Louis de Jaucourt) defines opera as follows:

> As to its dramatic aspect, an opera is the representation of a marvelous action. It is the divine of the epic turned into spectacle. Since the actors are gods or half-divine heroes, they must declare themselves to mortals through manners of action, diction, and vocal inflection that defy the laws of ordinary probability. They do things that look like wonders. The sky opens, chaos resolves, the elements show themselves in turn, a celestial being is wafted on a luminous cloud; an enchanted palace vanishes at a casual sign and transforms itself into a desert, etc.[1]

We may scratch our heads when we read this, because we're accustomed to thinking of opera in quite a different way. For Jaucourt, opera was the god-haunted domain of Lully and Rameau, a place of superhuman emphasis of passion and impossibly expensive stage effects. But our most popular operas concern not Juno and Hippolytus and Zoroaster but a Spanish gypsy, a French prostitute, a barber in Seville, a Sicilian roughneck, and a clutch of starving young artists in Paris. If these operas are expensive, it's mostly because good singers aren't easy to come by. The staging itself of *Carmen, La traviata, Cavalleria rusticana, La bohème,* and so forth doesn't require flying machines, collapsing palaces, or panoramas of chaos resolving itself into cosmos.

And yet, if Jaucourt were hauled into the twenty-first century, he might be able to argue his thesis. Carmen is a gypsy, but an unusually potent kind of gypsy, as Théophile Gautier noted in an 1872 poem:

> Carmen is thin,—a streak of black
> Circles round her gypsy eye.
> Her hair is dangerously black,
> Her skin, a devil burned it raw.

> The women say that she is ugly,
> The men are mad about her flesh:
> The archbishop of Toledo sings
> Upon devoted knees the mass.
>
> Her piquant, stinging ugliness
> Has a grain of that sea-salt
> From bitter seas where Venus rose
> Naked, with a sour smell.[2]

This poem concerns not Bizet's opera—Gautier died before its premiere—but the Prosper Mérimée novel on which Bizet's opera is based. But Bizet's Carmen is similar: a scruffy, sulky version of Venus herself. In the bourgeois opera, the characters are still gods, gods whose extraterrestrial intensity of feeling has been translated into some domain of the commonplace. They may wear ordinary clothes, but through the costumes they burn with an eerie glow.

Jaucourt further notes that operas are neither tragedies nor comedies, and are highly irregular in dramatic construction. We often complain of the unintelligibility or absurdity of the plots of such operas as *Il trovatore*, but as far as Jaucourt was concerned a sprawling, complicated, willfully knotted plot was just the sort of thing most appropriate for the genre. An opera isn't a play that observes the old unities of time, place, and action: an opera is a mishmash of miracles, designed only to produce awe. The word that Jaucourt uses is *epic:* "C'est le divin de l'épopée mis en spectacle."[3] ([An opera] is the divine of the epic rendered as spectacle.) An epic, of course, is pure sprawl, a poem that, in the case of the *Odyssey* and the *Aeneid,* covers many years of travel across the whole Mediterranean basin, including places that don't actually exist. Jaucourt seems to consider an opera a highlight reel excerpted from an epic, an anthology of stupendous moments, all chills and thrills without any of the boring intervening matter necessary to establish plausibility, logic, and so forth.

So according to Jaucourt's theory of opera, Meyerbeer got it right and Wagner got it wrong. Wagner considered a Meyerbeer opera a series of effects without causes, "a monstrously piebald, historico-romantic, diabolico-religious, fanatico-voluptuous, frivolo-sacred, mysterio-jaunty, sentimento-knavish dramatic hodge-podge."[4] Exactly—Meyerbeer was the perfect opera composer. Wagner, on the other hand, by trying to impose on his gods the law of necessity, by putting them under the iron scepter of cause and effect, *dike,* had to pad out his operas with a great deal of low-intensity material designed to establish motive and provide an exposition of background. From a Jaucourtian point of view, nothing is more hostile to opera than the notion of a *Gesamtkunstwerk,* a music drama that fully integrates all its elements.

Now to Berlioz. We have been looking at one strand of the opera discourse of the world in which Berlioz lived. But Berlioz was far more attracted to a strand that completely contradicted it, the tradition of Gluck. Berlioz was so besotted with Gluck that he wrote what amounts to a book on Gluck's *Alceste* and devised the standard performing edition (still in use in some quarters) of Gluck's *Orphée et Eurydice*. According to the doctrine of Gluckian reform, opera should be swift, linear, and dramatically pointed. As Gluck (or his librettist Rainer Calzabigi) says in his preface to *Alceste* (published in 1769), "I have striven to restrict music to its true office of serving poetry by means of expression and by following the situations of the story, without interrupting the action or stifling it with a useless superfluity of ornaments. . . . I have sought to abolish all the abuses against which good sense and reason have long cried out in vain."[5] But what Gluck calls abuse, Jaucourt calls opera itself: a string of irrational, boggling marvels, whether marvels of vocal prowess or marvels of set design. Gluck has little to do with the epic: he is concerned with tragic drama and likes libretti based on actual Greek tragedies, preferably by Euripides.

For all Berlioz's admiration of Gluck, Berlioz was not by nature an instinctive Aristotelian. He was an instinctive epicist, drawn to operatic situations too huge and unwieldy to fit in an opera house: the action of *La damnation de Faust,* for example, zooms effortlessly from the plains of Hungary to Faust's study to will-o'-the-wisp-land to hell to heaven. It is hard to squeeze onto a stage, partly because Berlioz, barred from the only house in Paris that could have produced it, wrote it as a concert piece, and partly because the only opera that really attracted Berlioz was impossible opera. When Berlioz, aging and ill, took a dare from a princess and composed *Les Troyens* (mostly between 1856 and 1858), he did not compromise. He tried to realize on stage not just a miscellany of jaw-dropping epic effects, but the actual aesthetic of Virgil's *Aeneid,* as shown in two episodes (from Book II and Book IV) carefully chosen for the sake of stageworthiness.

I'm fascinated by Jaucourt's notion that the opera is epic rather dramatic in character, but it is nevertheless true that actual classical epics have been of limited interest to opera composers. Cavalli and Purcell wrote important Dido operas, and there are a number of settings of Metastasio's *Didone abbandonata*. Berlioz himself knew Piccinni's *Didon,* and some of the text of *Les Troyens* echoes lines from Piccinni's libretto.[6] But it's fairly easy to plunk the Dido episode onto a standard operatic template and cut it to shape, without trying to deal with its Virgilian context—though Cavalli's *La Didone* (1641), in its way as impressive an achievement as *Les Troyens,* has a number of epic features, including a hunter's present-tense narrative of the storm and the lightning-struck tree and the scurrying for shelter of all living things, including, of course, Dido and Aeneas. Opera is epic in its desire to present stupendous passion, but opera has traditionally shied away from other aspects of the epic: its recitedness, its ease of movement through time and space, its immense cultural comprehension.

Homer's epics are oral and formulaic in character: the stock epithets ("rosy-fingered dawn," "wine-dark sea") are metrical blocks easily chunked into the poem, to allow the reciter a moment's pause while he thought about what to sing next. Because Homer is telling the story all by himself, he can range freely over the zodiac of his wit, moving effortlessly from the past to the future, from

Phaeacia to the clouds above Olympos. Virgil, on the other hand, did not rely on oral transmission to produce the *Aeneid:* it is a sort of literary simulation of an oral epic. He wrote it, and, if his executors had carried out his command to destroy the poem, it would be as if it had never existed at all.

Berlioz took this process one step further: there are signs in *Les Troyens* that he conceived the opera as an operatic simulation of a literary simulation of an oral epic. In a letter to Princess Caroline Sayn-Wittgenstein (12 August 1856), Berlioz prays that all of Virgil's gods assist him in the task of composing his opera, and signs himself "Your grateful and devoted Iopas."[7] Berlioz's identification with Iopas is interesting, because Iopas is the chief singer and myth maker of Dido's court, as Virgil has it at the end of the first book.

> The goblet goes around: Iopas brought
> His golden lyre, and sung what ancient Atlas taught:
> The various labors of the wand'ring moon,
> And whence proceed th' eclipses of the sun;
> Th' original of men and beasts; and whence
> The rains arise, and fires their warmth dispense,
> And fix'd and erring stars dispose their influence. . . .[8]

Iopas entertains Aeneas and Dido with these cosmological tales. Then Aeneas proceeds to tell Dido at length of the smuggling of the wooden horse into Troy and the havoc and ruin that followed. It's as if behind all the storytellers of the epic—behind Virgil, behind Aeneas—is the benign presence of Iopas, singing the universe into being, stating the great tale that comprises all lesser tales, even the *Aeneid* itself. On Atlas's shoulders the world rests; on Iopas's harp the world of language rests.

In *Les Troyens,* Iopas sings how the blonde Ceres makes the land fertile, how the timid bird and the silly lamb and the winds of the plain all sing her blessings (No. 34, "O blonde Cérès"). He sings with a certain effortless, formal aplomb. Dido finally interrupts him in order to hear more of Aeneas's exciting tales of the escape from Troy. But Iopas has done his work by calming Dido's anxious heart, by casting a spell of fertility, sexuality, on the queen. Just as Othello seduces Desdemona with his tales of marvels—the anthropophagi and the men whose heads do grow beneath their shoulders—so Aeneas seduces Dido through narrative. Iopas is a professional reciter, but Aeneas is a talented amateur: the characters in the opera are chock full of stories. Sometimes Berlioz's orchestra functions dramatically, in the Gluck mode, by reinforcing the emotional tonality of the actors in a scene. But in some of the score's memorable moments, the orchestra functions epically by illustrating a narrated event. A fine example occurs at Aeneas's entrance in Act 1 (No. 7, "Du peuple et des soldats"), as the hero tells how two great serpents rose from the sea, wound the priest Laocoön in their coils, and breathed fire on him. In this passage the orchestra itself is Iopas, supporting all finite tales with its infinite resources of expression, such as the queasy blats of the seasick lower brass. Much of the action in an epic is not direct action at all but virtual action, action embedded in stories narrated by the characters themselves. For example, the befooling of Polyphemus, the escape from Circe, the descent into Hades, and most of Odysseus's other famous adventures are told indirectly in stories Odysseus narrates at the Phaeacian banquet. In Berlioz's opera, the epic tissue that holds all the subordinate stories in place is the orchestra.

The three most important characters in *Les Troyens* are Aeneas, Dido, and Cassandra. But Cassandra is not herself a character in the *Aeneid*. She exists only as a virtual presence, a personage in Aeneas's tale to Dido about the last days of Troy. It was Berlioz's decision to promote her into an actual *dramatis persona*. She retains, however, certain vestiges of nonexistence. Berlioz gives her striking music, and she registers on the audience as a figure of power, as in the upsurging figure at the beginning of her great aria (No. 2, "Les Grecs ont disparu!") (figure 4.1).

On the other hand, she scarcely registers at all on the other characters in the opera. She's a sort of televised image so faint that it scarcely be discerned at all. Corebus is sick with love for her, but he might just as well be sick with love for a statue or a phantom. He pays no attention to what she says—this is of course the curse under which she labors—and he refuses to abandon Troy despite her potent pleas. Because no one listens to her, she is in effect a ghost while still alive. Even the upsurging figure at the beginning of the aria is music appropriate for the rising of an apparition out of thin air; it is music fit for a spectre of doom, not for a mortal woman. When Cassandra commits suicide at the end of Act 2, she is only taking a further step along her protracted journey into unreality.

Cassandra is also unreal in that her mind operates in a condition of extreme temporal destabilization—she is paranormal, paranoid, para-everything. Her grasp on the present instant is weak: before her eyes is a continual spectacle of catastrophe and a vision of the new Troy that Aeneas will establish in Italy. When her prophecy of ruin comes to pass, she snatches a lyre from a woman's hand and starts to sing. A captain sees her in full exultation, and calls her "a blue-eyed Bacchante drunk with harmony" (No. 16, Act 2 Finale). The boundary between singer and song is starting to blur: Cassandra, an artifact of song, herself becomes a rhapsode, an inspired bard chanting an epic. Not only is *Les Troyens* an epic, but its characters aspire to becom epicists themselves.

The threshold between the living and the dead is equally unclear. In a letter to Hans von Bülow (20 January 1858), Berlioz compares his labor on *Les Troyens* to that of Sisyphus: "Je continue à rouler mon rocher" [I keep on rolling my rock].[9] Berlioz's characters themselves seem to dwell in Hades. The voices of the dead are never far from Aeneas's ears. A music rhetoric of infernal prophecy takes shape as we hear the opera. At the beginning of Act 2, the shade of Hector appears to the dreaming Aeneas, chanting of the coming storm of flame and Aeneas' heroic death in faraway Italy (No. 12, "Ah! . . . fuis, fils de Vénus!") (figure 4.2). The shade sings each of his lines on a single note, descending through the chromatic scale, until the apparition vanishes and his voice is lost in the depths of the orchestra.

Figure 4.1. Berlioz: *Les Troyens,* Cassandre, from Hector Berlioz, *Les Troyens*, Grand Opéra en cinq actes, Partition chant et piano orientée à l'original de la Nouvelle Édition Berlioz d'Eike Wernhard, ed. Hugh Macdonald (Kassel: Bärenreiter, ca. 2003), 22. © 1969 by Bärenreiter. © Renewed. All rights reserved. Used by permission of European American Music Distributors LLC, sole U.S. and Canadian agent for Bärenreiter.

Figure 4.2. Berlioz: *Les Troyens,* "Ah! . . . fuis," from Hector Berlioz, *Les Troyens*, Grand Opéra en cinq actes, Partition chant et piano orientée à l'original de la Nouvelle Édition Berlioz d'Eike Wernhard, ed. Hugh Macdonald (Kassel: Bärenreiter, ca. 2003), 162. © 1969 by Bärenreiter. © Renewed. All rights reserved. Used by permission of European American Music Distributors LLC, sole U.S. and Canadian agent for Bärenreiter.

Hector is a figment of voice, a demipersonification of some huge imaginary speech—the talkiness of epic turned into a stage presence of noble gloom. Much later in the opera, in Act 5, Aeneas, torn between love of Dido and the command to recreate in Italy his extinct civilization, sings his big aria (No. 41, "Inutiles regrets"); immediately thereafter the specters of Hector, Priam, Corebus, and Cassandra form a kind of ghost box around him (No. 42, "Scène: Énée! . . . [Les ombres]"), hemming him in from all directions, constituting a little hell for the living hero. Cassandra even seems to lose her sex. Her ghost never sings except in tandem with Hector's, as if in the underworld there is no personal agency, only a common voice. Melodic movement has nearly vanished; the specters assail Aeneas in an impersonal monotone, a gray discourse, so quiet and urgent that it becomes a sort of talking silence.

Aeneas and Dido are recognizably operatic characters, thrilling in their bravery of passion, in the old Gluck tradition; but they do not feel inexhaustible, in the way that Orfeo or Carmen or Siegfried feel inexhaustible. Dido and Aeneas spend themselves and are quenched. Aeneas becomes unable to engage in further dialogue or action, patiently outwaiting Dido's contumely, while Dido sinks, out of breath, into quotation—a quotation of her love duet with Aeneas (No. 48, "Adieu, beau ciel d'Afrique, astres que j'admirai") (figure 4.3).

This might feel like the residue of a fast-evaporating mad scene in the tradition of *Lucia di Lammermoor,* but I hear it more as Dido's self-abandonment to old tunes and vain words. Her whole character was patched together from operatic remnants of pride, devotion, jealousy, and *amour fou,* but now the stitches are coming apart, and she is becoming phantasmagorical, even to herself. Like Cassandra, Dido loses her hold on her present situation and drifts into the future: she calls on an unborn Carthiginian, Hannibal, to avenge on Rome the harm that Aeneas did to her. And like Cassandra, she is a kind of ghost, a chimera of violent feeling, even while she is alive. In the last scene she seems to be losing melody, dwindling toward that single note that is the only pitch left to the dead.

Even during the great love duet in Act 4 (No. 37, "Nuit d'ivresse"), the most imposing and impassioned vocal music Berlioz ever wrote, Dido is conscious of her own literariness; she knows that she's a character in an epic. The love duet was the germ of the whole *Troyens,* the first music that Berlioz composed for this opera. He based his text not only Virgil but also on Shakespeare:

> The moon shines bright: in such a night as this,
> When the sweet wind did gently kiss the trees,
> And they did make no noise, in such a night
> Troilus methinks mounted the Troyan walls,
> And sigh'd his soul toward the Grecian tents,
> Where Cressid lay that night.[10]

Figure 4.3. Berlioz: *Les Troyens*, "Adieu, beau ciel d'Afrique, astres que j'admirai," from Hector Berlioz, *Les Troyens*, Grand Opéra en cinq actes, Partition chant et piano orientée à l'original de la Nouvelle Édition Berlioz d'Eike Wernhard, ed. Hugh Macdonald (Kassel: Bärenreiter, ca. 2003), 515. © 1969 by Bärenreiter. © Renewed. All rights reserved. Used by permission of European American Music Distributors LLC, sole U.S. and Canadian agent for Bärenreiter.

This is part of Lorenzo's courting of Jessica in *The Merchant of Venice*. Berlioz adapted it thus:

> *Dido.* Par une telle nuit, le front ceint de cytise,
> Votre mère Vénus suivit le bel Anchise
> Aus bosquets de l'Ida.
> *Aeneas.* Par une telle nuit, fou d'amour et de joie,
> Troïlus vint attendre aux pieds des murs de Troie
> La belle Cressida.[11]

> *Dido.* On such a night, her head enwreathed with blossom,
> Your handsome father lay on Venus's bosom,
> On Ida's mountain thicket.
> *Aeneas.* On such a night, mad with love and joy,
> Troilus waited by the lofty walls of Troy
> For the lovely form of Cressida.

Berlioz shares with Wagner a certain sense that sexual feeling is a state of parasympathetic arousal, most intense when you are half-asleep. Many of Berlioz's greatest sex scenes are nocturnes. The sinuous beauty of the melodies makes it hard to attend to the words, but the words are disturbing. Never mind that Shakespeare's text concerns a businessman wooing a usurer's daughter with an expensive and carefully planned musical show; it is enough to note what Dido and Aeneas are saying. *He* says that this night as a glorious as the night that brought Cressida to Troilus—Cressida a lover proverbial for faithlessness. *She* says that this night has just as much charm as the night when you, Aeneas, were conceived by your mom and dad. These are not necessarily the thoughts that lead to a happy night of sexual abandon.

One of Shakespeare's favorite tricks, when he writes plays set in classical antiquity, is to make his characters oddly aware of their status as proverbs. In *Troilus and Cressida,* there is a moment when Cressida tries to avert her own future ill repute:

O you gods divine,
Make Cressid's name the very crown of falsehood,
If ever she leave Troilus![12]

Shakespeare's Cleopatra is even conscious that some day she will become a character played on stage by a male actor, as if she has a foreglimpse of the Elizabethan stage:

the quick comedians
Extemporally will stage us, and present
Our Alexandrian revels; Antony
Shall be brought drunken forth, and I shall see
Some squeaking Cleopatra boy my greatness
I' the posture of a whore.[13]

Berlioz's Dido also sees herself through posterity's eyes, as a heroine of a love story walking in the footsteps of previous heroines of love stories. Just before her suicide, she declares, "Mon souvenir vivra parmi les âges." (My memory will last through all ages.) In *The Merchant of Venice* there's a passage from the Lorenzo-Jessica dialogue that Berlioz failed to translate:

Lorenzo. In such a night
Stood Dido with a willow in her hand
Upon the wild sea-banks, and waft her love
To come again to Carthage.[14]

But this unsung verse haunts Berlioz's whole love duet: Aeneas and Dido are small, sad, distant characters in their own rhetoric of rapture.

The epicizing of the opera is best shown by the ways in which the operatic sections keep losing voice, trailing off into pantomime. Berlioz was a Gluckist, but nevertheless he disliked Gluck's insistence that music was an adjunct to drama. As Berlioz wrote in an 1856 letter to Princess Caroline Sayn-Wittgenstein:

> The most difficult task is to find the musical *form*, this form without which music does not exist, or is only the craven servant of speech. This is Wagner's crime; he would like to dethrone music, and reduce it to "expressive accents," exaggerating the system of Gluck, who, fortunately, did not succeed in carrying out his ungodly theory. I am in favour of the kind of music you call *free*. Yes, free and proud and sovereign and triumphant, I want it to grasp and assimilate everything, and have no Alps nor Pyrenees to block its way; but to make conquests, music must fight in person, and not merely by its lieutenants; I should like music if possible to have fine verses ranged in battle order, but it must itself lead the attack like Napoleon, it must march in the front rank of the phalanx like Alexander. Music is so powerful that is can sometimes conquer on its own, and has a thousand times claimed the right to say, like Medea: "Moi, c'est assez." To want to tie it down to the old kind of recitation of the ancient choros is the most incredible, and, mercifully, the most fruitless folly ever recorded in the history of art.[15]

In his dramatic symphony *Roméo et Juliette* (1839) Berlioz created a *scène d'amour* in which the voices of Romeo and Juliette were represented purely by orchestral means. In *Les Troyens* the tenor and the soprano sink into darkness while the orchestra—like the voice of the epic reciter—continues to trace delicate figurations of caress. At the end, as a shaft of moonlight falls on Aeneas's armor, the pantomime figure of Mercury—or not quite pantomime, since he does sing a single word, "Italie!"—descends to remind Aeneas of his duty to depart. Berlioz abandons the operatic aspect in favor of epic narration via music, music marching in front of the phalanx of words.

At the beginning of Act 5, the young sailor Hylas falls asleep in the midst of his aria (No. 38, "Vallon sonore"). He dozes off before he can complete the refrain line "Ô puissante mer, l'enfant," with its last words, "de Dindyme!" (This refers to a mountain in Phrygia associated with the goddess Cybele, so prettily hymned by the Trojan virgins in Act 2). In Berlioz's opera, the singers can only sporadically maintain a hold on song. It is telling that the opera's most famous number is a pure pantomime scene, the "Royal Hunt and Storm" (No. 29), where Dido and Aeneas take shelter and consummate their love. The music illustrates the bursting into flames of a tree struck by lightning, and the mad dance of satyrs as they wave the burning branches.

Figure 4.4. Berlioz: *Les Troyens,* satyrs' dance, from Hector Berlioz, *Les Troyens,* Grand Opéra en cinq actes, Partition chant et piano orientée à l'original de la Nouvelle Édition Berlioz d'Eike Wernhard, ed. Hugh Macdonald (Kassel: Bärenreiter, ca. 2003), 351. © 1969 by Bärenreiter. © Renewed. All rights reserved. Used by permission of European American Music Distributors LLC, sole U.S. and Canadian agent for Bärenreiter.

This is the musical equivalent of a Delacroix painting, a study in swirling oils (figure 4.4). Earlier, in Act 1 (No. 6), we heard another pantomime, as Hector's widow and young son lay flowers by the altar to a sober simple clarinet melody—the musical equivalent of a frieze on a tomb (figure 4.5).

Other mime or dance scenes depict wrestling matches; celebratory processions of masons, sailors, and agricultural workers; and even a ballet of Nubian slave girls singing a made-up language (No. 33c). The orchestra and the mime scenes give us a good deal of Troy, the whole of Carthage, and something of the rest of Africa as well—sometimes excitingly, sometimes in a somewhat chill mode of silent recitation. If an epic is a poem about the coming into being of a civilization, its purchase on its values, then *Les Troyens* is a powerfully epic work. Just as the Trojan Horse looms over the set in some stagings of the end of Act 2, so the majesty and fret of civilization itself looms over the whole opera, reducing the size of the individual characters.

But if there are antioperatic aspects to *Les Troyens,* there are also antiepic aspects. Virgil wrote the *Aeneid* to praise Rome and Rome's emperor by establishing

Figure 4.5. Berlioz: *Les Troyens,* Andromaque, from Hector Berlioz, *Les Troyens,* Grand Opéra en cinq actes, Partition chant et piano orientée à l'original de la Nouvelle Édition Berlioz d'Eike Wernhard, ed. Hugh Macdonald (Kassel: Bärenreiter, ca. 2003), 76. © 1969 by Bärenreiter. © Renewed. All rights reserved. Used by permission of European American Music Distributors LLC, sole U.S. and Canadian agent for Bärenreiter.

a single chain of events linking Aeneas to Augustus. In Book 6, set in the underworld, the shade of Anchises shows Aeneas a haze of souls, those who will be reborn as Aeneas's children and grandchildren and remote descendants, all the way down to Virgil's present day. But Berlioz's own sojourn in Italy was not happy, and he thought Aeneas basically detestable: if Virgil's usual epithet is "pious Aeneas," Berlioz's usual epithet is "that hypocrite Aeneas." Within *Les Troyens,* Italy's future magnificence is only a mirage, whereas the destruction of Troy is vivid. Berlioz waves the banner of African civic glory throughout Acts 3 and 4—in fact my favorite of all national anthems is the anthem that Berlioz wrote for archaic Carthage (No. 18). But when Dido dies it seems that Carthage's soul is crushed, and the city grows hollow, scooped-out, threatened by a sort of implosion. A classical epic does not end with irony, with curses against an as yet nonexistent place; but that's how *Les Troyens* concludes.

And yet, not all epics are classical epics. In one kind of epic that I haven't yet mentioned, irony, sarcasm, lasciviousness, frivolity have a major role; collapse and undoing are part of the normal rhythm of things. I mean the romance epics of the sixteenth century, particularly the *Orlando Furioso* of Ariosto, in which naked women do a fair amount of writhing, and one fellow flies to the moon to try to recover Orlando's lost wits. The romance epic typically promotes a minor episode from the *Odyssey*—Odysseus's troubles with Circe, who turns his men into swine—into a central plot element. In *Orlando Furioso* the witch Alcina imprisons the hero, Ruggiero, in a castle on her magic island; in Spenser's *Faerie Queene,*

Figure 4.6. Berlioz: *Les Troyens,* "Stat Roma," from Hector Berlioz, *Les Troyens,* Grand Opéra en cinq actes, Partition chant et piano orientée à l'original de la Nouvelle Édition Berlioz d'Eike Wernhard, ed. Hugh Macdonald (Kassel: Bärenreiter, ca. 2003), 580. © 1969 by Bärenreiter. © Renewed. All rights reserved. Used by permission of European American Music Distributors LLC, sole U.S. and Canadian agent for Bärenreiter.

the witch Acrasia tempts Sir Guyon in the Bower of Bliss; and in Tasso's *Gerusalemme Liberata,* the witch Armida seduces, and actually falls in love with, the great hero Rinaldo. The right end to such a plotline is the destruction of the pleasure palace: either the hero rips and ravages to show his immunity to sexual charm, or the huffy witch herself destroys the palace. Composers who wrote operas on the Armida theme were especially fond of ending with a disenchantment scene, in which the palace collapses and the witch rides away on a flying chariot. That's why Jaucourt, in the passage I quoted at the beginning of this essay, mentioned "an enchanted palace that vanishes at the smallest sign and transforms itself into a desert." This scene was the gold standard of operatic special effects. It required musical special effects, too, growing more extravagant with each generation. It is interesting to compare the castle collapses at the end of Lully's 1686 *Armide* and Gluck's 1777 *Armide* (both to the same libretto, by Philippe Quinault) with the end of the second act of Wagner's *Parsifal* (1882), in which the sacred spear undoes Kundry's magic garden and Klingsor's castle—a scene that owes a good deal to the Armida tradition. I like the way that Gluck makes the beams and walls fall down in an orderly sequence, whereas Wagner's castle goes down in a zigzag heap, with bits of rubble bouncing up in diminishing arcs, a nightmare of ruin.

Acts 2 and 5 of *Les Troyens* both end in the collapse of edifices, although it's a chiefly metaphorical collapse in the case of Act 5. Berlioz had some trouble with this finale: he composed two versions. In the second version, the Carthaginians assert their hatred of Aeneas and of Rome-to-come, though their song is drowned out by the Trojan march, now understand as the anthem of Rome-to-come, as if the orchestra were mocking their semifutile resistance. The first version is looser and more interesting. In it Clio, the muse of history, appears on stage to sing a terse Latin motto, "Fuit Troja Stat Roma": Troy has been; Rome *is* (figure 4.6). (This motto is based on the line "Fuit Ilium," from a speech that Virgil gives to Panthus, a priest of Apollo.) We've been looking at *Les Troyens* mostly as a musicalization of the oral, recitational aspect of epic; but here Berlioz ends with an inscription, as if Clio were writing on a scroll, or as if a stonecutter were carving letters on a pediment. As the opera subverts itself into epic, it first becomes chant or pantomime or fading song; at last it becomes text. Berlioz ends Clio's utterance with an echo sung by two unidentified singers, a soprano and a tenor—the first echo comes *au fond du théâtre*, the second *encore plus loin*.

This finale is itself an echo of the finale of Act 1, in which Berlioz depicts the procession with the Trojan Horse with three different groups of offstage instruments, placed at varying distances from the audience. The drama, large though it is, takes place in a resonating cavity, the belly of epic. The undoing of opera leaves a vast, hollow space, to be filled by preechoes of coming things, by a history of something in one sense not yet written, something in another sense written many centuries ago, unforgettably *written*.

Chapter Five
Far Sounds in Zemlinsky and Schreker

Seated one day at the organ,
I was weary and ill at ease;
And my fingers wandered idly
Over the noisy keys.
I know not what I was playing

Or what I was dreaming then,
But I struck one chord of music
Like the sound of a great Amen.
It flooded the crimson twilight
Like the close of an angel's psalm,

And it lay on my fevered spirit
With a touch of infinite calm.
It quieted pain and sorrow
Like love overcoming strife;

It seemed the harmonious echo
From our discordant life.
It linked all perplexèd meanings
Into one perfect peace,

And trembled away into silence
As if it were loth to cease.
I have sought, but I seek it vainly,
That one lost chord divine,
Which came from the soul of the organ

And entered into mine.
It may be that death's bright angel
Will speak in that chord again;
It may be that only in heav'n
I shall hear that grand Amen.[1]

Alexander von Zemlinsky (1842–1900) lived during the great age of lost chords. When Zemlinsky was a little boy, Arthur Sullivan wrote set to music the famous poem about hearing a concord beyond all concords. But although Sullivan's piano mimics an organ swelling in rich modulations, I don't think that any specific chord could be considered a "lost" chord, or even that any chord formation would present the slightest challenge to the humblest student of

Simon Sechter or Heinrich Schenker. But the text, by the poet Adelaide Anne Procter, doesn't invite any particular search for occult harmonies. A "chord divine" that links "perplexèd meanings Into one perfect peace," a chord that is the grandest of Amens, has to be something familiar. There are plenty of lost discords, but there are no lost concords: nothing is ultraconcordant beyond the octave, the fifth, and the other very simple ratios. An Amen heard in heaven can't be more heart easing than an ordinary plagal cadence, unless transfigured ears can hear things we can't hear; a plagal cadence is exactly what Sullivan supplies at the end of his song. It is an incompetent organist who can't find a fine triad or two. In fact, the whole song sounds like a highfalutin' version of the story that Francis Toye tells about Giuseppe Verdi, who, as a little boy, kept fooling around with a dilapidated piano until he found a C-major chord, but became so upset when he couldn't figure out a way to make it sound again that he smashed the piano with a hammer.[2]

But during and after Sullivan's time, bolder composers sought lost chords of all sorts: vagrant chords, uncanny chords, delinquent chords, ruined chords, ecstatic chords, forbidden chords, supernatural chords, impossible chords, damned chords. And some composers found them. Probably the most famous examples of "lost" chords found are, first, Richard Wagner's "Tristan" chord, and second, Alexander Scriabin's mystic chord. Scriabin's found chord, like the unfound chord in Sullivan's song, has an unearthly, apocalyptic quality, as if it were best heard in heaven. Indeed, in its prime version, it consists entirely of fourths, though it is so oversaturated with augmented and diminished fourths that it doesn't fall into any Pythagorean sort of consonance. One might think of it as a single celestial fourth forced to shine through a sort of sound prism, revealing the full spectrum of fourthness. Scriabin hoped that this chord—heard, for example, just before the end of *Prometheus* (1910), on the brink of resolving into an F♯ chord—would help to hasten the end of the world. But that is to ask a great deal of a chord, even of a quite wonderfully contrived one.

Most composers who set out *à la recherche des accords perdus* are symbolists, for whom some bizarre concatenation of notes will give a shiver of the transcendental—an image in sound of something unhearable, outside the sensuous world entirely. Some of these composers were synesthetes who thought that odd ricochets from light to sound, from sound to light, would provide an intuition of an intense spiritual vibration out of the range of either eye or ear. In fact, Scriabin scored *Prometheus* for a color organ as well as an orchestra, as if a confusing pileup of bright light and loud sound would translate the hearer into some domain of metaphysical shock. Much of the attractiveness of a certain kind of modernist music comes from this straining of sound to get to a place beyond sound.

But there are distinctions to be made among composers of symbolist music. Some symbolists are confident in their abilities to capture some distant trembling in the ether—sometimes a chord, sometimes a strange progression, sometimes a single weird note. Scriabin was confident and audacious. So was Schoenberg:

I might mention the hammer-stroke chord containing all twelve notes, when inspiration falls like an epileptic fit on the artist in *Die glückliche Hand* (1912); or the melismatic interweave of extremely high soprano voices near the end of the *Jakobsleiter* fragment (1917–22), climbing up to the God who dwells at the end of the overtone series; or the representation of the burning bush in *Moses und Aron* (1930–32) (see chapter 6) as a labyrinth of speaking and singing voices, an audition of God as singular and plural at once, *Elohim, Adonai*. Sometimes Schoenberg could use a single sound to provide a frisson of primal creative force, as in *Kol Nidre* (1938), where the great declaration "Let there be light" is given audible form by the flexatone, a sort of musical saw. In 1941 Schoenberg compared his discovery of the twelve-tone system with that divine fiat. He was not a modest man.

Both Scriabin and (to some extent) Schoenberg were theosophists, as were Yeats, Kandinsky, and many others. Theosophy provided them with a system of graduated emanations of the spiritual into the material. This philosophical undergirding may have bolstered their self-confidence as artists. However, other composers were equally drawn to the notion of mystical seizures of the unhearable but were much less confident in their ability to provide acoustic images of these intuitions—and much less confident in the wisdom in chasing such chimeras of sound.

For a long time writers and composers had felt a certain fear that faint, distant music called forth feelings of yearning and wonder so extreme that they were akin to madness—or that madness itself was felt as strange music. In 1814 E. T. A. Hoffmann wrote a passage that strongly anticipates the aesthetic of Baudelaire, Scriabin, and Schoenberg:

> Nicht sowohl im Traume, als im Zustande des Delirierens, der dem Einschlafen vorhergeht, vorzüglich wenn ich viel Musik gehört habe, finde ich eine Übereinkunft der Farben, Töne und Düfte. Es kömmt mir vor, als wenn alle auf die gleiche geheimnisvolle Weise durch den Lichtstrahl erzeugt würden und dann sich zu einem wundervollen Konzerte vereinigen müßten.... Der Duft der dunkelroten Nelken wirkt mit sonderbarer magischer Gewalt auf mich; unwillkürlich versinke ich in einen träumerischen Zustand und höre dann wie aus weiter Ferne die anschwellenden und wieder verfließenden tiefen Töne des Bassetthorns.

> Not only in dreams, but also in that state of delirium which precedes sleep, especially when I have been listening to much music, I discover a congruity of colours, sounds, and fragrances. It seems as though they are all produced by beams of light.... The fragrance of deep-red carnations exercises a strangely magical power over me; unawares I sink into a dream-like state in which I hear, as though from far away, the dark, alternately swelling and subsiding tones of the basset-horn.[3]

But Hoffmann ascribed this meditation to the angular, lurid, eccentric, not to say insane Kapellmeister Kreisler—a man who intends to commit suicide by stabbing himself with an augmented fifth.[4] It seems that at the edges of perception, where the half-heard, half-glimpsed, appears to us in half-sleep, lurk dangerous intoxicants. In Hoffmann's stories, distant music tantalizes, horrifies, delights, as in Kreisler's report of Chrysostomus's tale of the fading lute music that lures a woman to a bloody death.[5] In Hoffmann's opera *Undine* (1816) we hear the soft watery voice of the mermaid weeping in the depths before she wriggles from the fountain to give her lover the fatal embrace.

The crazed mind is obsessed by faint sound. In Poe's short story "The Fall of the House of Usher" (1840), Roderick Usher suffers from such acute hyperesthesia that he needs to live in almost complete silence. And yet he needs music, piano to pianissimo. The narrator hears Usher chant a poem, "The Haunted Palace," accompanied by a guitar:

> I have just spoken of that morbid condition of the auditory nerve which rendered all music intolerable to the sufferer, with the exception of certain effects of stringed instruments. It was, perhaps, the narrow limits to which he thus confined himself upon the guitar, which gave birth, in great measure, to the fantastic character of his performances. . . . I fancied that I perceived, and for the first time, a full consciousness on the part of Usher, of the tottering of his lofty reason upon her throne.[6]

Oddly parallel to the ultraquiet mad music of Roderick Usher is a passage in an actual string quartet—Bedřich Smetana's autobiographical First String Quartet in E minor (*From My Life,* 1876), whose hectic finale stops dead, except for one high violin note. Whereas Usher suffered from too-acute hearing, Smetana had become totally deaf in 1874. But he was haunted by a sort of tinnitus, for he constantly heard a single high E natural, a noise supplied by his inner ear. (The syphilis that deafened him eventually drove him mad as well, and he died in an asylum.) Perhaps it is not heaven but hell that entertains us with teasing wisps of sound: as Samuel Beckett was to put it much later, in his story "First Love" (1945):

> It took a long time, my lifetime so to speak, to realize that the colour of an eye half seen, or the source of some distant sound, are nearer to Giudecca in the hell of unknowing than the existence of God, or origins of protoplasm, or the existence of self, and even less worthy than these to occupy the wise.[7]

Giudecca is the name Dante gave to that ultimate region of hell where Satan forever chomps down on Judas and Brutus. Incomprehensible fringe sounds may turn out to be vanity, perplexity, pathology, not revelation.

The beckoning of eerie sounds on the threshold of audibility turned out to be a good subject for composers of overripe romantic operas. It is a sort of sequel to the Orpheus story and has similar ambiguities. Orpheus's song had the power to make trees dance, to make rocks move, to free his wife from the confines of hell; yet it led Orpheus to a gruesome end when the Maenads tore him apart limb from limb. Similarly, the pursuit of lost chords might lead the pursuer to salvation or damnation or some odd combination of the two. It is an Orpheus myth without Orpheus, in which a gang of male Eurydices stretches toward some hallucination of a harp. Claude Debussy wrote a libretto and some music for an opera based on Poe, *La chute de la maison Usher*, in which Roderick Usher is haunted, wracked, by the far-off voice of his sister, neither quite living nor quite dead, singing "musiques à damner les anges!"

Czech composers were especially attracted to the theme of the phantom siren, the spectral hush that conduces to doom. Leoš Janáček was a master at this: the gypsy ghost trio that lures the boy who was never heard from again in *The Diary of One Who Vanished* (1919) (No. 9, "Ruky sejpala"); or the sound of the Volga, represented by an eerie chorus heard just before the heroine of *Káťa Kabanová* (1921) plunges to her death—she asks "What are they singing?" Similar sorts of ravishings, light touches of ectoplasmic hands, can be found earlier in the works of Smetana.

But German and Austrian composers did more to place this theme on center stage. Franz Schreker, for one, wrote several operas in which the protagonist madly seeks for the source of some occult or liminal music. The purest is *Der ferne Klang* (1912), in which the young Fritz abandons his loving sweetheart, abandons his comfortable home, in order to pursue an acoustic will-o'-the-wisp, a *ferner Klang* that he compares with the sound that the wind makes when playing over the strings of a harp. Thinking that her father has gambled away her hand in marriage, Franz's sweetheart, Grete, also flees their hometown. Neither Fritz nor Grete prospers. The embittered Fritz believes that he has frittered away his life in search of a phantom, and tries to return to Grete. But when he finds that she has become a prostitute, he flees in horror and sets out once again in search of nowhere. In the last act we see the aging Fritz as a playwright, still haunted by the far clang. He reconciles with Grete, but dies, lamenting that his play is still unfinished.

We see that the distant sound takes on several guises, first as an Aeolian harp, finally as the inspiration for Fritz's writing, a muse plinking in the inner ear. Schreker's way of characterizing the distant sound by orchestral means keep changing, too. In the opera's prelude, it's just a monotonous set of arpeggios (figure 5.1).

Figure 5.1. Schreker: *Der ferne Klang*, prelude, from Franz Schreker, *Der ferne Klang*, Klavierauszug (Vienna: Universal Edition, 1911), 3. Used with kind permission of European American Music Distributors LLC, sole U.S. and Canadian agent for Universal Edition.

But by the "Nachtstück" interlude in the third act, it has become much more interesting. The monotony continues, but it is now decorated with all sorts of strange trillings and chirps, a nightscape in which tree frogs and crickets and a buzz of moonlight fill the spaces of the ear (figure 5.2). It is not far from this *site auriculaire* to the night music from Bartók's *Out of Doors* (1926), or the *Andante religioso* in his Third Piano Concerto (1945), or the *Music for Strings, Percussion and Celesta* (1936).

But whether Aeolian harp or representation of night, the orchestra seems to insist that the distant sound is still part of nature and therefore basically right and good. Fritz, however, isn't quite so sure: as he listens, at once bemused, rapt, and despairing, he thinks that he hears, not birds, but bells—not nature, but something unnatural (Act 3, scene 11: "Mir ist so seltsam zumut!") (figure 5.3).

Figure 5.2. Schreker: *Der ferne Klang*, Nachtmusik, from Franz Schreker, *Der ferne Klang*, Klavierauszug (Vienna: Universal Edition, 1911), 281. Used with kind permission of European American Music Distributors LLC, sole U.S. and Canadian agent for Universal Edition.

Figure 5.3. Schreker: *Der ferne Klang*, "Mir ist so seltsam zumut!" from Franz Schreker, *Der ferne Klang*, Klavierauszug, (Vienna: Universal Edition, 1911), 259. Used with kind permission of European American Music Distributors LLC, sole U.S. and Canadian agent for Universal Edition.

Sure enough, Schreker has moved the arpeggios from harp to celesta—still urgent, still insistent, but far more harmonically vagrant, and with some deep disturbances in the bass. In a sense the distant sound is still monotonous, but the monotony is eerie and unearthly, not the monotony of strings moved to sympathetic vibration by the wind.

We have heard this dream trauma of little bells earlier in the opera, in the ballad of the glowing crown from Act 2 (Act 2, scene 6, "Doch aus der Tiefe klingt es wie Zimbeln"). This ballad concerns the king of an unnamed land perhaps not too far from Goethe's Thule. Eager to be rid of the burdens of rule, he throws his burning crown into the sea, but a pale woman rises from the depths and drags him down. She is a late version of all those undines, melusines, nixies, and loreleis that haunt the romantic imagination—mermaids sometimes naïve, sometimes witchlike, but almost always accompanied by a music that grows more delicately weird with each passing generation.

In fact this is the sort of sonority that would soon be fixed in the modernist codebook as the sign of the extraterrestrial, the sonority of "Neptune, the Mystic" in Gustav Holst's suite *The Planets* (1918). In this famous movement, the cool looming of a gas giant at an immense distance from the sun is suggested by the imperturbable little bells orbiting slowly from E minor to G♯ major and back to E minor (figure 5.4).

Figure 5.4. Holst: *The Planets,* "Neptune," from Gustav Holst, *The Planets,* arranged for two pianos by the composer (London: J. Curwen, 1991), 100.

Colder still is the atmosphere in Holst's song "Betelgeuse" (*Twelve Humbert Wolfe Settings,* Op. 48, 1929), to a poem by Humbert Wolfe:

On Betelgeuse the gold leaves hang in golden aisles
For twice a hundred million miles,
And twice a hundred million years
They golden hang and nothing stirs,
On Betelgeuse.

Space is a wind that does not blow
On Betelgeuse and time is a bird,
Whose wings have never stirred
The golden avenues of leaves
On Betelgeuse.[8]

Betelgeuse is a red star, but here, beyond space and time, its heat has so dwindled that it has turned into a planet, a planet beyond the event horizon. Here the bronze shimmer and vitreous edges of "Neptune" vanish into music's absolute zero, not a temporary stasis but a stasis that seems to preclude the possibility of movement. We are inside a domain of lost chords and far sounds, inhabiting vast, evacuated spaces where nothing happens and we shiver at the happening nothingness. If the *ferne Klang* that entices Fritz pertains to the affable sounds of nature, it might be well worth following; but if it pertains to Neptune or Betelgeuse, as the music comes to suggest, Fritz has followed it at his peril. Well might the dying Fritz address "du tolles Getön" (you mad sound) and ask it to leave him in peace: "Gib Ruh'—o gib Ruh."

At the end of the opera, Fritz compares the sound that drives him on with the music of the spheres. According to Plato, the planets whirl on steel spindles; on the outer surface of each planet is perched an astronomical siren singing a single note, so that the ensemble makes a perfect concord. The philosopher Iamblichus said that only Pythagorus himself was able to hear this highest and deepest music. But clever sound images of this contraption of nested gyroscopes, reverberations of metal and quartz, and women's voices have been provided by a number of modernist composers. They feel air from other planets. For the most part they breathe this ozone seriously, but sometimes the new air creates a certain giddiness, as in Janáček's *Výlet pana Broučka do měsíce* (Mr. Brouček's Excursion to the Moon, 1917). Mr. Brouček, a man fond of sausage and beer and wenches, flies off to the moon and scandalizes the thin-blooded aesthetes who dwell there. Just before the complacent Brouček is translated into the sky, Janáček represents the flood of moonlight on Prague as a kind of empyrean hilarity (Act 1, "Zda ve snu říš mne k sobě—Cha-cha-cha-cha"). Sometimes the atmosphere of the outer planets is all helium, inert and rarefied, but on occasions it seems full of nitrous oxide.

Dwarf Sounds

Five years before Schreker's *Der ferne Klang,* Alexander von Zemlinsky had prepared an opera on a similar theme, *Der Traumgörge.* Here, too, a young dreamer refuses the satisfactions of a homey, comfortable life to chase after the ghost of a sound. In Zemlinsky's case the *Klang* was so *fern* that the composer almost never got to hear it at all. Through a series of misfortunes, the opera, already in rehearsal in the summer of 1907, was abandoned, and Zemlinsky was never able to find a public to hear the sonorities he had invented to represent the ear dreams of his hero.

At the beginning we see a playful Görg, improvising little fairy tales so that he can invest his boring village with a fantastic glamour. He tells his fiancée Grete that the local cat isn't a commonplace, dull cat but a cat baron, the leader of the cat parliament, the priest of the cat religion. She will have none of this nonsense. But later, when Görge describes his encounter with a fairy-tale princess, who appeared in a consort of sunlight and silver harps, Grete and the other villagers are somewhat impressed in spite of themselves (Act 1, "Sie kam, und der Wald") (figure 5.5).

When Görge mentions the princess's crown and her shimmering dress, we hear a motive in the orchestral that we soon hear again when Görge describes how the apparition vanished: "Ein Hauch—ein Lied—wohin, woher? Aus Luft gewoben" (figure 5.6).

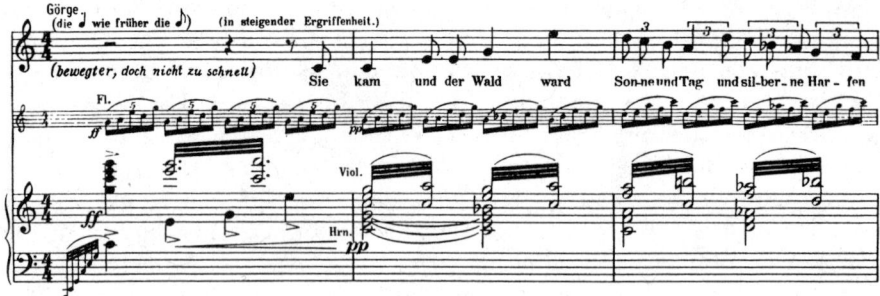

Figure 5.5. Zemlinsky: *Der Traumgörge,* "Sie kam," from Alexander Zemlinsky, *Der Traumgörge,* Oper in zwei Akten und einem Nachspiel, Text von Leo Feld, Klavierauszug (Milan: Ricordi, ca. 1991), 50.

Figure 5.6. Zemlinsky: *Der Traumgörge,* "Ein Hauch," from Alexander Zemlinsky, *Der Traumgörge,* Oper in zwei Akten und einem Nachspiel, Text von Leo Feld, Klavierauszug (Milan: Ricordi, ca. 1991), 54.

This tune—Burkhard Rempe calls it the *Traum* motive—belongs to that class of ideas in which the melody outlines first one triad, then another. Wagner was fond of such themes, such as the *Walküre* motive (which turns into its own mediant, translated into the major) and the *Siegfried* motive.

Indeed there are certain points of resemblance between the *Traum* motive and Siegfried. Both Görge's dream (in its "Aus Luft gewoben" form) and Siegfried thrust up from the tonic, cresting on the (flatted) submediant major (figure 5.7). But

Figure 5.7. Wagner: *Siegfried,* the name Siegfried, from Richard Wagner, *The Ring of the Nibelungen,* Third Part, *Siegfried,* Complete Vocal Score in a Facilitated Arrangement by Karl Klindworth (New York: G. Schirmer, n.d.), 194.

Zemlinsky darkens the chord with a seventh, makes it move in a manner more furtive than triumphant. Nevertheless, we are still very much in the musical domain of the *Naturthema*—a theme constructed from intervals easy to play on a horn—and therefore the music pronounces a kind of benediction over Görge and his dreams, just as the Aeolian-harp figures in *Der ferne Klang* suggest to Fritz that all is well.

Like Fritz, Görge will sacrifice his worldly goods and his peace of mind to chase after a breath, a song woven of air, until he becomes destitute and bitter, a useful idiot (in Görge's case) to a band of revolutionaries—useful because his verbal gifts make him an effective propagandist. But before his world falls into ruin, he hears, in addition to the princess's song, another sort of occult music. He leans over the stream where his mother used to read stories to him, and listens to the amiable voice of the water. He asks the friend under the waves if he still remembers his mother (Act 1, "Wer das verstünd,' dein ewiges rauschen"). This is one of the most widely admired passages in Zemlinsky's music: the opening is nothing but a playing with the scintillae of a D♭ chord, quicksilvering from major to minor and back (figure 5.8).

Figure 5.8. Zemlinsky: *Der Traumgörge,* rustling, from Alexander Zemlinsky, *Der Traumgörge,* Oper in zwei Akten und einem Nachspiel, Text von Leo Feld, Klavierauszug (Milan: Ricordi, ca. 1991), 57.

Some critics have compared it, plausibly enough, to the *Waldweben* in Wagner's *Siegfried*, but I'd like to add another term of comparison, this one from Smetana, the opening of *Má vlast*, part 4: *From Bohemia's Woods and Fields* (*Z českých luhů a hájů*). Zemlinsky made a recording of Smetana's *Moldau*—indeed the wetness of Görge's brook makes it seem one of the Moldau's tributaries—and I imagine that he knew well the whole of *Má vlast*. The opening of *From Bohemia's Woods and Fields* (1875) is one of the nineteenth century's most spectacular feats of orchestration. This is not nature as respite, nature as fostering mother, but nature as overwhelm, a wall of athematic sound. The huge oscillation is from tonic minor to tonic major to relative major. Here, as in *Der Traumgörge*, the music seems to have tapped into a sort of power generator, the earth's own alternating current. In Smetana's tone poem, this blank glory slowly decomposes into various cheerful audibilities, but the loud, beautiful incoherence at the beginning seems like another way of imagining Smetana's recent deafness, an intricate roar in which all the world's melodies are submerged. Zemlinsky provides a somewhat quieter version of this roar, a-twittering, a-trembling, gorgeous, but going nowhere. Görge is caught in shivers of sound that seem to promise everything, but in fact enclose him in a kind of cage, since the chord patterns simply keep circling back to where they started, in the manner of early Philip Glass. The music hypnotizes Görge, a suggestible sort of man.

We hear this *rauschen*—this rustle, this roar—again in Act 2, when Görge tries to heal himself of fever and fret by recalling the stream and his mother; and again in the Epilogue, when he and Gertraud—the woman whom he has accepted, acquiesced to, as the closest thing to an earthly version of the princess—listen to the stream one last time and dream together. The stream sounds almost exactly the same in each of these three cases; perhaps Görge hasn't really changed, or learned anything, after all his vicissitudes. I agree with Antony Beaumont that this happy ending is deliberately unconvincing—Zemlinsky was a master of the false ending.[9] Just before the final appearance of the stream music, Görge announces,

Nie find' ich den Berg im flammenden Braus,	For me, no mountain in a storm of flame,
Kein Wunderschwert werd' ich führen,	For me, no wonder-sword to wield,
Doch zwing' ich mein Leben und schirm' ich mein Haus,	But if I master my life and shield my home,
Dann fühl' ich den Gruß der Walküren![10]	It's as good as a valkyrie calling to me!

Zemlinsky provides any number of exciting, dimly Wagnerian themes here, but the Valkyrie triads seem so aimless and underpowered that we suspect that no Brünnhilde will ever appear to deliver a *Todesverkündigung* to Görge (figure 5.9). The dream princess was a more potent Siegfried than Görge himself could ever be. The whole opera seems to be a weak man's fantasy of unworldly strength and ecstasy.

Figure 5.9. Zemlinsky: *Der Traumgörge*, valkyrie, from Alexander Zemlinsky, *Der Traumgörge,* Oper in zwei Akten und einem Nachspiel, Text von Leo Feld, Klavierauszug (Milan: Ricordi, ca. 1991), 198.

Still Smaller Music

In Schreker's *Der ferne Klang*, the teasing music slowly altered its character from pleasant nature arpeggios to some sort of extranatural tintinnabulation. I think that in *Der Traumgörge* Zemlinsky made sure that the music that impels Görge stays strictly in the semantic realm of the natural. But when Zemlinsky took up the theme of distant impulse music in his later operas, he moved increasingly toward the uncanny and incomprehensible, toward toneless overtones. Indeed he went much further in the direction of Neptune or Betelgeuse than Schreker was ever to go.

In Oscar Wilde's story "The Birthday of the Infanta"—the basis for the libretto of his one-act opera *Der Zwerg* (1921)—Zemlinsky found a plot that gave his peculiar talents the freest possible scope for development. Wilde's fable concerns a princess who receives a gift from a dwarf, an unusual dwarf in that he grew up in the forest and has never seen a mirror. But after he is brought to the court and falls in love with the princess, he comes across a mirror and sees his hideous image, wishes that his father had murdered him instead of selling him, and dies of a broken heart. The princess regrets the loss of one of her playthings, but is happy to keep on playing.

In the opera version, the princess is not only unthinking but actively malicious; in fact, malice comes at the dwarf from all sides. His entire life has been a practical joke. Far from being a wild child, he has spent most of his life in society, but all mirrors have been removed from his presence, and he has been encouraged to think himself a gifted, handsome fellow. Eventually the princess commands her attendant to show the dwarf his image in a mirror, after he has resisted her attempts to demote him from a human being into a toy. And it's true that when we first hear of the dwarf, he sounds rather like a wind-up manikin that's missing part of one leg ("Das schönste ist scheußlich") (figure 5.10).

Figure 5.10. Zemlinsky: *Der Zwerg*, abominable beauty, from Alexander Zemlinsky, *Der Zwerg:* ein tragisches Märchen für Musik in einem Akt, Op. 17, Text von Georg C. Klaren, frei nach Oscar Wildes *Der Geburtstag der Infantin,* Klavierauszug, neu herausgegeben von Antony Beaumont (Vienna: Universal Edition, ca. 2006), 45. Used with kind permission of European American Music Distributors LLC, sole U.S. and Canadian agent for Universal Edition.

But soon the music corrects this false impression. Far from being a doll or a droll puppet, the dwarf is the most human agent in the opera ("Der Sultan sandte einen Zwerg") (figure 5.11).

This seems to me the most beautiful theme that Zemlinsky ever wrote—its pensive passage from D minor to B♭ minor depicts a whole world of melancholy, and of appeasement of melancholy through sheer loveliness of expression. The music tells us, then, that dwarf is a human being in the guise of a toy.

The princess, on the other hand, is a toy dressed up to resemble a human being. When the princess and her playmates first appear ("Das Gras ist warm"), we hear a bundle of eerie gestures belongs clearly to the class of *ferner Klang* music: something at the threshold of hearing, at the threshold of intelligibility, a spacey fugitive kind of E major, glittering with odd feints at remote keys (figure 5.12).

Figure 5.11. Zemlinsky: *Der Zwerg*, freak of nature, from Alexander Zemlinsky, *Der Zwerg: ein tragisches Märchen für Musik in einem Akt*, Op. 17, Text von Georg C. Klaren, frei nach Oscar Wildes *Der Geburtstag der Infantin*, Klavierauszug, neu herausgegeben von Antony Beaumont (Vienna: Universal Edition, ca. 2006), 47. Used with kind permission of European American Music Distributors LLC, sole U.S. and Canadian agent for Universal Edition.

Figure 5.12. Zemlinsky: *Der Zwerg*, warm grass, from Alexander Zemlinsky, *Der Zwerg:* ein tragisches Märchen für Musik in einem Akt, Op. 17, Text von Georg C. Klaren, frei nach Oscar Wildes *Der Geburtstag der Infantin*, Klavierauszug, neu herausgegeben von Antony Beaumont (Vienna: Universal Edition, ca. 2006), 12. Used with kind permission of European American Music Distributors LLC, sole U.S. and Canadian agent for Universal Edition.

It is a somewhat Straussian passage, and may have been inspired by the music for the Phantom Lover in Strauss's recent *Die Frau ohne Schatten*. Soon the picturesque girls are dancing and singing in the meadow and ("Tanzt, tanzt auf der Wiese"). The meadow is an agreeable, sunny place, but the music is distinctly unnatural in character, as if the princess were from some land not far from that of "Laideronnette, Impératrice des Pagodes," in Maurice Ravel's *Ma mère l'oye* (1910). Zemlinsky's Spain is clearly west of Ravel's Pagodaland and somewhat softer, less brittle, but both places are toy kingdoms, inhabited by characters that run on music-box springs. It is precisely because the princess is herself a toy that she can imagine no role for the dwarf beyond that of *Spielwerk*. (Her toylike character is equally apparent in the music that Franz Schreker wrote for Gustav Klimt's 1908 spectacle *Die Geburtstag der Infantin*, based on the same Oscar Wilde story as *Der Zwerg*.)

The limit of Traum-Zemlinsky's chase after unearthly sonorities occurs in his last opera, *Der König Kandaules* (composed in short score by 1936, but unfinished at Zemlinsky's death in 1942). In this opera about a king who possesses a magic ring that confers invisibility on its wearer, the main form of elusiveness is visual, not auditory, but many of the tropes are teasing half-audibilities. The plot concerns Kandaules' peculiar need to display the beauty of his wife, Queen Nyssia, to the public at large. She is a modest woman, and protests that she'd like to remain hidden, but Kandaules insists that she unveil herself before the men of his court, a band of aesthetes and flatterers, *précieux*, idle, tediously witty. Nyssia reluctantly consents, but during the revealing dinner a courtier finds in the fish a ring that turns out to be magic—it renders its wearer invisible. Kandaules wishes to meet the fisherman who caught the fish—Gyges, a poor, crude, assertive fellow who likes to mind his own business. Gyges is puzzled by the king's strange warmth toward him, and still more puzzled when Kandaules insists that he put on the ring of invisibility and ogle the naked Nyssia. But during this odd scene, Kandaules finds that a still odder thought keeps flitting just beyond the edge of his consciousness—Zemlinsky embodies the elusiveness of this idea with remarkable musical precision (Act 2, "Lauter, sprich lauter, mein jüngster Gedanke!") (figure 5.13).

As it turns out, this quiet, perverse insinuation, the idea that Kandaules is trying to formulate, is that Gyges should not only see Nyssia, but have sex with her.

Why? This is the main question that the opera poses. In the source for the libretto, a none-too-successful play by André Gide, it is likely that there's an unspoken homosexual infatuation of *le roi Candaule* with Gyges, a piece of rough trade—an infatuation that gets displaced into a sort of voyeuristic transference of identity. Candaule, unable to confess his love for Gyges, requires that Gyges *become* Candaule, at least for a night. But I suspect that Zemlinsky wasn't interested in any homosexual subtext. For Zemlinsky, the libretto was useful because it was the final chapter in the studies of weakness that constitute his main achievement as a dramatist. Zemlinsky found his greatest strength through the depiction of weak men.

Figure 5.13. Zemlinsky: *Der König Kandaules*, recent thought, from Alexander Zemlinsky, *Der König Kandaules*, Drama in drei Akten von André Gide, deutsche Umdichtung von Franz Blei, Klavierauszug von Antony Beaumont (Munich: Ricordi, ca. 1993), 97.

Kandaules is so weak, so lacking in any core, that his own experience isn't real to him unless someone else experiences it for him. He may derive more sexual pleasure from the vicarious thrill of watching Gyges having sex with Nyssia than he can get from sleeping with her himself. Just as Nyssia isn't really beautiful to him until the courtiers comment on her beauty, so Nyssia isn't really voluptuous until Gyges enjoys her sexual charms. Kandaules becomes disturbed that Nyssia enjoyed her night of passion with Gyges better than she had enjoyed any night with Kandaules himself, but that only tends to confirm the sense, powerful throughout the opera, that Gyges is an actual human being, whereas Kandaules is an inauthenticity and an unreality, so low in definition that he's half-invisible even before he obtains the magic ring. The extravagant, sick hush that represents his half-formed idea that Gyges should sleep with Nyssia is one of many signs in the opera of Kandaules's incoherence, nonexistence. Bass lines that peter out into the void, clusters of tremoli with far too many notes—these are the symptoms of Kandaules' disease. By contrast, Gyges is a simple, if not simple-minded character. His motive appears often in the opera, notably in Act 1, just before the words "Also bist du Gyges?" This is the same sort of stomping-thirds music that Strauss used to represent the three deformed brothers in *Die Frau ohne Schatten* (as at the beginning of Act 1, scene 2). You can rely on clomping, earthbound thirds. They are the exact opposite of the fairy music of Strauss's empress, or of the music of Kandaules, all queasiness and fake shimmer. In *Der König Kandaules* Zemlinsky concludes more firmly than ever before that the pursuit of the invisible, the inaudible, the extraterrestrial, is a fools' game; music, real music, is the domain of the vulgar, the coarse, the lacking-in-imagination. Exiled in New York and strapped for cash, Zemlinsky felt that he was cheapening himself by writing popular songs and school exercises for instrumentalists. But I suspect that he felt with despair that advanced music, ultrachromatic harmony and unearthly timbre, *ferne Klänge*, had in some sense failed him—or that he had failed it. Zemlinsky seems especially confident when writing music for hard labor, hard play—I think that's one reason that he was attracted to the poets of the Harlem Renaissance, as in his *Afrikanischer Tanz*, Op. 27, no. 9 ("Grollen die Tom-Toms"). This is the exact opposite of dream music in the *Traumgörge* sense: it is not fugitive or tantalizing but overt, even blatant—muscle music, like Gyges's theme in *Der König Kandaules*. It is music for sweaty people who have little occasion to dream, for people who have given up on all pleasures except the simplest.

The last theme that I want to explore is the possibility that Zemlinsky felt that he himself was hollow, inauthentic—that his compositions were simply vanities, tracings on the void. In 1897, when Zemlinsky was entering his artistic maturity, Gustav Mahler "noted his 'incredible technique,' but found his music 'full of resemblances and plagiarisms.'"[11] Mahler seems to have felt that Zemlinsky was no one in particular, that his music was a kind of anthology of bits and pieces of other people's music.

The charge of plagiarism is strong and worth examining. In his early work, Zemlinsky seems promiscuously to quote other composers, not for the sake of allusion or witty adaptation, but simply through some defect of the inner censor that keeps most composers chaste. Near the beginning of *Der Traumgörge*, for example, during Görge's tale of the cat preacher ("Ringsum kein Laut, and keiner miaut"), we hear a little cobbling gesture straight out of Wagner's *Meistersinger* (heard, for example, near the end of Act 1, "brächt ein mit morgen die neuen Schuh"). This is a piece of very petty larceny, but elsewhere Zemlinsky steals from Wagner at climactic moments. For example, during the waving of the banner of victory in his first opera, *Sarema* (1897), the heroine sings "Du siehst nicht unser Siegespanier" to a melody taken directly from the lips of Wotan (*Die Walküre*, Act 2, "Ein Held dem helfend nie"). As Antony Beaumont has noted, this is only one of many Wagnerisms in the score of *Sarema*.[12] And after the première many listeners applauded Zemlinsky for his skill in handling Wagnerian material. But still, Zemlinsky may have had a certain anxiety about the colorlessness of his creative personality.

In his later work, borrowings and thefts are still a striking feature, though he may borrow more cannily, deliberately, as at the fearful moment in *Der Zwerg* when Ghita broaches the subject of mirrors, and the dwarf asks, "Mirror, what is that?" Ghita replies gravely that you can't believe your friend, but you can believe the mirror ("Und hast du einen Freund"). At this moment we hear a little moaning figure straight out of the final monologue in Strauss's *Salome* (1905) ("Ah! Ich habe deinen Mund geküsst"). But it could be argued that Zemlinsky intended this. *Salome*, like *Der Zwerg*, is based on a text by Oscar Wilde, and Zemlinsky may be subtly calling attention to the fact that Salome, gazing on Jochanaan's severed head, is also gazing into a sort of mirror, an image of her own repulsive fanaticism. In fact, Wilde makes much of the ways in which Salome and Jochanaan are doubles of one another.

There is nothing postmodern about Zemlinsky. None of his operas is a bricolage in the way that Schnittke's *Doktor Faustus*—or, for that matter, Mozart's

Die Zauberflöte—is a bricolage. Zemlinsky's quotations, his radical shifts in musical language, are never abrupt, never unmodulated. There's an incomparable smoothness to his gear changes from the harmonically lush to the rhythmically spare, from the decadent to the naïve, from something like Schoenberg to something like *Des Knaben Wunderhorn*. Not even Strauss's musical engine has an automatic transmission quite so plush as Zemlinsky's.

Alfred, Lord Tennyson once said, "There can have been since Shakespeare no such master of the English language as I. To be sure I have nothing to say." I can imagine Zemlinsky thinking something similar, though he did have something to say, something important, but pertinent to futility, ugliness, self-disgust. When I think of Zemlinsky, I think of Thomas Mann's early story *Enttäuschung* (1896), concerning a man who has come to nothing, a man who has tasted the dregs of disillusionment because poets have told him that there were supreme emotions of overwhelming love, of overwhelming hate. But the man says that these poets lie, that in fact joy doesn't give much pleasure, and pain isn't particularly awful. Human life is trivial, but we puff it up in order to flatter ourselves:

> Ich bin umhergeschweift, um die gepriesensten Gegenden der Erde zu besuchen, um vor die Kunstwerke hinzutreten, um die die Menschheit mit den größten Wörtern tanzt; ich habe davor gestanden und mir gesagt: Es ist schön. Und doch: Schöner ist es nicht? Das ist das Ganze?[13]

> I have traveled around and visited the most widely praised regions of the earth, in order to walk up to the art works around which mankind dances with the biggest words; I have stood in front of them and said to myself: That's beautiful. And then: But not more beautiful? That's all there is?

Or, as Francis Picabia once wrote, there are fewer things in heaven and earth than are dreamt of in your philosophy.[14] Zemlinsky, like Mann's protagonist, chased after some faint tremor or some great earthquake of beauty, but found that beauty wasn't adequate to his purposes.

Several composers in the history of music have seemed to feel a certain disgust with themselves, or disgust at the art of music itself. Giacomo Carissimi is thought to be the composer of an oratorio written around 1650, *Vanitas vanitatum II*, in which some of the phrases terminate in sudden silence, as if to show that music itself is a vanity. As soon as a sound appears, it passes, and is as if it had never been. Self-disgust as a compositional mode is quite rare, but as it happens that the most expert composer in this vein was one of Zemlinsky's first heroes, Johannes Brahms.

In the cantata *Rinaldo* (1869), his closest approach to opera, Brahms set a poem by Goethe based on a story from Tasso. The great Christian knight Rinaldo falls under the sexual spell of the Saracen witch Armida and cannot leave her island. Rinaldo is saved after his companions give him a diamond shield that shows him his own reflection:

Chor. Nein! Nicht länger ist zu säumen!	*Chorus.* No! No longer can we linger!
wecket ihn aus seinen Träumen,	Wake him! Wake up the dreamer,
zeigt den diamantnen Schild!	Show him the shield of adamant!
Rinaldo. Weh![15]	*Rinaldo.* Woe!

Some of Brahms's best music, especially "Denn alles Fleisch ist wie Gras" from *Ein deutsches Requiem* (1868), pertains to the nullity at heart of human existence. All flesh is grass; when I look at my face I see shame, depravity.

Brahms, like Zemlinsky, was a man who seemed born old, and Rinaldo's despair at his image in the mirror is an extraordinarily Zemlinskian moment. It is the same plot as *Der Zwerg*, the man who thinks himself an elegant hero but learns to see himself as a contemptible, twisted thing. Brahms, too, once chased fugitive sounds, as in the song "An die Äolsharfe." To some extent Zemlinsky's career recapitulates Brahms's, in a still darker key.

There is a Zemlinsky, then, who develops certain perversions found in Brahms; and there is also a Zemlinsky who anticipates certain perversions found in Kafka. Antony Beaumont has noted a connection, via Walter Benjamin, between Zemlinsky's song "Das bucklichte Männlein" and the spool man Odradek in Kafka's "Sorge eines Hausvaters";[16] I would like to try my hand at another one. In "Der Bau," left incomplete at Kafka's death in 1924, the only character is some sort of burrowing mammal who has dug himself a great underground labyrinth in order to defend himself from predators and to store the food he kills during his rare excursions to the surface world. He is prey to ceaseless anxiety: he fears that the burrow has been misconstructed from the beginning, and, far from rendering him immune from harm, has left him all the more vulnerable to it. At one point he starts to hear a mysterious hissing, a sound that first intrigues him, then obsesses him. He hypothesizes that it's the noise of innumerable small critters making their way through the earth; he wonders whether it's just his own heartbeat ringing in his ears. But finally he surrenders to terror:

> Aber was helfen alle Mahnungen zur Ruhe, die Einbildungskraft will nicht stillstehen und ich halte tatsächlich dabei zu glauben—es ist zwecklos, sich das selbst abzuleugnen—, das Zischen stamme von einem Tier und zwar nicht von vielen und kleinen, sondern von einem einzigen großen. . . . Ich kann mir das Zischen nur so erklären, daß das Hauptwerkzeug des Tieres nicht seine Krallen sind, mit denen es vielleicht nur nachhilft, sondern seine Schnauze oder sein Rüssel, die allerdings, abgesehen von ihrer ungeheuren Kraft, wohl auch irgendwelche Schärfen haben. Wahrscheinlich bohrt es mit einem einzigen mächtigen Stoß den Rüssel in die Erde und reißt ein großes Stück heraus, während dieser Zeit höre ich nichts, das ist die Pause, dann aber zieht es wieder Luft ein zum neuen Stoß. Dieses Einziehen der Luft, das ein die Erde erschütternder Lärm sein muß, nicht nur wegen der Kraft des Tieres, sondern auch wegen seiner Eile, seines Arbeitseifers, diesen Lärm höre ich dann als leises Zischen.

What good all these admonitions to be calm, my imagination will not rest and I actually hold the belief–it is futile to try to deny it—that the hissing stems from a beast and not indeed from many small beasts but from one single great one.... I can only explain the hissing in this way, that the beast's main tool is not its claws, which it perhaps uses only as a secondary aid, but its snout or proboscis, which, leaving aside its monstrous strength, must come to a sharp point of sorts. Probably it bores with a single mighty thrust of its snout into the earth and tears out a great hunk, during this time I hear nothing, that is the pause, then it draws air in again for a new thrust. This indrawing of air, that must be an earth-shaking noise, caused not only by the beast's strength but also by its haste, its zeal for work, I hear this noise then as a light hissing.[17]

Perhaps this was the story that Zemlinsky sought all his life to turn into a opera: a creature that hunts a *ferner Klang* only to flee from it, destroy his own burrow in a great implosion of being. The sonorities of Kandaules' inner voices might be a good representation of the hissing; maybe even better the single high note E in the Smetana E-minor quartet, the noise of the hearer's own nervous system, the noise of deafness itself.

Chapter Six

Butchering Moses

There is no Moses, only a whole tribe of Moseses. In the course of his life he undergoes many shape changes: an abandoned child drifting down a river; the leader of a slave revolt; a guide through the wilderness; a miracle worker; a lawgiver; a literary man writing the Pentateuch; a figure of disappointment, gazing from the mountaintop at the land of milk and honey he will never be permitted to enter. It is to be expected, then, that artistic representations of Moses would be vague and contradictory.

There is a small tradition of memorable musical Moseses. For example, in Carl Philipp Emanuel Bach's oratorio *Die Israeliten in der Wüste* (1768–69), Moses is little more than a chorister promoted to soloist, the voice of his people praying to God for rescue. The main event is the miracle of the spring that suddenly flows from the rock. Bach set a text by Daniel Schiebeler, perhaps with some assistance from the redoubtable Friedrich Gottlieb Klopstock, author of *Der Messias;* and Moses as a precursor of the Messiah was the only Moses here present. A century later, in Max Bruch's oratorio *Moses* (1895), Moses' character has almost reversed: Bruch's Moses is a Jewish Wotan, thundering invective on his own people as idolators. Far from being at ease as a member of the chorus, he outshouts the whole multitude in a great antiphony, in the oratorio's one impressive passage at the end of Part 1, "Abtrünnige, kam es dahin mit euch?" Moses was always more at home in oratorio than in opera, where his lack of a dramatic sex life was a handicap; but Rossini, in *Mosè in Egitto,* perches Moses uncomfortably on top of a love story involving the Egyptian pharaoh's son and a Hebrew girl. It is always a perplexity when the lead character in an opera has no particularly intense personal relation with the other characters; sometimes such a libretto encourages the composer to identify the lead character with the orchestra, and this is exactly what happens in *Mosè*. Moses is a faceless torso of power who summons God's revenge in the form of great orchestral interludes: the plague of darkness at the beginning, the parting of the Red Sea at the end. Rossini didn't add Moses' magnificent prayer *Dal tuo stellato soglio* until 1819; in the 1818 original, Moses had little of interest to sing—he was merely the conductor of the divine instrumentalists in the pit.

Representing Moses has been a trial for visual artists as well. They are vexed by the Vulgate's mistranslation of the Hebrew verb *qaran*, which can mean either "grow horns" or "shoot out rays"; by choosing the former definition, the translators

First published in *The Opera Quarterly* 23 (2007): 441–54.

of the Latin Bible enjoined artists to outfit Moses with a fine pair of horns on his forehead. Michelangelo knew how to sculpt Moses as an image of clenched, potent wrath, despite the horns. But Tintoretto and other painters equivocated between the two definitions of *qaran* by plunking onto Moses's head two narrow yellow triangles, an effect that gives the impression of a defective halo. In this way the traditional iconography of Moses became entwined with the traditional iconography of fauns, satyrs, and cuckolds—and, worse, devils. Indeed, Joseph Kiselewski's graceful terracotta Moses, unveiled in 1965 at Syracuse University, eventually provoked members of the Latino American Law Student Association, the Black Law Student Association, the Women's Law Caucus, the Lambda Law Student Association, and the Jewish Law Student Association to complain against depicting Moses as a demon.[1]

The visual Moses, then, was often at the threshold of burlesque. But in *Moses und Aron* (1930–32), Arnold Schoenberg was the first composer to imagine a musical Moses of this sort. Schoenberg's Moses doesn't sing (except for one brief, optional phrase). His music-speech has pitch indications, but these pitches are gestic improvisations, not very closely related to tight unfurlings of the twelve-tone row that determines the real music in the opera. Moses is at once the opera's central force and a songless creature trying to shove and bully his way into a spectacle in which he doesn't belong. Far from conducting the orchestra, as in Rossini's opera, Schoenberg's Moses is helpless in the presence of music. The origins of Moses's *Sprechstimme* lie in Engelbert Humperdinck's fairy-tale opera *Königskinder* (1895–97) and in the fairy tale of nature redemption (the wild hunt of the wind) at the end of Schoenberg's *Gurrelieder* (1901–10): *Sprechstimme* is a kind of fairy speech. Schoenberg perfected the technique in 1912 for the peculiar cabaret show *Pierrot lunaire*. Moses is, from one point of view, a slapstick figure, God's clown.

The traditional mask known as a Pierrot (or Petrushka) is a sad clown—the weeping clown who never gets the girl, who remains helpless in the face of superior force. You might understand the following exchange as part of a Pierrot skit:

The Burning Bush. Take off your shoes.
Moses. My tongue is stiff.

—except that this is one of the most sacred moments in the entire culture of the West. Here Schoenberg promotes Pierrot's futility, his sense of inadequacy, his puzzledness, into the general buffoonery of mankind before an unfathomable God—Elohim, Adonai, Yahweh, at once singular and plural, a labyrinth of speech, a vertigo of song, an unsolvable sound knot. This is the opera's opening scene. Later, Moses is stronger, more assertive and blustering, but he nevertheless remains a curiously impotent presence. In Schoenberg's rewriting of Exodus, the miracle worker is not Moses but Aron, who turns the rod into a snake and makes water gush from the rock. In Bertolt Brecht's *Das Badener Lehrstück vom Einverständis* (1929), a gigantic clown complains of aches in his various limbs, and his straight men promptly saw them off, one by one. When Aron withers Moses's hand into a leprous thing, he is as much a black comedian as anyone in Brecht. By this way of thinking, *Moses und Aron* is a farcical quarrel between a stage magician and a schlemihl. An evil stage director could even present the shattering of the Tables of the Law as an act of petulance, with Moses sticking out his lower lip in a comic grimace: "No one wanted these wonderful laws in the first place, and I'm taking them away [sniff] and going home." Maybe one reason for Schoenberg's inability to write music for the third act was his difficulty in conceiving a genuinely powerful Moses who could demote Aron into nonentity with a wave of his hand.

Throughout the opera, Moses is a figure of heroically obsessive befuddlement. The victim of the incomprehensible command of an incomprehensible God, he imitates the divine unmeaning as best he can by speaking sentences that swallow their own tails, like the serpent of eternity. He tells the Golden Calf, "Vergeh, du Abbild des Unvermögens, das Grenzenlose in ein Bild zu fassen!" (Perish, you image of the impossibility of grasping the dimensionless in an image!) But one suspects that God himself knows much finer paradoxes: Moses is only fooling around in the margins of the ineffable. For Moses, speech is a domain of stutters and growls and gnomic grievances; as for music, it is hard to know whether his ear can hear it at all. If Elliott Gyger is right in believing that the other characters can't hear Moses's *Sprechstimme*,[2] then Moses is a sort of metaoperatic phantom who stalks and glowers on a level of reality on which the other characters don't exist at all. They are his hallucination and he is theirs.

Nietzsche considered that Socrates's whole philosophy was vitiated by his dislike of music—that is, until in the final days of his life, when he asked for music lessons. Moses the thinker can't sing and may not even be able to hear correctly; he may be the first tone-deaf operatic lead. What he hears is mostly a kind of tinnitus in the fashion of the decaying Smetana, or a kind of mute vibration in the fashion of Beethoven, biting a stick and putting one end on the piano. Moses' *Sprechstimme* sounds like botched singing, as if Moses dimly understood that everyone else was sticking to the score, and only he was unable to follow the melody and the rhythm. And the sound of the Burning Bush—voiced by six singers and six speakers intricately subdivided—may represent the gibberish that a musically illiterate man hears when confronted with modernist music. The Burning Bush resembles the Golden Calf in that it is an image of the impossibility of confining the dimensionless in an image, but Schoenberg's music, teasing, elusive, shapeless, tries to avoid any implication that the impossible might be possible after all. If it is music, it is impossible music.

In writing this scene, Schoenberg may have conceived Moses along the lines of those music critics—not necessarily hostile to Schoenberg's artistic goals, but certainly bewildered by them—who left Schoenberg's concerts scratching their heads, but with tongues far from stiff. Think of Moses as Beckmesser. Sometimes Moses seems puzzled by music, sometimes (especially when Aron sings) he seems antagonistic to it: Moses' antecedents include the snare drum that tries, with its improvised pitchless urgencies, to overwhelm and punish the orchestra in Nielsen's Fifth Symphony (1921–22), and the baritone who puts a stop to the proceedings in Beethoven's Ninth Symphony (1824)—"O Freunde, nicht diese Töne"—though that baritone turns out to be a good deal more genial than Moses.

The high point of the first act of *Moses und Aron* is the opening scene, with its phonic simulation of something beyond music, and its somewhat deaf auditor. In the rest of the first act, Schoenberg accustoms us to the shape of melodies directedly derived from the tone row: the first forty-eight notes that Aron sings, at the beginning of Act 1, scene 2, comprise the row, its inversion, its retrograde, and its retrograde inversion. As the act proceeds, the row gets subdivided into more and more epigrammatic and comprehensible (comprehensible, and therefore fallen) forms: at the beginning of Act 1, scene 3, a girl marvels at Aron, a flame going forth to the waste land—she sings a retrograde version of the row (R10), but repeats the first four notes three times; then a boy replies that Aron passed by like a shining cloud—he sings a retrograde inversion of the row (IR7), but also repeats three times the first four notes. In this way the first four notes of the retrograde become a striking and memorable melodic figure: we easily hear the boy as an upside-down girl. As the music descends from the realm of the divine to the realm of opera—Aaronic tenor charisma—it becomes more and more preoccupied with graspable figures and intelligible procedures, though of the sort more often found in instrumental music than in vocal.

When we come to the great orgy that occupies most of the second act, we have music for the first time in the score, music that anyone would understand as music. It opens with a procession of camels, asses, and horses bearing sacrificial gifts for the Golden Calf, and a "Dance of the Butchers," who carry long knives. Glissandi seem to imitate the panting of animals, and to anticipate the lubriciousness of the upcoming revels. At the section marked *Rascher* (m. 371), Schoenberg starts up (of all things) an accompaniment figure in monotonous arpeggios of stacked fifths, one sequence beginning on D, the other on C (figure 6.1). As Elliott Gyger has commented, these figures stand out strongly because the perfect fifths are so idiomatic for the strings that the listener becomes aware of violins and violinists instead of "a subtly varying reservoir of disembodied timbres."[3]

Above these arpeggios a xylophone starts playing a catchy fragment of the row (6): many of the notes from the row are omitted, because they have been demoted to the accompaniment, but the row's notes 8 to 10 (F–G♭–A♭) become obsessively repeated, always terminating with a repetition of the A♭ and a falling sixth (to C♭), strong on the first beat, weak on the second—the C♭ is from note 11 of the row.

Figure 6.1. Schoenberg: *Moses und Aron*, xylophone, from Arnold Schoenberg, *Moses und Aron*, Oper in drei Akten, Klavierauzug von Winfried Zillig (Mainz: B. Schott's Söhne, n.d.), 210. © 1957 by Gertrud Schoenberg. © Renewed. All rights reserved. Used by permission of European American Music Distributors LLC, sole U.S. and Canadian agent for Schott's Music.

After the xylophone, the trumpet takes up the catchy fragment, and notes 8 to 11 (F–G♭–A♭–C♭) start to seize control of the whole texture: their rhythm (dotted eighth, sixteenth, eighth; strong eighth, weak eighth) infects figures composed of different pitches (figure 6.2). All this is part of the introduction to the "Dance of the Butchers."

The Dance of the Butchers proper begins with two fortissimo chords: the first consist of the notes D, B♭, and G, the second of D♯, B, and F♯ (figure 6.3). The first may be gathered together from row (R11), the second from row (IR2); the first is a D-minor triad, the second a B-major triad, astonishingly abnormal in the context of this formidable opera.

This passage could be straight out of Strauss's *Elektra* (1909). Indeed, it is possible to hear the bellowing of the sacrificial animals and the fall of the butcher's axe, a sound not far from the crack of the axe on Agamemnon's head so often recalled in Strauss's opera. After this peremptory beginning, the dance proceeds, a fugato of trumpet figures in rhythms similar to those just described. Schoenberg provides a good deal of what might be called pseudoretrograde, for example at measure 446, where the rising notes B–(A)–D♯–C are followed by the falling notes C–E♭–B♭. The phrase seems to aim for B, but to miss it by a half step (figure 6.4).

Everywhere the music suggests something energetic, clumsy, crackpot, an act of blasphemy against the row. I once played this passage for my friend the composer and theorist Robert Morris, who responded with one word: craven.

The glissandi, the clumped vigor, the trumpet, the xylophone—all these suggest jazz, and Schoenberg may have intended it as a parody of pop music, like the ghastly stuff that comes out of the radio in Schoenberg's previous opera, *Von heute auf morgen* (1930). But I wonder whether Schoenberg's indictment of music might reach much farther.

Figure 6.2. Schoenberg: *Moses und Aron,* trumpet, from Arnold Schoenberg, *Moses und Aron,* Oper in drei Akten, Klavierauszug von Winfried Zillig (Mainz: B. Schott's Söhne, n.d.), 211. © 1957 by Gertrud Schoenberg. © Renewed. All rights reserved. Used by permission of European American Music Distributors LLC, sole U.S. and Canadian agent for Schott's Music.

There are passages in the grand classical tradition that have something of the sonority and constructive procedure as the Dance of the Butchers. A notable example is the hair-raising fugato in the first movement of Liszt's *Eine Faust-Symphonie* (1854), at rehearsal letter Z (*Sehr langsam*). It is made up mostly of sequences of rising augmented triads displaced over the whole gamut; but Liszt doesn't hesitate to include other sorts of triads when it suits him. Earlier examples can be found in Beethoven: the first movement of the Fifth Symphony (1808) fills up the entire phonosphere with a single figure, but that figure is much more stable than Schoenberg's. A better example is the final movement of the "Tempest" sonata, Opus 31, no. 2 (1801–2), in which the obsessive four-note figure keeps distending or contracting its intervals, reconfiguring itself, leaping around the keyboard, but always retaining a recognizable shape.

Schoenberg staked his career on the primacy of pitch over every other musical variable. The twelve-tone system assumes that the well-tempered scale is a

Figure 6.3. Schoenberg: *Moses und Aron*, triads, from Arnold Schoenberg, *Moses und Aron*, Oper in drei Akten, Klavierauzug von Winfried Zillig (Mainz: B. Schott's Söhne, n.d.), 213. © 1957 by Gertrud Schoenberg. © Renewed. All rights reserved. Used by permission of European American Music Distributors LLC, sole U.S. and Canadian agent for Schott's Music.

Figure 6.4. Schoenberg: *Moses und Aron*, pseudo-retrograde, from Arnold Schoenberg, *Moses und Aron*, Oper in drei Akten, Klavierauzug von Winfried Zillig (Mainz: B. Schott's Söhne, n.d.), 237. © 1957 by Gertrud Schoenberg. © Renewed. All rights reserved. Used by permission of European American Music Distributors LLC, sole U.S. and Canadian agent for Schott's Music.

universal fundamental, like pi; and that music is a body of procedures for relating twelve different pitch classes to one another. But in Beethoven, in Liszt, and especially in Wagner and Richard Strauss, a contrary line of thought can be found: that the rudiment of all music is the figure, the cell, the gesture; and that this figure, though composed of pitches, is not subservient to them. Often Wagner or Strauss will take a theme and completely alter its intervallic nature—and yet the theme retains its identity. In fact, in *Der Ring des Nibelungen* Wagner composed *Leitmotive* (Nibelungs, or Hagen) so intensely rhythmic in character that you can recognize them when they are tapped out by a single kettledrum.

I don't know if Schoenberg quite articulated this to himself, but I see this sort of gestic music as a threat to Schoenberg's hegemony. In the Dance of the Butchers, Schoenberg uses the very compositional procedures I have just described: he retains enough of the tone row to appease his conscience, but he makes the butchers jog to continuously permutating music shapes that are remarkably independent of the intervals that compose them. In other hands (Beethoven's, or Verdi's—I'm thinking of "Dio mi potevi scagliar" from *Otello*), such music might indicate a suppleness of conception, a plasticity to altering emotional states; but in Schoenberg's hands it is merely diabolic slither.

This pandering has many ramifications. It is a concession to opera in the bad sense of the word—in Alexander Rehding's words, "You want a love story? Okay, I'll give you a love story. Here, have some sex and violence."[4] But such pandering disparages the thing it condescends to—and it condescends not only to opera, but to the whole gestic-dramatic means of development prevalent in instrumental music. If the "Dance of the Butchers" constructs music from unstable cells in order to indict music constructed from unstable cells, it is proscribing a good deal of the music we hear in our concert halls. But it is possible that Schoenberg's accusations extend to everything we commonly call music. According to Schoenberg's *Harmonielehre* (1911), all music that has ever been composed and ever will be composed is sleeping inside a single note:

> The primitive ear hears the tone as irreducible, but physics recognizes it to be complex. In the meantime, however, musicians discovered that it is *capable of continuation,* i.e. that movement *is latent within it.* That problems are concealed in it, problems that clash with one another, that the tone lives and seeks to propagate itself.[5]

To think in terms of cells and gestures, independent of pitch, is to overlay an arbitrary form over the music derived from the spectral study of a note. Furthermore, Regina Busch has called attention to a strange but important passage in *Totentanz der Prinzipien* ("Death Dance of the Principles," 1915), where Schoenberg notes that bells keep ringing even after the twelfth stroke is finished:

One sound! Without any differentiation.... We recognize that it lives; by its pallor and insipidity; by its wealth of indistinctnesses;... by the fact that its pallor and insipidity now resolve themselves into colours and shapes.... It disintegrates more and more and is in motion.... So much and every individual thing seems important.... Now it sings; each one sings something different, thinks that he sings the same, and really in one direction it sounds in unison; (in amazement) in another polyphonic. In a third and fourth it sounds different again; but that cannot be expressed.[6]

It is as if silence, or a reverberation impinging on silence, can slowly gather its vaguenesses together, clasp itself into *tönend bewegte Form,* form made of moving sounds. This sound shape can appear as one note or as a complicated composition according to where the listener stands with respect to it. A single note is always in the act of becoming all sounds; a complex web of sound is always in the act of refining itself down to a single note. The infinitely varied and the ultimately simple are two faces of the same thing. Therefore the God of *Moses und Aron* expresses his monotheistic character by whispering and shouting and singing all the notes at once: white noise has all frequencies, just as white light has all colors.

Music, then, is a motion that expresses a stasis. There is something deeply Parmenidean in Schoenberg's musical makeup. Parmenides taught that the world is an unchanging whole, and change is only an illusion created by the defects in our sense organs. Parmenides' pupil Zeno tried to confirm this belief through his celebrated paradoxes: the arrow shot by the archer never leaves the bow, because in a single instant it could travel no distance at all, and, since time is nothing but a heap of instants, the sum of a sequence of zeroes must remain zero. Schoenberg's music is astonishly complicated, dense in event, but it keeps alluding to a transcendental plainness. In the end, perhaps all music is contaminated and compromised by its very audibility, its motility, its lack of changelessness. Perhaps unheard melodies are not only sweeter, but the only music worth attending to.

Schoenberg was fond of music that leaves off on nothingness: the accelerating vanish of the shiver at the end of *Erwartung* (a piece described by Schoenberg as an instant of time turned into a half-hour spectacle); the soprano voices that climb to the threshold of hearing in *Herzgewächse* (1911) and the *Jakobsleiter* fragment (1917–22). In the latter work, the Angel Gabriel says,

Tritt näher du, der auf mittlerer Stufe ein Abbild ist und den Glanz besitz;	You on the middle level, step closer, who are a likeness and possess the radiance;
der einem Viel-Höheren ähnlich ist, wie dem Grundton der ferne Oberton;	who are similar to one Much Higher as the distant overtone is similar to the fundamental;

während andere, tiefere, selbst fast Grundtöne,	while others, deeper, themselves almost fundamentals,
ihm wie der helle Bergkristall,	are more foreign to him, as the bright rock crystal
fremder sind, als Kohle dem Diamanten!⁷	is more foreign to diamond tha coal is.

Jacob's ladder is a *Tonleiter*, a scale: and God is the limit point at the top of the overtone series. In a perspective drawing there is always a vanishing point exactly opposite the eye, toward which all parallel lines lead. Schoenberg seems to have conceived music similarly, as an art in which all sounds point upward toward some single sound far above the threshold of hearing. *Moses und Aron* begins with God-music, an audible omnipresence, passing human understanding; it ends with a single prolonged F♯, as if all music had folded itself back up into that single note in which all music is latent. This is God's other face, the unitary simplicity on the far side of all complexity, the grace that comes (in Kleist's phrase) when we eat a second time from the fruit of the tree of knowledge.

But *Moses und Aron* is a work of art, not a theological tract, and the ending is trickier than it first seems. What drives Moses to despair is the sight of his people following an image: not the Golden Calf, but the Pillar of Cloud by day, the Pillar of Fire by night. To oppose magic is one thing when the magician is your oily brother Aron; it is another thing entirely when God himself stoops to miracle. The happy populace marches behind the Pillars to repetitive, clunky music with a high rhythmic profile, a dumbed-down version of the procedures we heard in the "Dance of the Butchers." (We heard this same music at the end of Act 1. It's as if, after all the sex and glitz and suicide, after the production of the Ten Commandments, after the destruction of the Ten Commandments, nothing has happened at all.) Moses feels himself an unwitting accomplice in God's own incentives to idolatry.

The last few bars are among the most widely admired of Schoenberg's achievements, partly because of the overwhelming beauty of the unison melody, partly because Moses and the orchestra seem no longer at odds with one another (figure 6.5). The strings play the last seven notes of the row (IR4), but get the row wrong by reversing the B and the C♯, as if the row were acquiescing in the general error of the human condition, allowing itself to *express* Moses's despair instead of representing a glassy mathematical transcendence in which Moses could play no part.

In every way the music, like God himself, seems to be trying to accommodate human frailty.

I spoke earlier of the *Sprechstimme* of *Pierrot lunaire* as a kind of clown speech, but that wasn't quite right. The performer doesn't represent Pierrot himself; she recites little poems *about* Pierrot's antics and impersonates Pierrot from a great distance. If the parallel with *Moses und Aron* is exact, Moses is not himself the clown but a narrator telling us about the behavior of a superior clown, namely God. Schoenberg was

Figure 6.5. Schoenberg: *Moses und Aron,* end of Act 2, from Arnold Schoenberg, *Moses und Aron,* Oper in drei Akten, Klavierauzug von Winfried Zillig (Mainz: B. Schott's Söhne, n.d.), 300. © 1957 by Gertrud Schoenberg. © Renewed. All rights reserved. Used by permission of European American Music Distributors LLC, sole U.S. and Canadian agent for Schott's Music.

not a frivolous man, but there are some odd features to his theology. The only work of Schoenberg's that closely resembles (texturally speaking) *Moses und Aron* is his very last composition, the unfinished *Moderner Psalm* (1950). A speaker intones a prayer over orchestral and choral accompaniment, thanking God for not paying any attention to his prayers—the pleasure lies in the praying itself, not in the expectation of blessing. A deaf God who amuses us (amuses himself?) with inventing rules and then making exceptions to them; who dazzles us and ignores us; who craves our love and yet craves nothing—such is the clown God, the clown Schoenberg.

Chapter Seven

Elliott Carter and Poetry

Listening to, Listening Through

Poets have always been listening. The meanings they seek to convey in their poems often seem to lie half outside the words, in the rush of wind or water, in the thunder, in the cries of birds, as if poets were trying to translate into human language a poetry that preexists in the whole body of the world's sounds. Composers also listen. When they read poems, they listen both to the music of the words themselves, and to the music on the far side of the poems, the music that the poets themselves were attending to. So when Haydn sets a passage in *The Seasons* in which frogs appear, he sets the orchestra a-croaking. The philosopher Schopenhauer greatly deplored this tendency in Haydn, on the grounds that music should strive to align itself with the deep urgencies hidden in the heart of things, and not to imitate external phenomena. But it's futile to try to argue Haydn out of his ribbits, or Beethoven out of his cheep-cheeps in the song "Die Wachtel" ("The Quail"). In a poem about sound, the external sound is an irresistibly potent metaphor for the poem's meaning. Imagine a composer trying to set this passage from a poem from 1646 by Richard Crashaw, concerning a nightingale:

> There might you hear her kindle her soft voice,
> In the close murmur of a sparkling noise,
> And lay the groundwork of her hopeful song,
> Still keeping in the foreward stream, so long
> Till a sweet whirlwind (striving to get out)
> Heaves her soft bosom, wanders round about,
> And makes a pretty earthquake in her breast. . . .[1]

Only an extraordinary chaste composer could resist the temptation to embody in the music something of the dynamic of the whirlwind and the earthquake, the immense pressure trying to escape through the small orifice of the bird's throat. The meaning of the poem may not be exactly identical with tornado, tremor, or throb of song, but it would be difficult to convey the poem's meaning without some audible allusion to these things.

Elliott Carter is a composer particularly gifted at listening to and listening through poetry. As a sample of his skill at listening to, one might consider a setting he wrote in 1938 of Shakespeare's song "Tell me where is fancy bred."

This lithe and elegant tune is perhaps the only twentieth-century setting of a Shakespeare song that would have given sure pleasure to Shakespeare himself if he had been able to hear it. The contour of the melody, expertly adjusted to the poem's rhythm and breathing pattern, does all the work of expressing the shadowed simplicity of the text.

But of course Carter is famous for text settings of a very different kind. For a long time during the middle of his career, Carter abstained from writing vocal music, and when he resumed he began to write in a style that adapted some features of the strikingly original instrumental style he developed in the 1950s. Two relevant features of Carter's mature style are, first, what Carter calls in a 1959 essay "emancipated musical discourse," extending Schoenberg's idea of the emancipation of the dissonance to a thorough liberation of every aspect of music;[2] and, second, Carter's preoccupation with a sort of utopian polyphony involving the careful coordination of wildly independent strands of music—in his words, "distinct, simultaneously evolving, contributory thought-processes or musical characters."[3]

In Carter's first three compositions for voice and instrumental ensemble—*A Mirror on which to Dwell* (1976), to poems by Elizabeth Bishop; *Syringa* (1978), to a poem by John Ashbery; and *In Sleep, in Thunder* (1982), to poems by Robert Lowell—we can hear a radical rethinking of the notion of setting words to music. When Carter was young, he composed a "Madrigal Book," from which he published a few selections, such as the cheerfully Morleyesque "Harvest Home" (1937). I suspect that the madrigal is for Carter the fundamental musical form for dealing with words. I'm not sure whether to describe the style of the Bishop, Ashbery, and Lowell settings as a sort of antimadrigalism or as a sort of madrigalism pushed to its limit. In the seventeenth-century Italian madrigal, the staggering of voices is typically a device for intensifying the central emotion, as if feeling were heightened to such a pitch that one voice reels off dizzyingly into a small band of reinforcements. (The opening of Monteverdi's *Vago augeletto* provides an good example.) But in Carter's work the accompaniment may reinforce the main line—when there *is* a main line. It may also qualify, resist, question, or contradict the main line. Such features occasionally occur in old madrigals, and quite often in opera: as Carter himself said in a 1960 critique of Shostakovich's *Lady Macbeth of Mtsenk*, "The relation of the music to the action is unaccountable, ranging from opposition, as in the scene in which the heroine and her lover strangle her husband . . . to a lively dance tune, to the more familiar underlining of action and mood."[4] Carter rather disapproved of this opera, which he called "makeshift and callous," a "'comic' book."[5] But he himself was to spend a good deal of time investigating the ways in which music could resist a text, not in a haphazard or arbitrary manner, but by teasing out the text's internal voices of self-resistance. Carter's approach is essentially deconstructive. In a sense, he's Mikhail Bakhtin's or Jacques Derrida's dream composer in that he searches for the implied polyphonies of meaning within the poetry he sets. Carter listens to the text, and he listens *through* the text for ironies and false notes, for veiled meanings that can realize themselves in half-hidden or ambiguous lines in the instrumental accompaniment.

Figure 7.1. Carter: *A Mirror on which to Dwell,* "Sandpiper," from Elliott Carter, *A Mirror on which to Dwell: Six poems of Elizabeth Bishop,* for soprano and chamber orchestra (New York: Associated Music Publishers, ca. 1976), 44. © 1976 (Renewed) by Associated Music Publishers, Inc. (BMI). International copyright secured. All rights reserved. Used by permission.

For this reason Carter often chooses texts in which self-excoriation, bad faith, doubt, or sheer puzzledness is prominent. For a simple example of listening through the text, a passage from the Bishop poem "Sandpiper" might be useful:

The roaring alongside he takes for granted,
and that every so often the world is bound to shake.
He runs, he runs to the south, finical, awkward,
in a state of controlled panic, a student of Blake.

The beach hisses like fat. On his left, a sheet
of interrupting water comes and goes
and glazes over his dark and brittle feet.
He runs, he runs straight through it, watching his toes.

—Watching, rather, the spaces of sand between them
where (no detail too small) the Atlantic drains
rapidly backwards and downwards. As he runs,
he stares at the dragging grains.[6]

This is as literal as Carter gets (figure 7.1). The oboe is obviously imitating the piping of a bird, and the whooshes of the piano are probably imitating the waves. But I think that the oboe is imitating, more than the sound of the bird, the motion of the bird, its hectic jerky gait; Carter is creating a cock-eyed, off-kilter, titubated sort of rhythm. The sandpiper is a student of Blake because Bishop is thinking of Blake's famous lines, "To see a World in a Grain of Sand / And a Heaven in a Wild Flower" ("Auguries of Innocence"); but Blake elsewhere wrote,

Mock on Mock on Voltaire Rousseau
Mock on Mock on tis all in vain
You throw the sand against the wind
And the wind blows it back again

And every sand becomes a Gem
Reflected in the beams divine
Blown back they blind the mocking Eye
But still in Israels paths they shine

The Atoms of Democritus
And Newtons Particles of light
Are sands upon the Red sea shore
Where Israels tents do shine so bright[7]

According to Blake, some folks see grains of sand as gems, whereas others see only inert bits of dead matter. Bishop compared herself to the sandpiper, as she once said: "All my life I have lived and behaved very much like the sandpiper—just running down the edges of different countries and continents, 'looking for something.'"[8] She was clearly looking for gems—"quartz grains, rose and amethyst," according to the end of "Sandpiper," but maybe she was to find only sand. I wonder if Carter caught a glint of self-mockery in this poem. The staccato pecking of the oboe and the voice, atomizing the music, breaking it down into irregular blips and

Figure 7.2. Carter: *A Mirror on which to Dwell,* unheard band, from Elliott Carter, *A Mirror on which to Dwell: Six poems of Elizabeth Bishop,* for soprano and chamber orchestra (New York: Associated Music Publishers, ca. 1976), 70. © 1976 (Renewed) by Associated Music Publishers, Inc. (BMI). International copyright secured. All rights reserved. Used by permission.

peeps, has a somewhat scattered or scatterbrained quality. As an expression of that paradoxical condition, intent aimlessness, the music could hardly be surpassed.

A more complicated example of listening through can be found in another song from the Bishop sequence, "View of the Capitol from the Library of Congress," in which Bishop—then the poetry consultant for the Library of Congress—watches the Air Force Band in the distance, but can't hear it:

> On the east steps the Air Force Band
> in uniforms of Air Force blue
> is playing hard and loud, but—queer—
> the music doesn't quite come through.
>
> It comes in snatches, dim then keen,
> then mute, and yet there is no breeze.
> The giant trees stand in between.
> I think the trees must intervene,
>
> catching the music in their leaves
> like gold-dust, till each big leaf sags.
> Unceasingly the little flags
> feed their limp stripes into the air,
> and the band's efforts vanish there.
>
> Great shades, edge over,
> give the music room.
> The gathered brasses want to go
> *boom—boom.*[9]

Carter is especially attracted to poems about screening. This poem concerns an almost unheard band—and Carter must have relished the challenge of writing music to describe an inaudibility (figure 7.2). We strain our ears to listen through the blocking foliage for the oompahs on the other side, but all we hear are acoustic ghosts: a muffled snare drum, a few faint, defective fanfares from piccolo, oboe, and clarinet (marked *quasi da lontano*, "as if afar"), often with leaps not likely to be encountered in Sousa, such as an upward major ninth. But as the song continues, the direction *quasi da lontano* starts to be found in the parts of the violin and cello, instruments not usually heard in a marching band. It's as if the specter of the band, the imaginary band constructed out of memories of other bands in other places, is itself becoming the screen that blocks the real band's sound. The band is at once everywhere and nowhere. Ultimately the singer has to supply the band's noise herself by saying out loud the syllables *boom—boom,* "intensely whispered," according to the score. From the age of sixteen Carter knew the composer Charles Ives, who was quite fond of musical evocations of distant brass bands. As Carter wrote in a 1946 essay on Ives, "The effects of acoustical perspective made by placing instruments and even whole bands in antiphonal, opposing position on the village green were also tried."[10] Anne Shreffler has consulted Carter's notes and manuscript drafts for "View of the Capitol" and has argued, with great precision and subtlety, that in certain passages Carter is organizing his music into two distinct simultaneous bands, one fast, one slow.[11] But maybe one can hear innumerable spectres of bands. Wisps of pseudobrass seem to come from every direction at once, a metaphor for a sort of ubiquitous nonexistence of sound. I think that Carter, unlike Ives, isn't dealing with too many bands, but with too few. There aren't many precedents in music for portraying a missing sound, but Debussy tries the experiment at the end of his piano prelude "Feux d'artifice" ("Fireworks"). The refrain of the *Marseillaise* ("Aux armes, citoyens") lingers in the air like the memory of a lost tune; as Keats said, unheard melodies are sweeter. Incidentally, Elliott Carter was five years old when Debussy composed that piece.

"Sandpiper" deals with audibly complicated meanings, but "View of the Capitol" deals with an absent meaning. This concern with a meaning that isn't quite there is a strongly modernist aspect of Carter's art. At the climax of T. S. Eliot's *The Waste Land* the thunder speaks the saving syllable, the magic syllable—DA—that ought to bring rain to the desert and heal the broken heart. The poem explains, more or less, that *da* is the root of Sanskrit words meaning "give," "sympathize," and "control." Giving, sympathizing, and controlling are surely all fine things, but it's not clear that they're enough to ease the predicament of modern man. The poem ends polyphonically, in a celebrated piece of gibberish blending Italian and Latin and French and Sanskrit: *uti chelidon nel fuoco à la tour abolie shantih shantih shantih,* to squash the ending even more than Eliot did. The thunderword of *The Waste Land*, and the still more interesting thunderword that appears on the first page of Joyce's *Finnegans Wake,*

> Babadalgharaghtakamminarronnkonnbronntonnerronntuonnthunntrovarrhounawnskawntoohoohoordenenthurnuk!

are desperate, vaguely comical attempts to find a word that can convey ultimate meaning. (Joyce concocted this word out of roots meaning *thunder* in a great variety of different languages.) The supremely meaningful and the absolutely meaningless are strangely intimate with one another in twentieth-century art. This is a sort of aesthetic that tries to listen through the text to hear, in effect, the voice of the universe itself, a voice that may turn out to have nothing to say. As the century progressed, and the modern drifted into the postmodern, the conviction grew that there was a general absence of meaning in texts of all sorts, from the English language to the genetic code. Art becomes a set of inscriptions and doodles and little noises posed on top of a vacuum. I know of no artist more gifted than Carter at making elegant traceries that hint at something missing underneath.

In "View of the Capitol," most of the music represents not what we want to hear, but the screen that prevents us from hearing it, the thick frazzle of leaves disabling the sound of the band. In the next and last song of the Bishop sequence, "O Breath," the instrumental music is unusually static, representing the sleeping woman's slow breathing, but it is full of odd soft tremoli and scurryings and half-audible iridescences of a suspended cymbal and the occasional low muffled blat, as if hinting that the woman's sleep is uneasy, perhaps troubled by nightmare:

> Beneath that loved   and celebrated breast,
> silent, bored really   blindly veined,
> grieves, maybe   lives and lets
> live, passes   bets,
> something moving   but invisibly . . .
> (See the thin flying   of nine black hairs
> four around one   five the other nipple,
> flying almost intolerably   on your own breath.)
> Equivocal, but what we have in common's   bound to be there. . . .[12]

Or maybe the disturbances aren't in the sleeper but in the listener's nerves. At this level of intimacy it's hard to say where the listener stops and the sleeper begins.

Breath can be taken as one of the ultimates of art, an origin and a terminus, since all speech, much music, is but a breath of air. An aura of the sacred surrounds the word *breath,* since words for the human soul—*spiritus, pneuma, ruach*—are often words for breathing. But this is a poem about equivocation, about evasions in love, about shortness of breath, so to speak. Bishop was an asthmatic. The illness curtailed her schooling and sometimes hospitalized her; the breaks in the lines represent a kind of panting. The sleeper breathes, but the singer seems deranged from breathlessness. The melismas of Carter's vocal line are so fretful, so interrupted, that they suggest a singer who continually snatches for air; the song is a tissue of holes. We still listen through the song, but the only thing to be heard on the other side is silence. The florid soprano scribbles on air; but the missing object here is oxygen.

The Lowell sequence repeats many of the themes and devices of the Bishop sequence. Parallel to "Sandpiper" is Lowell's "Across the Yard: La Ignota." In the Bishop setting we hear through the poem to the sandpiper; in "La Ignota" we hear through the poem the voice of a soprano who practices Wagner in a dilapidated house.

> The soprano's bosom breathes the joy of God,
> Brunhilde who could not rule her voice for God. . . .
> She has to sing to keep her curtains flying. . . .
> She flings her high aria to the trash like roses. . . .
> When I was lost and green, I would have given
> the janitor three months' rent for this address.[13]

The unruled voice is represented by a trumpet *quasi da lontano,* in an odd reversal of instrument and voice: the actual tenor we hear singing seems only to be providing a critical commentary on some more potent vocal music that half eludes his hearing (figure 7.3). As in Bishop's "View of the Capitol," there is

Figure 7.3. Carter: *In Sleep, in Thunder,* Brünnhilde, from Elliott Carter, *In Sleep, in Thunder: Six poems of Robert Lowell*, for tenor and 14 instrumentalists (New York: Hendon Music, 1984), 17.

a certain muffling, a screening out of sound, though the curtains here are far less effective than the leaves in the earlier song. I hear no specific allusions to Wagner in the trumpet line, but it can be understood as a bending out of shape of any number of things in *Die Walküre*. The most likely thing, perhaps, for a ruined, retired, or wannabe Brünnhilde to be practicing would be "Hojotoho," as sung at the beginning of Act 2 (figure 7.4).

Figure 7.4. Wagner: *Die Walküre*, "Hojotoho," from Richard Wagner, *The Ring of the Nibelungen*, Second Part, *Die Walküre*, Complete Vocal Score in a Facilitated Arrangement by Karl Klindworth (New York: G. Schirmer, n.d.), 82.

Figure 7.5. Wagner: *Die Walküre*, Valkyrie motive, from Richard Wagner, *The Ring of the Nibelungen*, Second Part, *Die Walküre*, Complete Vocal Score in a Facilitated Arrangement by Karl Klindworth (New York: G. Schirmer, n.d.), 81.

Her first big whoop consists of an augmented G-major triad, progressing into E major, then F major, then F♯ major. The delirious excitement is produced by semitonal upward creeping of the harmony. Wagner's Valkyrie music is marked by a strong tendency to outline triads, but then to violate them, bend them by brute force into a new shape. The Valkyrie motive itself (as first heard at the end of the prelude to Act 2) is built up from a C major triad, but instead of the expected culmination on the octave, the tune lands a little below, on B, the major seventh, making the melody lurch violently into E major (figure 7.5).

In other words, Wagner, like Carter, gives us botched fanfares, but Wagner finds a way to repair the fracture. This swerve to the mediant is the same electric shock that Ravel gives you at the climax of *Boléro*, though Wagner doesn't make you wait fifteen minutes to get it.

A study of the trumpet part in "La Ignota" reveals all sorts of distorted bugle calls, including, at measures 15–16, a fractured Valkyie-like fanfare, and even a quick flash of the G-major augmented triad of "Hojotoho." Later (mm. 34–35) we hear the phrase shape, but not the notes, of "Hojotoho." But of course these Wagnerisms don't sound particularly Wagnerian, since Carter not only deprives them of harmonic support, but also provides the "wrong" support, so that they spike out into all sorts of peculiar shapes. Carter is playing a game similar to the game that Schoenberg played in his 1929 opera *Von heute auf morgen*, whose plot concerns the marital difficulties of a modern composer, not wholly unlike Arnold Schoenberg. At one point the composer's wife flirts with a Wagnerian tenor, who quotes his favorite line from *Die Walküre*, "Schmecktest du mir ihn zu?" ("Will you taste it first for me?" This is the exhausted Siegmund's request to Sieglinde, after she's brought him some water). In Schoenberg's opera, the composer's wife offers the tenor a cup of coffee, and the tenor replies, "Coffee! O sweet Hebe, poured out by *you!*—or, as I sing it as Siegmund, 'Will you taste it first for me?'—café au lait would certainly taste like gin!" What is strange is how easily Wagner's music fits into the atonal texture of Schoenberg's opera; similarly, in "La Ignota" the allusions to Wagner are modest and inconspicuous, in the distance in several senses.

Now much of the story of modernist music consists of various extensions and subversions of Wagner. As a founding father of modernism, Wagner might represent some primary meaning dimly audible behind the occlusions of the twentieth century, some rock, like the great E♭ chord at the beginning of *Das Rheingold*, on which the dizzying experiments of later periods might ground themselves. But as we listen through "La Ignota" to Wagner, we don't find any such place of refuge. Drifts of fake or forgotten Wagner float effortlessly through the song. It's difficult to know whether the Brünnhilde can't sing right or the poet can't hear right, across the yard and through the veils of the curtains. Carter doffs his hat to Wagner, but he doesn't adore him. Wagner provides pleasure, but for Carter, unlike Lowell, Wagner doesn't seem to have anything to do with the voice of God, the trumpet of judgment.

So far we've looked at a number of teases in Carter's music—sound-glimpses of some domain of meaning that is touched on but never fully entered. But in "Syringa," Carter does seem to enter a second world, to expose some deep stratum of meaning beneath the words of a poem. As he explains in his note to the score:

> The idea of accompanying the singer of Ashbery's text with another singer whose part would express the subliminal background that might be evoked in the mind of a reader, very soon suggested itself. Indeed, lines near the poem's end: "In

whose tale are hidden syllables / Of what happened so long before that" led to the idea that the second singer could have a text that reflect some of the sounds, ideas, and feeling of the Ashbery poem in "hidden syllables"—the "hidden syllables" of classical Greek, since the poem was about a classical myth.[14]

Ashbery's poem is difficult, but I construe it as follows: behind the poem lies some experience of loss that the poet can't describe directly, since the pointed facts of a specific man's pain are finally unspeakable, beyond the range of art. So the poet chooses to write not about his own loss but about Orpheus's loss of Eurydice, a well-understood, easily available story. But as he writes his Orpheus poem Ashbery discovers that Orpheus too was a sort of prevaricator, inventing stories because he couldn't deal with the pain of *his* loss, either. The poem reels backward from the truth, in an endless deferral of meaning; it's less a poem than a description of what a poem would look like if it were so fortunate as to exist. Everywhere Ashbery keeps probing the possibility of a secret language adequate to our feeling, like "the language of the birds" that a horse boasts that he can understand; but the poem isn't optimistic about the possibility of holding on to either the people we love or to the love itself or even to the expression of that love in words. At one point a poem streaks by, "its tail afire, a bad / Comet . . . The singer / Must then pass out of sight."[15] Neither the poet nor the poem can hope to endure, can hope to say much.

But Carter counterpoises all this palaver about how life runs off into places we can't find, how life petrifies into snapshot and microfilm, with texts from classical Greek, including a creation song ascribed to Orpheus himself; lines by Sappho of the utmost erotic intensity; and Plato's peculiar story of the phantom Eurydice that followed Orpheus from the underworld—a phantom, not the real woman, because the gods figured that a musician was too craven actually to die for love. Classical Greek is a language little known to the public at large. Any language you don't understand is a plausible version of the language of the gods. Robert Morgan, in his wonderfully wide-ranging article, points out that in the nineteenth century writers spoke of music as "a second Sanskrit" (E. T. A. Hoffmann) or "a mysterious language [revealing] that which is most mysterious" (Ludwig Tieck); but the notion of juxtaposing two musical languages, one discursive and prosaic, the other esoteric, perhaps began after Hoffmann's time.[16]

In some sense "Syringa"'s whole premise of realizing a secret language somewhere behind a vocal line is a monstrous expansion of a device Carter used in his Frost song "The Line Gang" (published 1975, evidently written 1942), concerning the destruction of forests to provide telephone and telegraph lines. Here Carter taps out a bit of Morse code, as if to provide an occult second language in counterpoint to the text. We listen through the poem into a language of pure rhythm—or at least an allusion to such a language. If this rhythmically active, aroused beep speech were given to a singer, it would sound rather like "Syringa."

Figure 7.6. Carter: *Syringa*, Eros, from Elliott Carter, *Syringa*, for mezzo-soprano, bass, and guitar, with 10 instruments (New York: Associated Music Publishers, ca. 1980), 48. © 1980 by Associated Music Publishers, Inc. (BMI). International copyright secured. All rights reserved. Used by permission

The sonority of the mezzo-soprano singing Ashbery's poem is usually quite distinct from that of the bass singing the Greek (mm. 159–82) (figure 7.6):

But it isn't enough
To just go on singing. Orpheus realized this
And didn't mind so much about this reward being in heaven
After the Bacchantes had torn him apart, driven
Half out their minds by his music, what it was doing to them.
Some say it was for his treatment of Eurydice.

Eros, once again,
unloosens my body
torments me
bitter-sweet
irresistible monster. . . .
The seed of fire
preserving. . . .[17]

As Lawrence Kramer once pointed out in a fine article, the distance between the mezzo-soprano and the bass keeps shifting; but in general the mezzo-soprano is conversational, easy-going, as if she were reading the text out loud, whereas the bass yelps, yodels, agonizes.[18] Carter himself was inspired by Cavalieri's *Rappresentazione di anima e di corpo*,[19] but in some ways the effect is closer to that of Monteverdi's narrated epic *Il Combattimento di Tancredi e Clorinda* (1624), except that the narrator and the impassioned characters often sing at the same time. We listen through the mezzo-soprano to the hyperexpressive sound world of the bass, revealing the true affect hidden beneath the often prosaic surface of Ashbery's text. In most settings of the Orpheus story, there is a musical dialectic between beauty and terror. In Gluck's *Orfeo ed Euridice* (1762), Orpheus sings a lovely song to the furies, while the furies threaten him and Cerberus howls. Stravinsky's *Orpheus* (1948) begins with the plinks of Orpheus's lyre and climaxes with the Bacchantes' ripping Orpheus into pieces. But in "Syringa," beauty and terror, lamentation and dismemberment, all belong to the emotionally intense world of the bass, the undersong; the mezzo-soprano doesn't seem to know much about them.

In some ways Carter's strategy, ingenious as it is, betrays the effect that Ashbery sought. Instead of an unspoken x at the core of the poem, Carter provides an articulate musical speech; where Ashbery frames an absence, Carter fills the hole with an opera. As soon as music's secret language becomes audible, it isn't a secret any more; the bass's voice becomes simply one more line in the whole polyphonic collection, distinct only insofar as it offers unusually legible codes of affect. On the other hand, if Carter is trying to demonstrate that there isn't really anything there on the far side of music—if he is exposing the folly of trying to listen through music to something real, something miraculous, beyond the surface—then maybe "Syringa" accomplishes his goal. When I hear it, I feel disillusioned. Beyond the web of sound there seems to be nothing but an excited bass showing off.

Perhaps there's a clue in "Syringa" itself that the limitation of music, its inability to reach distant goals, is Carter's true theme. When the bass sings of the phantom Eurydice and the cowardly Orpheus, he suggests that under the aspect of eternity neither the singer nor his grief counts for very much; and all the bass's ululating and whooping may be read not as woe or horniness or exaltation, but as fear—the fear that all these expressive gestures may reel off into nothing. By revealing in song the secret meaning of Ashbery's poem, Carter makes it ordinary.

If I'm right about this, the true sequel to "Syringa" is his *Symphonia* (1998), subtitled *Sum fluxae pretium spei* ("I am the prize of flowing hope"). The line is from a Latin poem, "Bulla" ("Bubble"), by Richard Crashaw, the seventeenth-century Royalist and Roman Catholic convert. The motto of the amazing final movement, *Allegro scorrevole,* is also taken from Crashaw's poem:

Sum venti ingenium breve	I am the genius of the gust,
Flos sum, scilicet, aeris. . . .	And the sure flower of air. . . .

This movement is the most prolonged act of vanishing in music: it is a playful representation of sheer nihil. Carter isn't the first composer to deal with nothingness as a theme for music. For example, at the end of Schoenberg's *Erwartung* (1909), the music glides away into a faint, fast prickling of zero. And we can find similar things in much earlier music. In Crashaw's age—in fact in Rome, the very city where Crashaw held a minor clerical post—a peculiar subspecies of oratorio arose called the *vanitas*. In one such oratorio, *Vanitas vanitatum II,* attributed to Carissimi, pompous music depicting the pomp of royal life suddenly collapses at the mention of the word *vanity,* like a balloon pricked with a needle:

Sceptres, crowns, purple pomp,
triumphs, laurels, honors, decorations,
glories, even games, and delights,
and feasts, and riches, all
is vanity and a shadow.[20]

The simplest meaning of the word *vanity* is "emptiness." This oratorio is exactly equivalent to those seventeenth-century still lifes in which a skull and a housefly were somber signs of the transience of all things mortal. Carissimi even builds long rests into the music, as if the listener were to contemplate the fact that of the things that pass away, nothing passes away so quickly as music, which makes its little noise and then is as if it never was. In the twenty-first century, silence stands as one of the austere ultimates of experience, along with meaninglessness and death, those Easter Island statues that loom over the art of the age. But Carter seems to smile as he contemplates the silence that is the only certain thing that lies on the far side of sound. Again and again in his later work appear musical realizations of the dissolving and dissipating of all things: *solvet saeclum in favilla* (all the ages dissolve in ashes). In William Carlos Williams's poem "Lear," which Carter set in his *Of Rewaking* (2003), one passage describes how Williams dreamed of a throng of solid-seeming men and women:

> but as we approached down the paved
> corridor melted—Was it I?—like
> smoke from bonfires blowing away[21]

The poem may be called "Lear," but the music would be right for that speech in *The Tempest* where Prospero describes how

> The cloud-capp'd tow'rs, the gorgeous palaces,
> The solemn temples, the great globe itself,
> Yea, all which it inherit, shall dissolve,
> And like this insubstantial pageant faded
> Leave not a rack behind. We are such stuff
> As dreams are made on, and our little life
> Is rounded with a sleep.[22]

Carter is sometimes thought of as a rather abstract composer, and this essay may have made him seem all the more abstract, if not abstruse. But I want to end with a notion that Carter is in one sense a remarkably concrete composer. I've argued that we listen through the music and find absence, breathlessness, silence; but from another perspective we listen through the music and hear an extraordinarily complete representation of the way it feels to have a body. If I attend closely to the rhythms of my body and count up how often my heart beats in a minute, how often I breathe, I find that these frequencies have no relation to one another. Pulse and breath seem to operate on independent arithmetical systems. If I factor in other data, such as the oscillations of eyeballs, the twitches of head and arms, not to mention blinking, I find that on the most concrete level my life as a mammal is a polyphony. In a note in the score of *Partita* (1993), which became the first movement of *Symphonia,* Carter wrote,

> During and after composing Partita . . . my musical intention was to present the many changes and oppositions of mood that make up our experience of life. In general, my music seeks the awareness of motion we have in flying or driving of a car and not the plodding of horses or the marching of soldiers that pervades the motion patterns of older music. At the time I was reading poems

of the English Jacobean poet Richard Crashaw, and was fascinated by . . . *Bulla* (Bubble), which at one point personifies a floating bubble. . . .[23]

Carter sees his music as something like a jet plane performing aerial maneuvers. I see his music as a description of the sheer multifariousness of the motor and perceptual nervous system, the buzz and shimmer of living in a world where independent phenomena bombard us from all sides. But in either case Carter is a realist of the deepest human senses—muscular clench and balance, coenesthesis. You should hear not only elegant inflections, but bone and blood.

Chapter Eight

Sophoclean Opera

Everyone knows that opera arose at the end of the sixteenth century as an experiment in recapturing the music of Greek tragedy. But strangely, the composers of the first operas had little use for the actual texts of Greek tragedies. Jacopo Peri's *Euridice* (1600) and Claudio Monteverdi's *Orfeo* (1607) were both based on the story of Orpheus as known principally from Ovid's *Metamorphoses* X, with certain details taken from Virgil's *Georgics* IV and Angelo Poliziano's terse drama *La favola di Orfeo* (1480). There is no extant Greek tragedy starring Orpheus, but the early opera writers were so enamored of the tale that they created a sort of fake Greek tragic text especially suited to the fake Greek tragic music they were composing.

Ovid was far more congenial than Aeschylus. Music is the art of change. Metamorphoses, endless reshapings of fields of sensation, were more appealing to the early opera composers than Aeschylus's rough-hewn rhetoric of heroic steadfastness. In Aristophanes's *Frogs*, Euripides denounces Aeschylus—both of them are in hell—as a

> creator of crude characters, stubborn-mouthed,
> he's got an unbridled, uncontrolled, ungated mouth
> uncircumlocuitous, brag-bundle-voiced. . . .
> [A] dozen bullish words
> With eyebrows, crests, some awful witch-faced things,
> Unknown to the audience.[1]

There is enough truth in this caricature to show why Aeschylus's rugged, orotund plays were unsuited to an art that prized (at least at its beginning) delicacy of emotional transition. Early opera is overwhelmingly Ovidian: the fifth intermedio from *La pellegrina* (1586, composed by Malvezzi and Peri) retells Ovid's story (*Fasti* II) of Arion and the dolphin. Marco da Gagliano's *La Dafne* (1608) retells the famous tale of Daphne's metamorphosis into a laurel tree (*Metamorphoses* I).

In fact, at the beginning of Ottavio Rinuccini's libretto to *La Dafne*, Ovid himself descends from Elysium to warn the spectators that they're about to see a play about the dangerousness of love: beware, you might fall in love with a girl only to find her turned into a tree. Immediately after this brief prologue, Apollo kills a dragon with his bow and arrow. The whole protocol of this opening is all wrong by the standards of Greek tragedy. If there is a prologue, it is a god (as in Euripides' *Hippolytus*), not a poet. Monsters are killed offstage and enter the play as a form of narrative (also as in the *Hippolytus*). The early opera writers quite liked combats with monsters. In the third intermedio from *La pellegrina* (music by Luca Marenzio), Apollo slays the monster at Delphi. To some extent we might say that opera labored to bring into the theater what the Greeks considered indecorous—obscene in the root meaning of the term, that is, incapable of being presented onstage. Ovid's poetry seemed to offer opportunities for sex and violence beyond what was permitted in serious Greek or Roman drama.

In later times, actual Greek tragedy made its way onto the operatic stage, but hesitantly and in much altered form. The most important Greek tragedy, for operatic purposes, was Euripides's *Alcestis,* the subject of substantial operas by (among others) Lully, Handel, and Gluck. I suspect that several reasons for this popularity were: (1) the fact that the plot—a harrowing of Hades for a beloved wife—was the closest thing in Greek tragedy to the story of Orpheus, the gold standard in operatic story lines; and (2) the story had a happy ending, unlike that of Orpheus. However, with some wrenching and hammering, a happy ending for Orpheus was usually contrived. Monteverdi's *L'Orfeo* had an unhappy ending according to the published libretto of 1607, but not according to the published score of 1609. A third reason for the popularity of *Alcestis* was that the luxury-uxorious aspect of the tale flattered an increasingly bourgeois taste. Here was a G-rated opera fit for the whole family. Of course, Euripides wrote his share of X-rated material as well, such as the leeringly incestuous *Hippolytus*. It was daring of Rameau to write *Hippolyte et Aricie* (1733), his first *tragédie lyrique,* based, at a great distance, on such material.

Nietzsche was exquisitely sensitive to the rationalistic nature of Euripidean tragedy, at once matter of fact and driven to spectacular effects. In *The Birth of Tragedy* (1872) he reviles the first opera composers for continuing the castration of Greek tragedy begun by Euripides: harmless sensitive shepherds carving the names of their beloveds into tree trunks, instead of the black Dionysiac revels, the panic fury, the fury of Pan. Even in the Hades of *The Frogs,* Aeschylus disdains Euripides for collecting the low talk of low people:

you gossip-gathering
beggar-making son of a rag-stitcher[2]

It seems that Euripides' work is full of ordinary things and commonplace characters, without the grit and might of the older drama.

My present project is to study how the older tragedies were assimilated into the world of opera. It would be possible to include Aeschylus as well as Sophocles, but Aeschylus has enjoyed little love among musicians. Beethoven's ambitious ballet *The Creatures of Prometheus* and Liszt's excellent *Prometheus-Cantate* have little to do with Aeschylus. Taneyev's *Oresteia* is a chiefly a curiosity. In general it is difficult to see that Aeschylus had much influence in Western dramatic music until Darius Milhaud's *Agamemnon* (1914) and *Les Choéphores* (ca. 1916) and a few later works by Carl Orff and Iannis Xenakis. On the other hand, in the 1850s Wagner considered writing a Prometheus opera, and recent critics have shown that there's a good deal of occult Aeschylus in *Die Walküre*.

The case of Sophocles is richer. Few operas are adaptations of his plays. It is telling that Michael Ewans, in his close study of opera and tragedy discusses at any length no Sophoclean operas written earlier than the twentieth century (though he treats Strauss's *Elektra* and Enesco's *Oedipe* as fully as they deserve).[3] And yet Sophocles looms up behind the whole genre as a sort of conscience of the race of dramatic composers, an ideal of both propriety and expressive power. To write music for Sophocles is, in a sense, to accept a dare, to try to bend a corrupt, compromised genre, full of idly virtuosic displays of singing, into some conformity with the noble ideals with which opera began. This is not true in every case: Antonio Sacchini, Théodore Gouvy, and others wrote tasteful and unstrenuous Sophoclean operas. But I'm concerned with composers who seem aroused, even made nervous, by the challenges that Sophocles presented.

I want to begin with the opening chorus of *Antigone:*

Shaft of the sun, fairest light of all that have dawned on Thebes of the seven gates, you have shone forth at last, eye of golden day, advancing over Dirce's streams! You have goaded with a sharper bit the warrior of the white shield, who came from Argos in full armor, driving him to headlong retreat.

He set out against our land because of the strife-filled claims of Polyneices, and like a screaming eagle he flew over into our land, covered by his snow-white wing, with a mass of weapons and crested helmets.

He paused above our dwellings; he gaped around our sevenfold portals with spears thirsting for blood; but he left before his jaws were ever glutted with our gore, or before the Fire-god's pine-fed flame had seized our crown of towers. So fierce was the crash of battle swelling about his back, a match too hard to win for the rival of the dragon.[4]

After the banishing of Oedipus, his sons Eteocles and Polynices decided to be alternate kings, first a year of Eteocles, then a year of Polynices, and so on. But at the end of his term Eteocles refused to abdicate, so Polynices gathered a band of Argives—foreigners, the Seven against Thebes—to attack his own city. This chorus describes the terror of the war, which ended when Polynices and Eteocles killed each other in single combat. Then Creon, Oedipus's brother-in-law, assumed the throne and commanded that the traitor Polynices' body be left unburied. Antigone refused to let her brother become food for crows and wolves, with many unhappy consequences.

Composers have treated this chorus in diverse ways. In 1772 Tommaso Traetta's opera *Antigona* was first performed, ten years after Gluck's great reform opera *Orfeo ed Euridice*. Just as opera had begun with Ovid, so it was reformed—made spare and swift, incisive—by means of Ovid. Traetta was as, far as I know, the first composer to see how Sophocles could be sung to Gluck's tunes, how this text could be crammed into the moulds of Gluckian dramaturgy. Traetta's librettist, Marco Coltellini, sent the text of *Antigona* to the lucid monarch of Prussia, Frederick II, along with a letter pointing out that instead of "simple allegories and fulsome praises" Coltellini had made use of "those two most powerful resources of the tragic theatre—Pity and Terror."[5] In this way we see that Aristotle accompanied Sophocles on the Enlightenment's path to tragic opera.

Traetta and Coltellini were willing to follow Gluck's precedent by greatly expanding the role of chorus, but they could not see the wisdom of putting near the beginning of the opera a great choral recapitulation of the battle, as Sophocles did. Instead, the opera opens with, of all things, a ballet, in which the competing armies dance a "Pyrrhic dance" in preparation for the single combat of Eteocles and Polynices. The first singing we hear consists of choral antiphony, as the opposing warriors cheer their champions on. Traetta skillfully intensifies the fight music just before the double murder, when Creon of Thebes and Adrastes of Argos cry "No!" in horror. His modulations of key and of emotional tenor, at once abrupt and supple, show how chunk-style baroque opera is quickly breaking down into a flexible dramatic discourse. But Sophocles was himself a composer of numbers operas, so to speak, with his careful articulation of his plays into episode versus chorus, his careful articulation of his choruses into strophe, antistrophe, epode. Traetta here uses the advanced tools of Gluckian dramatic rhetoric not in the service of Sophocles, but in the service of hauling onstage a combat that Sophocles relegated to choral reminiscence—in the service of making the obscene scenic (as earlier, I mean *obscene* in its root meaning of "not fit to present on stage"). Traetta's choristers aren't engaged in fancy acts of memory. They are active participants in the paradrama teased out of choral narrative. It is as if the singers in Sophocles' chorus got so caught up in the tale of the Seven against Thebes that they became Civil War reenactors.

Some of Traetta's choruses behave in a more orthodox Sophoclean manner as norms, commonplace folks, spouters of received ideas. For example, after Creon is acclaimed king, he utters his terrible edict concerning the corpse of Polynices, and the chorus assents piously: "Così finiscano" ("So perish all traitors—let their pale shades naked gather on Lethe's black marge"). This choral music is almost embarrassingly close to Gluck's music for *Orfeo*'s Furies (Act 2, "Chi mai dall'Erebo"), who challenge Orpheus for entering the realm of the dead—though Traetta's Lethe has a few more whirlwinds than Gluck's Styx.

Gluck's great achievement in Act 2 of *Orfeo* was to create a way of dramatizing the opposition between an individual and a mob. Orpheus pleads, the Furies refuse and refuse and refuse—and relent. Traetta understood the need for finding a way of incarnating conflict in music, but the only procedure for achieving this that he really understood was the method of Act 2 of *Orfeo,* so his choruses tend to sound like persecuting Furies even before anyone challenges them, as in this case. The arresting scenes in *Antigona* usually consist of chorus versus Creon, or chorus versus orchestra. For many conflicts in the text that don't pertain to the chorus, Traetta falls back on old conventions of *Affekt:* the plaintive Ismene, the raging Creon, the resolute Antigone, striking enough at times, but without any structure of dialectic. Even in the opening chorus, the Argive soldiers and the Theban soldiers sing exactly the same material. Expressing enmity in different kinds of musics doesn't come easily to Traetta, unless there's a conflict between chorus and soloist.

For a second treatment of the opening chorus of *Antigone* I turn to Felix Mendelssohn. In 1841 Mendelssohn wrote extensive incidental music for *Antigone* at the request of Friedrich Wilhelm IV of Prussia, who was trying to recreate the experience of Greek tragedy as precisely as the conditions of nineteenth-century Germany permitted. Mendelssohn toyed with some radical ideas for this music. Jason Geary quotes Mendelssohn's friend Eduard Devrient:

> His first thought was to have the choruses sung—if not spoken—entirely in unison recitative and in part by solo voices to an accompaniment of only those instruments that are believed to have been in use during Sophocles's time: flutes, tubas, and harps in place of the lyre. Opposed to this initial suggestion, I noted that the vocal part would be unbearably monotonous, but without achieving an understanding of the words. . . . Felix nevertheless made an attempt at this manner of recitative but confessed to me after only a few days that it could not be carried out.[6]

If Mendelssohn had continued in this vein, he might have repeated in a Biedermeyer key the whole labor of Caccini, Vicenzo Galilei, and the rest of the Florentine Camerata. But if the outcome of his work was more timid than his initial plan, he accomplished some remarkable things.

The avant-garde aspect of his *Antigone* music lies in his insistence that the crucial matter for modernizing Sophocles lies not in recognition and reversal, not in pity and terror, not in the instruments of his orchestra, not even in the interweave of chorus and dramatis personae, but in the meter. Jason Geary's article on Mendelssohn's Hellenizing of his musical style shows brilliantly how closely Mendelssohn hews to the prosody of Sophocles's text, as translated from quantitative to accentual meter, and from Greek to German, by Johann Jakob Donner: the pulse of the choriamb (long-short-short-long) informed Mendelssohn's musical thinking in many passages. And he devised a sort of *Sprechstimme* for the actors, notated with no pitch indication but with rhythmic precision, as when Antigone shudders as she anticipates her arrival in hell, unmarried or as the new bride of Hades (No. 4, "Lebend entführt Hades") (figure 8.1).

We will see soon just how modern, even modernist, Mendelssohn's procedure is. But first let us turn to Mendelssohn's setting of the initial chorus, the retelling of the story of the Seven against Thebes (No. 1, "Strahl des Helios, schönstes

Figure 8.1. Mendelssohn: *Antigone*, Hades abducts, from Felix Mendelssohn, *Antigone des Sophokles nach Donner's Übersetzung*, Op. 55 (Boca Raton, FL: Kalmus, n.d.), 38.

Licht"). The text speaks of elaborate horror; the music speaks of simple patriotic pride. The beast of war may glut itself with blood, but if the music has any military aspect it is that of soldiers on parade, glorifying city and king with displays of pomp.

Mendelssohn isn't deaf to Sophoclean terror, and sometimes his music expresses it well. But Mendelssohn's vision of ancient Greece is still to a large extent that of the Enlightenment, in which his grandfather participated so ably. When Mendelssohn reads the opening chorus, what he first thinks is not, Description of Gruesome Events, but Hymn to the Sun, since the text begins "Strahl des Helios, schönstes Licht" ("Ray of Helios, loveliest light"). The sort of music that comes to his mind is that of Sarastro in Mozart's *Magic Flute*. The Enlightened scholar Johann Joachim Winckelmann taught that the chief characteristics of Greek art were *Heiterkeit* and *Allgemeinheit*, cheerfulness and generality. This is why the slightly insipid features of the Apollo Belvedere sometimes intrude oddly into the tragic catharsis, diarrhea. Mendelssohn wants to give the tragedy its full measure of pain, but where he can find pretext for good cheer, he goes for it.

The other great piece of Sophoclean experimentalism in Mendelssohn's age, Giaocchino Rossini's gargoyle of a cantata *Edipo a Colono* (written before 1817), will show what I mean. This is a setting for baritone, men's chorus, and orchestra of some of the choruses in *Oedipus at Colonus*, as translated by Giambattista Giusti, Rossini's old teacher. Giusti was keen to revive Greek tragedy with as little compromise as possible; since he thought that only the choruses were sung in ancient times, that precluded the composition of an opera in the usual sense.

Rossini's decision to have much of the music sung by a solo baritone can be justified in terms of Greek theater, since Sophocles's chorus often seems to whittle itself down to a single speaker. But Rossini's normal habits of text setting tend to make the baritone into a strange amalgam of a voice denouncing Oedipus, a voice pitying Oedipus, and Oedipus himself. The baritone seems to float among the dramatis personae missing from the cantata's text. Greek tragedy began with the singing of choral hymns at wine festivals in honor of Dionysus, then slowly evolved into staged fables with masked actors. In *Edipo a Colono* we can almost behold taking place the archaic transition from hymn to theater.

In Rossini as in Mendelssohn, the music often seems to conform to Enlightenment notions of Greek serenity and poise, even in places where we might expect something different. Here is Sophocles' final chorus, the words that accompany Oedipus into hell, as he vanishes through a cleft in the earth:

> Goddesses of the nether world and unconquered beast whose lair lies in the gates of many guests, you untamable Watcher of Hades, snarling from the cavern's jaws, as rumor has always told! Hear me, Death, son of Earth and Tartarus! May that Watcher leave a clear path for the stranger on his way to the nether fields of the dead! To you I call, giver of the eternal sleep.[7]

Or, in the superior music of William Butler Yeats:

> Nor may the hundred-headed dog give tongue
> Until the daughter of Earth and Tartarus
> The even bloodless shades call Death has sung
> The travel-broken shade of Oedipus
> Through triumph of completed destiny
> Into eternal sleep, if such there be.[8]

But Rossini's setting of this final chorus ("O tu dell'Orco custode indomabile") disconcerts us with its good cheer. The semantics of Rossini's serious operas are often hard to follow for those used to his comic procedures. Passages of the utmost gravity in, say, *Semiramide*, nevertheless can sound silly and happy. But even granted that Rossini intended this without any trace of burlesque, the music's tension level, its rhythmic verve, produce an odd feeling of inner hilarity. I find this end moving, and I suspect that Rossini had wonderful instincts for the life enhancement that lies at the heart of the tragic experience; as Yeats liked to say, Tragedy must be a joy to the man who dies.

Twentieth-century settings of Greek tragic choruses rarely sound as frisky or good natured as Mendelssohn's or Rossini's. For example, in his 1927 opera *Antigone*, Arthur Honegger set the same chorus that Mendelssohn set, in the hard-boiled translation of Jean Cocteau:

Les Argiens ont fui à toutes jambes sous ton oeil fou soleil. Ils étaient venus aux trousses de Polynice et de ses vagues prétensions. Jupiter déteste la vantardise. Frappés de sa foudre, les panaches et les armures d'orgueil, ses sept chefs qui marchaient contre nos sept postes ont abandonné leurs armes. Il n'est resté sur place que deux frères ennemis. Maintenant la victoire est assise dans Thèbes. Le peuple chante. Mais voici Créon notre nouveau roi.[9]

The Argives have fled at full speed under your eye mad sun. They came on the heels of Polynices and his empty pretentions. Jupiter hates boasting. Struck by his lightning the plumes of pride and armor of pride, the seven leaders who marched against our seven gates have abandoned their arms. Only the two brother-enemies are left dead on the field. Now victory dwells in Thebes. The people are singing. But here is Creon our new king.

This is a disturbing piece of music. It's hard to be sure whether the music sneers at the pretensions of Polynices, the cowardice of the Argives, or the complacency of the chorus itself, confident that all the local political problems have been solved once and for all: God is clearly on the Theban side. But sneer the music does.

The orchestral introduction to the chorus is based on a succession of four chords, the same figure that begins the opera and recurs so often that the first scene resembles a psychotic passacaglia (figure 8.2). The figure comprises two strands. One is a descending F-minor tetrachord, the other is a chromatic ascent. In other contexts, the broken tetrachord might seem lulling, but Honegger outfits it with such dissonance that it becomes a sort of rigid icon of disorder.

As the chorus proceeds, the figure is demoted to the dim background, to the communal unconscious. The foreground becomes filled with a brass theme, shapeless at first but stiffening into impudent tonics and dominants, a bad triumph. This theme is related to a trumpet theme in Honegger's Fifth Symphony (1950)—a symphony, written in 1950, "témoignage d'un homme malade et désillusionné, expression de sa ferme conviction d'une fin du monde prochaine"[10] ("witness of a sick and disillusioned man, expression of his firm conviction that the end of the world is near"). I hear this theme as (in Dryden's words) music to untune the sky, but a fake glory, sodden and perverse.

Twenty years after Honegger's setting, the opening chorus of *Antigone* attained the condition of pure modernist catastrophe in Carl Orff's *Antigonae* (1949); for his libretto Orff chose the black magnificent version by Hölderlin. Nothing could be farther from the bright-hearted Mendelssohn setting. This is the Sophocles of World War II, in which the peppy-sexy devices of *Carmina Burana*—thumping ostinati, elementary consonances—are deformed into an evocation of modern warfare, mortar shells, the whistle of falling things, tanks crushing human bodies, the cranking up of the whole infernal machine (figure 8.3).

Figure 8.2. Honegger: *Antigone*, icon of disorder, from Arthur Honegger, *Antigone: tragédie musicale en 3 actes*, paroles de Jean Cocteau, adaption libre d'après Sophocle (Paris: Éditions Salabert, ca. 1927), 16.

As Orff hears it, the eagle that shrieks through Sophocles's antistrophe is clearly a dive bomber. This is a version of Greek tragedy that Nietzsche, not Winckelmann, might approve: unserene, unluminous, disproportioned, full of ecstatic dismemberment, the tearing apart of worlds, the wisdom that it would be best never to have been born.

Orff's chorus may be an abyss, but it is an abyss of exact measure. Orff's hard evocations of the meters of Greek of poetry place him in the lineage of Mendelssohn, for whom prosody was such an important component of the Greek tragic experience. As a classicist and a connoisseur of rhythm, Orff was extremely skillful at ramming the syllables of Hölderlin's verse into eccentric positions of triplet subdivisions of quarter notes, so that the music sometimes skips along in dactyls, sometimes thickens (as at "Sieben Fürsten") into great, brazen clangs of trochees. And as a composer who began his career by writing adaptations of Monteverdi, Orff delighted in creating a modernist *stile concitato* fit not for the single combat of two champions but for the havocking slaughter of thousands. The huge, unison chant seems above or beneath harmonization in the normal sense. But at the climax, the simple C–D tone cluster expands into crashes of C-major triads with an added D, a note that seems borrowed from the G-major triad, as if an aggregration of notes could be tonic and dominant at the same time—functional harmony defunging into a single chord.

The antistrophe, as Orff sets it, is much lighter than the strophe and the epode that frame it; the whole chorus can be construed as a single, giant, metrical foot, an amphimacer (long-short-long), just as many of Orff's choral triplets have accents on the first and last syllable.

In his youth John Cage made many experiments with hypermeters, structures in which the rhythmic pattern of a single bar was echoed in large structural patterns. Music is rich in such rhymes of the large with the small: for example, Alfred Lorentz (if I remember correctly) proposed that the three acts of Wagner's *Die Meistersinger* could conceived as a magnification of the same stanza

Figure 8.3. Orff: *Antigone,* war, from *Carl Orff, Antigonæ: ein Trauerspiel des Sophokles;* [Übersetzung] von Friedrich Hölderlin; Klavierauszug (Mainz: B. Schott's Söhne, ca. 1949), 29. © 1949 by Schott Music. © Renewed. All rights reserved. Used by permission of European American Music Distributors LLC, sole U.S. and Canadian agent for Schott Music.

structure (the *Bar* form) that the old mastersingers themselves used: two identical Stollen followed by a nonidentical Abgesang. (Each of Wagner's first two acts ends in public consternation; the third act ends in general concord.) All these things manifest what mathematicians call self-similarity, the feature of the Mandelbrot set, where every detail is potent with the All. Sophoclean opera, as we shall see, is especially marked by such structures, at once archaic and the newest of the new—an art that prides itself on its capacity to instill the universe into each small part, in the manner of the microcosm, or the monad, or the fractal. The eon and the instant speak in the same rhythm.

The modernist who listened with the most acute ear to the quantity of classical measure was not Orff but Igor Stravinsky, who seems to have considered his Greek tragedy *Oedipus rex* (1927) a sort of metrical exercise. What is remarkable is how powerfully Stravinsky could summon up Melpomene, the muse of tragedy, by means of procedures that assigned little weight to plot, or character, or anything else Aristotle considered important, but extreme weight to meter. Stravinsky did what he could to deaden every aspect of Sophocles (via Cocteau's stripped, spare version) that would usually be considered dramatic:

> No one "acts," and the only individual who moves at all is the narrator, and he merely to show his detachment from the other stage figures. *Oedipus Rex*... is not at all operatic in the sense of movement. The people in the play ... do not turn to listen to each other's speeches, but address themselves directly to the audience. I thought they should stand rigidly, and in my original version I did not even allow them exits and entrances. My first conception was that the people of the play should be revealed from behind small individual curtains, but I realized later that the same effect might be accomplished more easily by lighting. . . . The singers should be illuminated during their arias and become vocally, though not physically, animated statues. Oedipus himself should stand in full view throughout, of course, except after the "*Lux facta est*" [Light dawns] when he must change masks. . . . I am often asked why I should have tried to compose a waxworks opera.[11]

The notion of a stage fractured into a number of private mini stages, each inhabited by one character, suggests just how far Stravinsky was willing to go toward a cubist tessellation of the concept of drama: he happily dismembered the stage, just as his music sometimes seems to tear the characters limb from limb.

Stravinsky's favorite staging of *Oedipus rex* was Cocteau's 1952 production; Stravinsky particularly liked Cocteau's "huge masks."[12] Cocteau's mask of the blinded Oedipus as a human snail, with eyes at the end of stalks spouting ropes of blood, may well have appealed to Stravinsky's dramacidal lust: Sophocles demoted to the gastropod level. Left to his own devices, Cocteau tended to be frivolous about Greek drama. A few years after *Oedipus rex* he wrote another play on the same theme, *The Infernal Machine,* in which the sphinx is a flirtatious femme fatale with long gloves à la Marlene Dietrich, and Jocasta is a giggly young widow who pouts to Tiresias (whom she nicknames Zizi) that it isn't fair that all the other girls get to go to dances, while she has to be in mourning. (Cocteau's libretto for Honegger's *Antigone,* though fairly straightforward, makes a few jokes too, as when Créon reproaches Antigone for insulting her brother Etéocle with her "hommages antipatriotiques"—the vocabulary of a fascist tyrant.) This sort of frivolity had no attraction for Stravinsky; yet Stravinsky too fools around in the musical margins of the drama, while taking care that dadaist hysteria doesn't destroy the impression of statuelike rigor and monumentality. Cocteau once wrote a poem to Stravinsky that contained the line "Je sculpte en rêve Igor ton audible statue"[13] ("dreaming I sculpt Igor your audible statue"). The whole of *Oedipus rex* is indeed a speaking statue, impressive yet bizarre. A talking classical marble isn't far from that talking, life-size statue of Abraham Lincoln that used to be at Disneyland.

Deadness clustered around *Oedipus rex,* but it has its sources of life as well. Life in Stravinsky's music tends to arise from rhythm, both metrical rhythm and the large-scale dramatic rhythm of conflict itself. The main conflict here doesn't arise from the interactions of the characters—waxworks figures aren't likely to have much passion—but from a simple antithesis of terror versus pity.

The opera opens with a loud five-note theme, B♭–C–A–B♭–A, followed by the soft declaration "Theba peste moritur" ("Thebes is dying of plague") (figure 8.4). Then the loud music returns, followed by a soft passage repeating the name Oedipus over groups of three eighth notes bouncing between the notes B♭ and D. Soft pleas for pity are sandwiched between stark, implacable musical figures; this sense of pity trying to find some room for expression between hard slabs of music is part of the generating dialectic of the opera. Often the pity music is formed in $\frac{6}{8}$, out of those bouncing groups of three eighth notes. Stravinsky wrote, "All of my 'ideas' for *Oedipus Rex* were in one sense derived from what I call the versification,"[14] in other words, from the metrical patterns of Greek poetry. Indeed, the structure of the opera's large units is also based on versification. The big rhythm of Terror-Pity-Terror (long-short-long) is itself a kind of hypermeter. Self-similarity is Stravinsky's organizational key, just as it is Mandelbrot's, or the early Cage's.

Now one of the basic Greek meters is the dactyl, long-short-short. The groups of three eighth notes (bum-bum-bum-BUM-BUM-BUM) seems a sort of continual allusion to the meters of classical poetry, even though Stravinsky pays no attention to the actual scansion of the words, which he misconstrues in every way possible. For example, in the second soft part of the opening, the chorus sings, "OE-DI-pus, oe-DI-pus," casually shifting the syllable length and the accent. Perhaps the most metrically intense passage in the chorus is the chorus's prayer to Apollo, "Delie exspectamus" ("We await you, Delian") (figure 8.5).

Figure 8.4. Stravinsky: *Oedipus Rex,* beginning, from Igor Stravinsky, *Oedipus Rex,* Opéra-Oratorio en deux actes d'après Sophocle par Igor Stravinsky et Jean Cocteau, Nouvelle révision 1948, Réduction pour chant et piano par l'auteur (New York: Boosey & Hawkes, 1949), 1.

There is a sort of fatal dactylic underrhythm beneath every choral plea. The chorus's desires are everywhere constrained by hard metrical facts that can't be evaded, no matter how strong the pleas for leniency. For the Greeks, the dactyl was a meter appropriate to epic, not tragedy—it's Homer's meter more than Sophocles'—but Stravinsky is interested only a general and pervasive sense of metricality, not in the words per se.

According to Aristotle, the best tragedies are marked by two features, *anagnorisis* and *peripeteia,* recognition and reversal. Recognition scenes themselves can be understood as a sort of reversal, a pivoting of lie into truth. Sometimes a lie is deliberately assumed, as when Orestes in *Electra* pretends to be a messenger announcing Orestes' death; sometimes a lie is simply a tacit condition of someone's

Figure 8.5. Stravinsky: *Oedipus Rex*, choral prayer, from Igor Stravinsky, *Oedipus Rex*, Opéra-Oratorio en deux actes d'après Sophocle par Igor Stravinsky et Jean Cocteau, Nouvelle révision 1948, Réduction pour chant et piano par l'auteur (New York: Boosey & Hawkes, 1949), 27.

whole life, as in *Oedipus Rex*, where the truth about Oedipus's parentage isn't completely understood by anyone until a number of facts come together. But in twentieth-century Sophoclean operas, the juxtaposing of truth music with lie music is a critical dramatic technique. In Richard Strauss's *Elektra* (1909), for example, Klytämnestra has the line "das ist wahr und das ist Lüge" ("what is true, and what is lies") (figure 8.6).

Truth is a clean little chirp of a fourth; lies are chromatic, thick, sick, hungover, a slosh of chords over a tritone. This is a miniature version of the whole opera's dialectic, juxtaposing Klytämnestra's involutions of musical neurosis and narcosis against Truth—for example, the octave figure that represents the shade of Agamemnon, which keeps looming out of Elektra's monologue "Allein, weh ganz allein" (figure 8.7).

Figure 8.6. Strauss: *Elektra*, truth and lies, from Richard Strauss, *Elektra*, Tragödie in einem Aufzuge von Hugo von Hofmannsthal, Op. 58, Klavierauszug von Carl Besl (London: Boosey and Hawkes, n.d.), 67.

Figure 8.7. Strauss: *Elektra*, Agamemnon's ghost, from Richard Strauss, *Elektra*, Tragödie in einem Aufzuge von Hugo von Hofmannsthal, Op. 58, Klavierauszug von Carl Besl (London: Boosey and Hawkes, n.d.), 23.

For Stravinsky, Truth is a matter of both rhythm and pitch. The oracle's deep stratum of truth is represented by the quiet dactylic pulse; other forms of truth are represented by other sorts of musical fundamentals, such as the triad and the scale. For example, Creon enters to a striking figure, singing, "Respondit deus" ("The god answers") (figure 8.8).

Figure 8.8. Stravinsky: *Oedipus Rex*, god's truth, from Igor Stravinsky, *Oedipus Rex*, Opéra-Oratorio en deux actes d'après Sophocle par Igor Stravinsky et Jean Cocteau, Nouvelle révision 1948, Réduction pour chant et piano par l'auteur (New York: Boosey & Hawkes, 1949), 15.

Figure 8.9. Stravinsky: *Oedipus Rex*, parentage revealed, from Igor Stravinsky, *Oedipus Rex*, Opéra-Oratorio en deux actes d'après Sophocle par Igor Stravinsky et Jean Cocteau, Nouvelle révision 1948, Réduction pour chant et piano par l'auteur (New York: Boosey & Hawkes, 1949), 67.

What does the god say? Perhaps that matters less than how the god says it, in a descending C-major triad. This sort of ultrasimple figure represents Authority. Creon freely tells everything he knows. Then Tiresias enters, "the fountain of truth" as the narrator calls him, knowing a great deal more, but refusing to speak: "Dikere non possum" ("I cannot say"). Most of the accompaniment here consists of empty octaves; and soon Tiresias sings another falling triad, this time in E minor. Truth, whether spoken or tacit, seems to be triadic in nature. When, in the second act, the Messenger at last announces the Truth, the horrible Truth—Polybus was *not* Oedipus's father—he sings it to a descending scale: "non genitor Oedipodis" ("not the father of Oedipus") (figure 8.9). Triads, scales, the rudiments that support tonal music, whether tonal music lies in its grave or still retains some force: these are the strong Doric columns that support the temple of the gods.

Figure 8.10. Stravinsky: *Oedipus Rex*, I will save you, from Igor Stravinsky, *Oedipus Rex*, Opéra-Oratorio en deux actes d'après Sophocle par Igor Stravinsky et Jean Cocteau, Nouvelle révision 1948, Réduction pour chant et piano par l'auteur (New York: Boosey & Hawkes, 1949), 9.

The notion that divine authority is best expressed by a falling, perhaps a smiting, scale is part of the old stock in trade of opera and oratorio composers: in *Athalia* (1733) Handel provides for Abner an aria on God's majesty, "When storms the proud to terrors doom," in which one of the most salient phrases is a falling scale. In Wagner's *Der Ring des Nibelungen*, Wotan's authority is grounded on the runes carved in his spear—whose *Leitmotiv* is a falling scale.

Inauthenticity is, of course, represented by music that is exactly opposite in character: shifty, florid music. At his first entry, Oedipus sings "Liberi, vos liberabo," "Just as I saved you from the sphinx I will save you from the plague" (figure 8.10).

Stravinsky referred to this as Oedipus's spreading "the tail feathers of his pride."[15] This is indeed preening, peacocky music. Show-off music requires the techniques of eighteenth-century opera, such as Handel's, the sort of opera designed for singers to display brilliant roulades and the whole battery of coloratura. I think it's significant that Stravinsky accompanies this opening aria with the iambic figures in the orchestra. The iamb is a satirical (and tragic!) meter in classical poetry; in fact, the word *iamb* is derived from the verb "to wound," and its skipping, short-long rhythm has a limping gait. In Greek, the name *Oedipus* means "swollen foot"—remember that Oedipus's feet were pierced when he was a baby—and Oedipus's music often has a hobbly sort of gait to it. Much of the orchestration of "Liberi, vos liberabo" is for winds, providing the accompaniment with a snide, snarky feel, as if the orchestra were sticking up its nose.

Another sort of inauthenticity can be found in Jocasta's music, in her famous aria "Nonne erubeskite" (figure 8.11).[16]

Figure 8.11. Stravinsky: *Oedipus Rex,* Jocasta, from Igor Stravinsky, *Oedipus Rex,* Opéra-Oratorio en deux actes d'après Sophocle par Igor Stravinsky et Jean Cocteau, Nouvelle révision 1948, Réduction pour chant et piano par l'auteur (New York: Boosey & Hawkes, 1949), 44.

This is some of the most dada music in the score—we don't often think of Stravinsky as a dadaist, but Stravinsky himself compared his music to a *Merzbild,* that is, to one of Kurt Schwitters's collages of urban junk—used railway tickets, cough syrup labels, bank advertisements, and so forth:

> Much of the music is a *Merzbild,* put together from whatever came to hand. I mean, for example . . . the fusion of such widely divergent types of music the *Folies Bergères* tune at No. 40 ("The girls enter, kicking") and the Wagnerian 7th-chords at Nos. 58 and 74. I have made these bits and snatches my own, I think, and of them a unity.[17]

What bit of music detritus has Stravinsky found for Jocasta's aria? Leonard Bernstein took special glee in describing it as "a hoochy-koochy dance,"[18] and that sounds just right to me: belly dance, striptease, any sort of hokey chromatic fake-Oriental scene you want to imagine. The sheer *wrongness* of the music for the text is Stravinsky's way of telling us that Jocasta, like Oedipus, lives in an unreal world, a fool's world. She keeps telling us that oracles can lie; but the only lies we hear are those coming from her mouth. She is a stock caricature of Woman as seductress, temporizer, nurse, just as Oedipus is a stock caricature of Man as arrogant, vainglorious problem solver: Don't you fret, little Thebans, I'll take care of everything.

Figure 8.12. Stravinsky: *Oedipus Rex,* dawning light, from Igor Stravinsky, *Oedipus Rex,* Opéra-Oratorio en deux actes d'après Sophocle par Igor Stravinsky et Jean Cocteau, Nouvelle révision 1948, Réduction pour chant et piano par l'auteur (New York: Boosey & Hawkes, 1949), 79.

The score seems to me as consistently excellent as anything in twentieth-century music, but the last ten minutes are remarkable even by Stravinsky's standards. When Oedipus is dazzled by the final revelation, his Handelian boasting vanishes utterly (figure 8.12):

Natus sum quo nefastum est,	I was born from one who should not have given birth,
Concubui cui nefastum est,	I married one whom I should not have married,
Kekidi quem nefastum est.	I killed one whom I should not have killed.
Lux facta est. [19]	Light dawns.

A haughty spirit goeth before a fall, and this is the fall: a descending B-minor triad in the vocal line moving toward a conclusive D-major resolution in the orchestra. Now, for the first time, Oedipus gets truth music of the sort that Creon and Tiresias and the Messenger sang earlier; but it is a truth that destroys. The final chorus returns to the mode of the opening chorus, in which terror keeps hemming in, circumscribing any possibility of pity: the Messenger keeps repeating his "four-word singing telegram"[20] "Divum Jocastae caput mortuum" ("the divine head of Jocasta is dead"), while the chorus tells of Jocasta's suicide and Oedipus's self-mutilation (figure 8.13).

Opera composers learned a long time ago that tragedy can best be expressed by a sort of refrain structure in which pity and terror alternate. The first tragedy in Western music that found a strikingly effective way of accomplishing this was, once again, Gluck's *Orfeo ed Euridice,* when the Furies shout to Orpheus not to enter hell, but he pleads with them to let him enter ("Deh! Placatevi con me").

Stravinsky's scene follows this model exactly, but backward: the soloist represents the inflexible boundary, and the chorus is the oppressed human presence that tries to cross it. The Messenger's great cry becomes a sort of hieroglyph of

Figure 8.13. Stravinsky: *Oedipus Rex*, telegram, from Igor Stravinsky, *Oedipus Rex*, Opéra-Oratorio en deux actes d'après Sophocle par Igor Stravinsky et Jean Cocteau, Nouvelle révision 1948, Réduction pour chant et piano par l'auteur (New York: Boosey & Hawkes, 1949), 84–85.

fate. Between its inexorable calls, the chorus keeps pushing out for room, a little bit, then a little harder, but finally collapses. It's the musical equivalent of the walls in the famous room in Poe's "The Pit and the Pendulum" that keep get closer and closer together, squeezing the occupant. Stravinsky called this chorus, quite wonderfully, a "mortuary *tarantella*."[21] The notion of dancing to this hectic, cheerful rhythm in a morgue is another example of Stravinsky's clowning with expression tropes at the margins of the sober text—just as he had dressed Jocasta in the musical equivalent of harem pants earlier. But you recall that the tarantella was so named after the Italian word for "tarantula." The purpose of the frenzied spasms was to rid the body of venom. The plague that infects Thebes infects the rhythm of the chorus as well, until the whole thing leaves off—"Vale, Oedipus, te amabam" ("Farewell, Oedipus, we loved you")—in the bouncing dactyls so often heard before. It is as if the opera trails away into a sort of

Figure 8.14. de Chirico: *The Disturbing Muses.* © 2009 Artists Rights Society (ARS), New York/SIAE, Rome.

empty meter, a surface on which a poet might inscribe a song if there were anything left to sing.

Oedipus rex was intended as a birthday gift for Serge Diaghilev, but the great impresario didn't much like it, and it had trouble finding its way into the twentieth-century canon. Those who hated Stravinsky—and incomparably the most talented hater of Stravinsky was Theodor Adorno—found in his works of the late 1920s fresh ammunition to be used against him. In the course of his astonishing book *Philosophy of Modern Music,* Adorno uses Stravinsky as a rag to shine Schoenberg's shoes. Adorno calls Stravinsky an acrobat, a civil servant, a tailor's dummy, hebephrenic, psychotic, infantile, fascistic, and devoted to making money. But there's one comment of Adorno's that I think goes far toward elucidating just what *Oedipus rex* is: "The completely shrewd, illusionless *I* exalts the *Not-I* as an idol"; a work by Stravinsky "maliciously bows to the public, takes off its mask, and shows that there is no face under it, only a knob."[22] If you think of *Oedipus rex* as an idol, a Greek statue that takes off its mask and shows only a knob, it makes perfect sense, though you don't need to find it quite so troubling as Adorno does.

What could Adorno have been thinking of when he compared a work by Stravinsky to a knob beneath a mask? I suspect he must have been thinking of the paintings of Giorgio de Chirico, such as *The Disturbing Muses* (1925), in which a red balloon is perched on top of a togated torso, itself mounted on a column (figure 8.14).

The notion of an effaced, worn-away classicism, in which the heads of statues have eroded into punching bags or the caps on top of newel posts, and the lucid space has cracked apart into competing systems of perspectives—it all seems perfectly appropriate for Stravinsky's *Oedipus Rex,* with its systems of competing mini stages and its oddly stylized, evacuated protagonists. In 1927, the same year that *Oedipus rex* appeared, Chirico painted *The Archaeologists,* whose knob-headed archaeologists have fragments of classical antiquity tucked away inside their torsos.

This is exactly how Adorno understood Stravinsky: an inhuman presence, contemptuous and contemptible, displaying the splinters and shards and broken pedestals he had scavenged from Handel and Verdi and other great composers of the past. Another gifted writer on music, the composer Ernst Krenek, explicitly compared Stravinsky's *Oedipus rex* with the paintings of Chirico:

> The classicism of antiquity in *Oedipus Rex* is just as problematic as de Chirico's landscape of ruins.... What is brought to light here looks more like excavations after an earthquake than like something freshly copied out of the atelier. Everything questionable in the age is engraved on the smooth façades erected here; and the ground, that bears the weight of the whole splendor, is furrowed by many uncanny rifts and fissures. The classicism of antiquity lives here anew and in the same shape in which it genuinely came to us: in the form of fragments. The torso, mutilated by invisible forces, has a more mysteriously intense

and charged life than the whole that it perhaps once was; in Neoclassicism (distinguished from the Renaissance in that it falls short of perfection because it lacks any intention for wholeness and illusion), the scars and fractures that a work carries with or without the intention of the maker, are not only its charm, but also represent its sole truth. . . . In the domain of the fragmentary the development of Neoclassicism is connected with *Surrealism,* which, more energetically destructive, lives in the montage of the ruins that it comes across.[23]

Krenek understood surrealism and neoclassicism as roughly the same thing, a way of reusing the past, not for the sake of glorifying the achievement of the past, not for the sake of aligning the present with the high standards of the past, but for the sake of flaunting in your face the degradation of the past, the pastness of the past. How can you demonstrate destructive energy? By displaying a destroyed thing. The Venus de Milo is exciting *because* she has lost her arms. We are all caught up in force fields that extinguish, snap off, stub out, rub away. Surrealist art sets itself the challenge of exhibiting these force fields. Surrealism, to Krenek, is simply entropy in visual plastic. It follows that *Oedipus rex,* like *The Waste Land,* offers us predecayed materials, flitter and rubble—for the only way to be truthful to the past is to recognize its lack of integrity. What we know of Greek tragedy is only a stump. The text is often garbled or full of holes; the music and the scenery have vanished almost utterly; so maybe the great theme of an opera faithful to Sophocles should be irrevocability itself.

Chapter Nine

Belletristic Music in the Twentieth Century

Every face of modernism is the face of Janus. To tell the story of modernism is to tell two stories simultaneously, in dissonant counterpoint—for each story makes itself felt against the antistory that shadows it. For example, one story of modernism concerns aesthetic purism, the strict partitioning of one medium from another. The great narrator of this story is the art historian Clement Greenberg, who writes, "To restore the identity of an art the opacity of its medium must be emphasized."[1] The puritan Greenberg resists the slightest erasure of the lines that divide one art form from another. He provides a simple criterion for success: a work of art is good to the extent that it displays the substantiality of its medium, without dissembling or fraud. Painting is a thrusting forth of pigment; sculpture is an extancy of metal, an inertia of stone; music is naked sound. The barrier between music and painting (or any other form of art) should be wholly impermeable.

Similarly, the puritan Theodor Adorno considers that Igor Stravinsky had defiled the art of music through what Adorno calls a *pseudomorphosis*, an attempt to organize a composition in one medium according to alien principles derived from a wrong medium. Adorno accuses Stravinsky of pretending to be a cubist painter: "the spatialization of music is witness to a pseudomorphosis of music to painting, on the innermost level an abdication"; "The trick that defines all of Stravinsky's organizings of form: to let time stand in, as in a circus tableau, and to present time complexes as if spatial—this trick wears off. It loses its power over the consciousness of duration."[2] Such purism is strongly antiromantic in that it contradicts Wagner's notion of the *Gesamtkunstwerk*, the total artwork in which the component media fuse into a single gigantic experience.

But every narrative of purism bears witness to a counternarrative that threatens to engulf it. Many composers of the twentieth century were impurists, paying little attention to the warnings of Greenberg; they continued to experiment in erasures of intermedia boundaries, in crossovers from music to painting and other media. One example is Ezra Pound's friend and music hero George Antheil, who liked to speak of his compositions as time canvases:

> In the *Ballet Mécanique* I used time as Picasso might have used the blank spaces of his canvas. I did not hesitate, for instance, to repeat one measure one hundred

times; I did not hesitate to have absolutely nothing on my pianola rolls for sixty-two bars; I did not hesitate to ring a bell against a certain given section of time or indeed to do whatever I pleased to do with the time canvas as long as each part of it stood up against the other. My ideas were the most abstract of the abstract.[3]

Another gifted worker in this field was Morton Feldman (1926–87), who felt that the dominant influences in his music came from the painters he knew:

Soon after meeting [Robert] Rauschenberg I met Jackson Pollock, who asked me to write music for a film about him.... In thinking back to that time I realize now how much the musical ideas I had in 1951 paralleled his mode of working. Pollock placed his canvas on the ground and painted as he walked around it. I put sheets of graph paper on the wall; each sheet framed the same time duration and was, in effect, a visual rhythmic structure. What resembled Pollock was my "all over" approach to the time-canvas. Rather than the usual left-to-right passage across the page, the horizontal squares of the graph paper represented the tempo—with each box equal to a preestablished ictus; and the vertical squares were the instrumentation of the composition....

Stasis, as it is utilized in painting, is not traditionally part of the apparatus of music. Music can achieve aspects of immobility, or the illusion of it: the Magrittelike world Satie evokes, or the "floating sculptures" of [Edgard] Varèse. The degrees of stasis, found in a [Mark] Rothko or a [Philip] Guston, were perhaps the most significant elements that I brought to my music from painting.[4]

Some of Feldman's early scores even have the Monopoly-board look of such Mondrian paintings as *Broadway Boogie Woogie* (1942–43), itself an example of the opposite pseudomorphosis, in which music flattens and congeals onto a visual surface.

But the boundary transgression I want to discuss now doesn't concern music and painting, but music and literature. All those sound glyphs cut into the time canvas can, from a certain perspective, look like the characters of an alphabet, as if a musical composition were simply a book reconceived according to different conventions. When I speak of belletristic music, I mean a transvestism between a musical composition and a spoken or written text—music that attempts not to illustrate a text, not to emphasize a text, but to *be* a text, to clench itself, to hump itself into some sort of writing—music that usurps the scepter of the logos.

The twentieth century is full of extraordinarily text-potent music. One doesn't have to look far to find music that goes far beyond the early seventeenth-century dream of melding of music and words into recitative. One of the developers of the genre of opera, Guilio Caccini, wrote that singing should be like "speaking musically," and composers have often written recitatives in which singers were encouraged to provide the inflections of speech. But the task of writing vocal lines that did not simply provide opportunities for speaking, but actually embodied spoken nuances, small pitch fluctuations, fell in part on the modernists.

Central European modernists also investigated the intersections of speech and music. One of the pioneers in this movement was Leoš Janáček (1854–1928), the late-blooming Moravian composer who had an almost sacred regard for the importance of speech, as if all authenticity in music sprang from a sort of heightened talkiness. The vocal lines in his operas, especially from *Jenůfa* (1903) on, were derived from a close study of the inflections of the Czech language. As he wrote in an article in *Hlídka* (Brno, 1905) on speech melody,

> The melodic curves of speech are an expression of the complete organism and of all phases of its spiritual activities. They demonstrate whether a man is stupid or intelligent, sleepy or awake, tired or alert. They tell us whether he is a child or an old man, whether it is morning or evening, light or darkness, heat or frost, and disclose whether a person is alone or in company. The art of dramatic writing is to compose a melodic curve that will, as if by magic, reveal immediately a human being in one definite phase of his existence.[5]

Some of the speech melodies that Janáček recorded in his notebooks are remarkably tuneful, such as the notation for "We reaped, where we reaped" ("Kde jsme žaly, tu jsme žaly"). For Janáček the content of speech is relatively unimportant; perhaps if I were speaking this essay instead of writing it you would be responding not to the meanings of the words, but to the shapes of pitch variation in my voice. The dictionary, then, is a useless tool for understanding the power of language, which lies, as Rousseau thought it lay, in the urgency, the general contagion, of melody within the voice of the speaker. A printed page can hope only to reproduce the dead husk of language; music can reproduce its living core. But this sort of speech music is like a printed page in that it renders an indelible record of language, real language. In "Signature, Event, Context," Jacques Derrida says that spoken discourse, just like written discourse, consists of graphemes: "This structural possibility of being severed from its referent or signified (and therefore from communication and its context) seems to me to make of every mark, even if oral, a grapheme."[6] And I think it follows that the tables of speech-music notation that Janáček compiled before writing his operas are properly considered as a sort of thesaurus of oral graphemes, a text inscribed on air.

Derrida's notion that a mark's status as a grapheme is contingent on its capacity to be severed from its referent suggests that a speech melody might be best able to display itself as a textual sort of entity if it could be abstracted from actual words. In the absence of words, a speech melody is, of course, *really* far from any conceivable referent.

The history of the evolution of speech melody after Janáček's time is another one of those two-part inventions I mentioned earlier. One story concerns the attempt of speech melody to embed itself more and more strongly in speech;

the antistory concerns the attempt of speech melody to disengage itself from any finite act of communication. One of the heroes of the first story is another Czech composer, Alois Hába, who in the 1920s developed a microtonal system of music in order to approximate more closely to the pitch structure of speech than the division of the octave into semitones permitted:

> The folksong-collectors Bartók (Hungary) and Plicka (Czechoslovakia) notated the perceived interval-deviations with a plus or minus sign (+, -). Older folksong collectors had notated all the intervals in the system of semitones, not observing the finer modifications of intervals. This first gained currency from the phonograph and tape recordings of folk music from various lands. . . . From folksong I learned to perceive melodic intervals a little smaller or greater than those of the semitone-system. . . . In my youth it oftened happened that the folk singers, who during the intermissions of dance festivals sang songs of "their kind," deviating from the semitone system, demanded that the first violinist of the Wisowitzer Kapelle play "their" melody just as they sang it. Once a temperamental singer threatened to strike the double bass player with a beer mug if he didn't "play along" with the song, exactly as he sang it.[7]

It is hard to exaggerate the strangeness of Hába's speech music. In Hába's cheerful peasant opera *Mother,* there is a passage in which a resilient second wife overcomes her husband's obtuseness. He sings, "Aha, it's long journey on foot, even if one's going to see his bride" ("Fu, fu, je to přeca daleká cesta pěšky, aj když ide člověk za svú nevěstú"), in a manner that fuses the transcendentally eerie with something earthy, coarse, maybe even clod hopping.

Still more interesting, perhaps, is the antistory, the distilling of speech melody into something at once verbal and beyond language. Hába plays a role here, too, but a more important figure is Arnold Schoenberg. Not long after the premiere of Janáček's *Jenůfa,* Schoenberg found ways of increasing the speech tension of music, but with rather different aesthetic goals. Schoenberg devised a notational scheme in which extremely chromatic lines (but without express intervals smaller than a semitone), combined with careful inflectional instructions to the performer, managed to simulate speech—not for the sake of simplicity or any naturalistic effect, but in order to heighten the artificiality, the eeriness of the music. Schoenberg states these instructions in his foreword to *Pierrot lunaire,* a setting of twenty-one poems by the symbolist poet Albert Giraud, concerning a clown who, among other things, tries in vain to wipe a spot of moonbeam off his coat; finds himself eating a bleeding heart in a mock eucharist; and drills a hole into another clown's skull and stuffs tobacco into it, in order to convert him into a living pipe. To imagine a music for this studied insincereness, this fun depravity, this blasphemy against expression, Schoenberg devised a style of vocal recitation called *Sprechstimme,* designed to be neither speech nor song but some hybrid of the two, a translunar synthesis. As Schoenberg writes

> The performer must closely guard himself from falling into a "singing" manner of speech-production. This is absolutely to be avoided. To be sure, there should be no striving at all for a realistic-natural manner of speaking. On the contrary, it should be plain that there is a difference between ordinary speaking and a speaking cooperative toward musical form.[8]

In 1627, Claudio Monteverdi wrote to Alessandro Striggio that musical expression should be concentrated "on the word and not on the meaning of the sentence" ("sopra alla parola et non sopra al senso de la clausula").[9] Schoenberg takes the minute examination of particular words to astonishing lengths, building (to take an example from the seventh song, "Der kranke Mond") a complicated apparatus of speech trills into the phrase droop of "todeskranker Mond" ("moon sick to death"). Here a word or an epithet is hoisted out of speech as we know it, out of song as we know it, into some expressive ether where it can attain the status of a phonic hieroglyph.

In the most imposing of all his Sprechstimme projects, the opera *Moses und Aron* (1930–32; see chapter 6), Schoenberg goes still further toward liberating speech-melody from common speech. With one brief exception, Moses never sings. He's a tongue-tied talker caught in a world of singers, a prophet frustrated that he can't make himself heard despite all his vehemence of speech. If the purpose of speech is communication, Moses is a speech-cripple, for he can convey none of his insight into the divine; the fluent cantilena of Aron is intensely communicative, but it falsifies everything that it utters, builds golden calves of discourse. Moses' very handicap—"Ich kann denken, aber nicht reden" ("I can think but not speak")—tends to isolate and abstract his words. Because all the other characters sing, Moses' stutterings of the incommunicable start to feel dimensionally defective, as if they existed as flat surfaces in an otherwise three-dimensional universe—or as if they were more like commandments written in an unintelligible script than like normal speech. In the parts of the opera that Schoenberg set to music, Moses's last act is to shatter the tables of the law that he brought down from the mountain. His last line is "O Wort, du Wort, das mir fehlt," ("O word, thou word that I lack") as his speaking crashes beyond the limits of speech into some transfiguration of communicative impotence (see figure 6.5).

Schoenberg worked closely with Wassily Kandinsky in the early 1910s, and both artists of course had strong tendencies toward abstractionism. Schoenberg disliked any sort of physiological response to music, and specifically deplored compositions that invited toe tapping. Schoenberg's speech gestures have something of the quality of the big numerals in some of Jasper Johns's paintings: figures elevated out of normal semiotics into aesthetic calligrams.

An antistory to Schoenberg's abstractions of speech can be found, oddly enough, in the music written by a California hobo who despised the abstract with all his heart. Harry Partch (1901–74) was a largely self-taught composer who had survived the depression as a migrant laborer picking grapes and plums. In 1930, he looked at the whole history of Western music and decided to discard it, with the exception of a few works by Giulio Caccini, Modest Musorgsky, and Leoš Janáček, because he thought he could do better. He marked this revolution by burning all his previous compositions. He thought that the human body, especially as expressed in the speaking voice, was the ultimate source of authority and virtue in music. All music that abstracted itself from the body, by engrossing itself in artificial procedures of counterpoint, development, and other formalities, was insipid and useless.

Partch's first mature compositions struggle to recenter the art of music on the speaking voice. But he felt that neither the twelve-note scale of Western music nor the instruments of the Western orchestra were viable tools for achieving a genuinely concrete music, a music attentive to the nuances of speech. A speaking sort of music needs to imitate intervals far smaller than the semitones to which most woodwind, brass, pitched percussion, and keyboard instruments are confined. So Partch devised his own forty-three-tone scale, which begins by achieving the major second (defined by a pitch ratio of $\frac{9}{8}$) as the termination of a widening series of near-unison pitch ratios ($\frac{1}{1}, \frac{81}{80}, \frac{32}{33}, \frac{21}{20}, \frac{81}{80}, \frac{16}{15}, \frac{12}{13}, \frac{11}{10}, \frac{10}{9}$ and at last $\frac{9}{8}$). He also devised his own instrumentarium in order to be able to play these pitches. The earliest novelties were stringed instruments such as the adapted viola (a viola with a huge neck grafted on), used to accompany the precisely notated intoning voice in *17 Lyrics by Li Po* (1931). Later, Partch used all sorts of technological junk, including artillery casings, light-bulb tops, airplane fuel tanks, and hubcaps, to create an enormous variety of instruments to which he gave whimsical names, such as diamond marimba, spoils of war, zymo-xyl, boo, harmonic canon, gourd tree, and cloud chamber bowls.

The ambitious Partch hoped to recreate William Butler Yeats's translation of Sophocles, *King Oedipus*, as an opera of speech. As Partch wrote in his project report to the Carnegie Foundation, "It is in no sense opera. The drama is paramount always—there is no attempt to reconcile it with musical form. It is drama heightened throughout, and finally purged, by music."[10] In 1934 a Carnegie grant enabled Partch to visit Dublin, meet Yeats, hear a performance of the play at Yeats's Abbey Theatre, and notate the pitches and rhythms of the actors' voices. Yeats was excited by Partch's method of speaking, often without melody, to musical instruments that employ "very minute intervals"; he wrote to Partch that "so far as I can understand your method [it has] my complete sympathy."[11] Yeats died in 1939, and it was not until 1952 that the finished opera was performed at Mills College in Oakland, California. Partch's *King Oedipus* remains one of the twentieth century's most compelling resurrections of the speech-oriented aesthetic of the earliest operas, those by Peri and Monteverdi.

Partch's later works continue his exploration of reviving Greek drama—what might be call the Partchian Renaissance—most notably in *Revelation in the Courthouse Square* (1962), loosely based on Euripides' *Bacchae*. In *Revelation*, Partch reimagined Dionysus as a rock singer. But in other works Partch investigated ways of writing a corporeal music less dependent on the human voice. In *Water! Water!* (1962), a satire about dam building in California, the text is gibberish. In such long, instrumental compositions as *And on the Seventh Day Petals Fell in Petaluma* (1963–66), he allowed the "sound-magic," the timbre collage of his strange instruments, to evoke the image of the dryness of wood, the heft of rock, the physical presence of the earth as it impinges on the human body. Few composers, either in vocal or instrumental music, have achieved such an intense witness of the reifying power of music, its textures of scrape and hit and pluck, its mouth feel. As Partch says, describing the superiority of folk and pop singers to refined, operatically trained voices:

> Frequently they break a word off short of its notated time and let it fall or rise in a gliding inflection regardless of the notation. Frequently they personify a directness of word appeal, characteristic of this age and this land, and characterized by suggestions of actual times, actual localities, actual identities, and actual human situations, all of which is the very antithesis of the Abstract concept.
>
> By mere control of the lips, mouth, tongue, palate, glottis, and diaphragm under emotional stimulus, the human voice is ready to express all the feelings and attitudes which the cumulative centuries have symbolized in words and poured into the dictionaryfrom joyful spite to tragic ecstasy, from ecstatic melancholy to hedonic fatuity, from furtive beatitude to boisterous grotesquerie, from portentous lechery to obdurate athanasia—prescience, felicity, urbanity, hauteur, surfeit, magniloquence, enravishment, execration, abnegation, anguish, riot, debauch, hope, joy, death, grief, effluent life, and a lot more.[12]

I don't know which phrase I like better: "obdurate athanasia" or the simple ending of "and a lot more." When I read this, I think of Roland Barthes's essay "Rasch," in which he described what he called *somathemes:*

> In Schumann's *Kreisleriana* (Opus 16; 1838), I actually hear no note, no theme, no contour, no grammar, no meaning, nothing which would permit me to reconstruct an intelligible structure of the work. No, what I hear are blows: I hear what beats in the body, what beats the body, or better: I hear this body that beats.[13]

But it could be argued that *Kreisleriana* is full of themes, grammar, meaning. Barthes' words apply better to the extremely somathematic music of Partch.

For the purposes of this essay, what is most important about Partch is his extraordinary fascination with novels and novelists. Indeed much of the theory of concrete music was derived from D. H. Lawrence, as Partch himself said:

> Contemporary visual art, and attitudes toward it, which arouse explosive resentment in D. H. Lawrence, in many ways parallel this situation in "serious" music. In viewing paintings, he maintains, we "are only undergoing cerebral excitation. . . . The deeper responses, down in the intuitive and instinctive body, are not touched. They cannot be, because they are dead. A dead intuitive body stands there and gazes at the corpse of beauty: and usually it is completely and honestly bored."
>
> And intuition died, declares Lawrence, because "Man came to have his own body in horror." We are afraid of the "procreative body" and its "warm flow of intuitional awareness," and fear is "poison to the human psyche." "We don't live in the flesh. Our instincts and intuitions are dead, we live wound round with the winding sheet of abstraction." . . .
>
> Finally [Lawrence writes]: "The history of our era is the nauseating and repulsive history of the crucifixion of the procreative body for the glorification of the spirit, the mental consciousness. Plato was an arch-priest of this crucifixion. . . . In the eighteenth century it became a corpse, a corpse with an abnormally active mind: and today it stinketh." . . .
>
> I am trying to hope that we are not entering an era where the only men of significance in music will be those facile at quoting Bach and Beethoven, Brahms and Tschaikowsky [*sic*]. . . . If we are entering such an age it is already dead. . . .[14]

But Partch was not concerned with novelists only for the sake of theory. Most composers are interested in speech-music for the sake of drama. Partch was not immune to the pleasures of writing music drama, but a surprising quantity of his speech-music sets inscriptions, letters, and artificial literary discourse. For example, in 1943 he wrote both *Barstow—Eight Hitch-hikers' Inscriptions from a Highway Railing at Barstow, California* and *Dark Brother—Final Two Paragraphs from Thomas Wolfe's "God's Lonely Man."* The next year, he wrote *Two Settings from Joyce's Finnegans Wake*. Partch liked not only to imitate real speaking voices, but also to provide fanciful realizations of the implicit voices of literary texts, by working at the scumbled margin between speech and writing. And by choosing *Finnegans Wake* for such treatment, Partch was bearing witness, as did so many other twentieth-century artists, to the amazingly concrete vocality of Joyce's novels.

Samuel Beckett, we remember, considered that in *Finnegans Wake* Joyce's prose had gone beyond representation into sheer incarnation of its subject matter:

> Here form *is* content, content *is* form. You complain that this stuff is not written in English. It is not written at all. It is not to be read—or rather it is not only to be read. It has to be looked at and listened to. His writing is not *about*

something; *it is that something itself*. . . . When the sense is sleep, the words go to sleep. . . . When the sense is dancing, the words dance. . . . : "To stir up love's young fizz I tilt with this bridle's cup champagne, dimming douce from her peepair of hide-seeks tight squeezed on my snowybreasted and while my pearlies in their sparkling wisdom are nippling her bubblets I swear (and let you swear) by the bumper round of my poor old snaggletooth's solidbowel I ne'er will prove I'm untrue to (theare!) you liking so long as my hole looks. Down." The language is drunk. The very words are tilted and effervescent."[15]

Note the bottle of Piper Heidsieck champagne hidden in the tangled hair of the phrase "peepair of hide-seeks." Not only a radical composer like Partch, but even a conservative composer like Samuel Barber (in *Nuvoletta*), found irresistible the idea of realizing the tilt and effervescence of *Finnegans Wake* by using music's rich vocabulary of wrongness: off-kilter rhythm, parodic or faintly offensive harmony (in Barber's case derived from *Tristan und Isolde*), or sung pitches that refuse to obey the even the mild rigor of the chromatic scale. For Partch, it's in the interstices between semitones that the truths of speech are hidden. In Partch's setting of the passage "In the name of Annah the Allmaziful, the Everliving, the bringer of all Plurabilities, haloed be her eve,"[16] the old-fashioned, tonal, triumphalist gestures are undercut by incomprehensible limping ploinks, as if the singer were a circus barker in the limbo of unborn children.

Two of the most exciting music-Joycing projects go far toward denarratizing Joyce's already somewhat denarratized verbal textures and toward reducing text and music alike to a state of static *écriture*, in which the planar flatness of the page is more audible than the stream of words inscribed on it. The first of these projects concerns not *Finnegans Wake* but *Ulysses:* Luciano Berio's remarkable *Thema (Omaggio a Joyce)*, written in 1958. *Thema* consists entirely of tape manipulations of the voice of Cathy Berberian (at the time his wife) reading the thematic catalogue at the beginning of the "Sirens" chapter. Her voice is so contorted, so overfolded, that it generates the percussive noises, the melos, even the harmony, that Joyce could only suggest in his prose. First she reads it straight, then the fun begins. As Berio piles one tape bit on top of another, the superimposition creates something of the instantaneous apprehension of reading a printed page, as if the ear were trying to do the work of the eye. In one especially loud, frantic passage it sounds as if Berio were fast-forwarding through Berberian's reading—thereby creating another sort of instantaneity by accelerating the text into a single blip of sound. I might note that Berio's work precedes by eight years the similar experiments of Steve Reich, though Reich's belletristic music, such as *The Desert Music*, seems to me less successful than his work with casual speech, as in *Come Out* or *Different Trains*, in which Reich teases out a sort of sacredness from the completely unpremeditated.

But perhaps the most impressive of all attempts to recreate Joyce in music is the second project, John Cage's radio play *Roaratorio: An Irish Circus on Finnegans Wake*

(1979). Cage was aware of Berio's *Thema*, though when an interviewer queried him about it, he evaded the question.[17] This piece combines most of the themes of speech-music that we've been regarding. Cage began by stringing out a set of isolated words from Joyce's text by applying to the whole novel a procedure he called mesostics. He wrote the letters JAMESJOYCE vertically down the center of a page, over and over indefinitely, and selected a word from *Finnegans Wake* containing a J not followed by an A, then one containing an A not followed by an M, then one containing an M not followed by E, and so forth to the end of time, until he had a manageable but wholly dismantled text, a pseudolibretto. Cage considered this an important work in its own right, and gave it the title *Laughtears*. Then Cage read it all into a tape recorder: "I gave up any thought of an Irish accent and began to slightly sing, sprechstimme."[18] Then he went to endless trouble to gather sound effects by having henchmen and henchwomen put tape recorders in randomly determined street intersections in various places mentioned in *Finnegans Wake;* by gathering in a sound library the calls of birds that Joyce named, and many similar sound effects; by commissioning Irish singers, uillean pipers, and bodhran players to record "Dark Is the Colour of My True Love's Hair" and other Irish ditties relevant to the text. At last he had a sound engineer splice together the voice track with the sound effects, with attack, volume, duration, and so forth determined by chance procedures from the *I Ching*.

Finnegans Wake was a sacred text to Cage, as much for its open, generous, here-comes-everybody-and-everything-including-the-kitchen-sink texture as for its daring experimentality. But it's clear that he preferred *Roaratorio* to the original, partly because he disliked the "militarized" linear sentence structure of Joyce's novel and enjoyed the way in which the mesostic procedure created a "demilitarization," something grammarless, punctuationless, a text of shreds and patches.[19] But mostly he approved of the *Roaratorio* because it activitated the reality music that could only be virtual in *Finnegans Wake* itself: "I am told, that Joyce said said that he didn't mean *Finnegans Wake* to be understood. He meant it as a kind of piece of music."[20] "I wanted [in *Roaratorio*] to make a music that was free of melody and free of harmony and free of counterpoint: free of musical theory. I wanted it not to be music in the sense of music, but I wanted it to be music in the sense of *Finnegans Wake*. But not a theory about music. I wanted the music to turn itself toward *Finnegans Wake*. And away from music itself."[21] This sense that Joyce's implicit speech-music can help to untie the straitjacket of formal rules of compositional procedures binding the composer strongly echoes the aesthetic of Partch on concrete music. Cage almost seems to quote Beckett's line that Joyce's prose is not about something but that something itself when he, Cage, speaks of music that turns itself toward *Finnegans Wake*. Perhaps Cage is saying that his music turns itself *into* Joyce's language, becomes a sort of extradimensional orthogonal sticking out of the text into acoustic space.

The dominant mode of *Roaratorio* is concreteness—Partchian concreteness, or the *musique concrète* of Pierre Henry's and Pierre Schaeffer's symphonies for sound effects. Cage explicitly tried to project the mysteriousness, the unconstruability, the resistance to the intellect, of Joyce's text: "It remains mysterious to me and expressive in a variety of ways. And that through this singing—rather than through this speaking. In a sense singing makes it more devoted to each letter and to each syllable."[22] The mouth feel of phonemes, rather than the mind feel of sememes, means everything. And yet, despite all Cage's resources of imagination, there is something slightly dogged about the concreteness of *Roaratorio*. Cage tabulates, concerning the first part of the radio play, the 6 thunderclaps, the 29 thunder rumbles and earthquake sounds, the 64 episodes of laughing and crying, the 5 farts, the 32 bangs of guns and explosions, the 56 cries of animals and "particular birds," the 64 occasions of singing (including "Largo al factotum"), and so forth. All these noises are completely relevant to Joyce's text, and yet all these thunderclaps and sea sloshes and songs can feel more illustrative than genuinely incarnational—a skeleton key to implied sounds, a guide to interpretation rather than a devastating apprehension of the text. For example, it is helpful to compare the beginning of Part IV, as read by Cage in *Laughtears*, with the same passage outfitted with sound effects in *Roaratorio*, where Cage responds to the resurrectional themes of Joyce's text by providing us with babies' wails, cockadoodledoos, and so forth. Cage obviously hoped that by providing an acoustic referent for Joyce's words, he could create a condition in which signifier and signified would attain an ideal unity—as if a signifier could swallow up its signified in the manner of a python gulping down a pig. But I'm not sure that he, or anyone else, could succeed in this enterprise. Perhaps here belletristic music has extended itself beyond its limits, and must retreat.

There are other sorts of belletristic music that have nothing to do with speech music: for example, some musical compositions posit or are based on pictographs, glyphs, or non- or quasi-alphabetical symbols. Stravinsky himself often conceived his music in terms of strange visual symbols:

> After working late one night I retired to bed still troubled by an interval. I dreamed about this interval. It had become an elastic substance stretching exactly between the two notes I had composed, but underneath these notes at either end was an egg, a large testicular egg. The eggs were gelatinous to the touch (I touched them).... I woke up knowing that my interval was right.[23]

Later composers sometimes write about their music as if it were a much more painful sort of inscription. Here is Iannis Xenakis on his *Persepolis*:

> "Persepolis" is neither a theatrical spectacle, nor a ballet, nor a happening. It is visual symbolism, parallel to and dominated by sound. The sound, the music absolutely prevail. The music corresponds to a rock tablet on which hieroglyphic or cuneiform messages are engraved in a compact, hermetic way, delivering their secrets only to those who want and know how to read them. The

history of Iran, fragment of the world's history, is thus elliptically and abstractly represented by means of clashes, explosions, continuities and underground currents of sound. The listener must pay for his penetration into the knowledge of the signs with great effort, pain, and the suffering of his own birth.[24]

And here is Wolfgang Rihm on his *Chiffre I* (1982–83):

There is enigmatic, sketchy art. Arte cifra. Chiffre is . . . a cipher. Perhaps a compact sign, not deciphered. The piano is enclosed by a resonant instrumental body: the seven instruments. Into this surrounding, the sound of the piano engraves itself like cuneiform script, leaving wounds, signs. [. . .] But these are thoughts that must come to me now for the programme booklet. They are wrong.[25]

The program note, like the music itself, manages to unwrite itself before it concludes, in a touch reminiscent of the end of Beckett's *Molloy*. There is, then, a kind of inscriptive music that is deliberately illegible, except insofar as it reproduces the scars left by whip and cudgel on human flesh. The infernal machine in Kafka's "In the Penal Colony," that gashes random marks instead of legible commandments into the body of the condemned prisoner, became an ideal compositional tool by the end of the twentieth century.

But this story also comprises its antistory, for certain musical compositions, instead of creating illegible symbols in the mind of the auditor, are themselves created from illegible symbols. To describe how this happens I must appeal to what might be called the theory of the squiggle, and especially to the work of the all-time master squiggler, Jackson Pollock. It was once thought that Pollock's squiggles were generated by a sort of broadcast of pouring paint, and a movie of Pollock at work seemed to confirm that; but recent art historians have suggested that many of the squiggles are in fact carefully drawn simulacra of such pourings. Any sort of handwritten squiggle tends to look like the alphabet of some unknown culture. Some of the power of Pollock's paintings comes from their twin evocation of natural processes—trails of snail slime, drips of maple sap, lashes of an anteater's tongue, webs of incompetent spiders—and of a sort of translunar Arabic. Often there is little background, as if the whole pictorial surface is so dense with signifiers that a whole illegible encyclopedia might lie compressed on the canvas.

To any squiggle there are three possible reponses: to assess the aesthetic quality of line; to ask what it means; and to ask how it is pronounced. Every painting that alludes to *écriture* also potentially alludes to speech. Part of the task of music in the later twentieth century was to find ways of voicing mysterious symbols. In music, the materialism of the signifier was advocated by John Cage, who insisted on listening to a sound as mere sound, not as one-third of a triad or as any other component of a preestablished musical system. Cage was so devoted to the notion of phonic objectivity that he wrote a piece called *Cartridge Music*, performed by scraping a phonograph cartridge over various surfaces, as if the meaning of a velvet dress or an ironing board or a chunk of rock lay strictly in the kind of cry it could be made to utter if attacked with a sound-conversion device.

I think of music—all music—as a teasing of the linguistic areas of the brain, a teasing that neither terminates in a finite language nor completely frustrates the mind's attempt to hear speech. Graphism in painting corresponds to writing as music corresponds to language: a teasing of our faculty to find meaning in a sign that yields only tantalizingly incomplete results. It therefore follows that musicians would be extraordinarily attracted to pictorial graphism. This sort of music exists in Europe, too; but Stockhausen's notational experiments seem to carry a far greater burden of vehement, impeded-speech expression than the stressless graphisms of some American composers.

The composers of the New York School—Cage, Morton Feldman, Earle Brown, and Christian Wolff—have been draftsmen as well as musicians. In 1952, Brown began a series of graphic scores called *Folio*, mostly consisting of horizontal and vertical lines of varying length and thickness; the performer had to figure out how to translate this deviant notation into pitches and durations and phrases. As graphic notation evolved in the later twentieth century, it became increasingly attractive to the eye, shapely and iconic, alluding only obliquely to the standard vocabulary of musical notation. It freed itself from the concept of sound symbol and entered the domain of plastic sign. In Brown's *For Ann* (after 1970), the score consists of a long, thin rectangle subdivided into smaller rectangles and densely but irregularly crosshatched. The score of Wolff's *Edges* (1969) consists of a lot of white space, figured erratically with thin snaky curves, plus signs, brackets, an asterisk, inverted carets, an arrow, the numerals 3 and 10, and a few bits of music-notational detritus—a crescendo sign, a *ppp*, a *ff*, and the word *singing* (figure 9.1).

Wolff once taught classical languages at Harvard, and his score seems to be a hitherto unknown sort of Cretan script, a Linear X in which the performer must be the Michael Ventris, or the Oedipus, who solves the riddle of these unknown letter shapes. Or perhaps the music is figured not in the squiggles but in the large white spaces between. Perhaps the squiggles only represent boundary lines, horizons of attention, where the music stops, or changes, or adjusts its focus.

Cage, Brown, and Wolff all insist that their graphic scores aren't invitations to improvise, but instructions, however cryptic, to be interpreted, demanding complete concentration on the visual form. Brown has furthermore said that his enigmatic graphics "extend and intensify the ambiguity inherent in all graphic representation and in every response that the composer, the performer, and the public can make to it."[26] The most detailed score by Beethoven or Stravinsky is also a visual design that needs to puzzled out by the performer; Brown claims

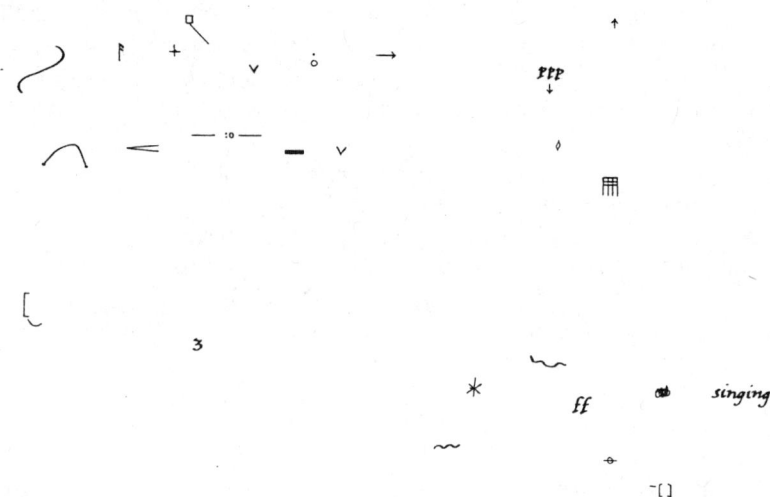

Figure 9.1. Wolff: *Edges*. © 1969 by C. F. Peters Corporation. Used by permission. All rights reserved.

only to be heightening the peril of an always perilous task. Music is a heap of sounds endlessly deferred from the collection of print traces in the score, traces that only point to other traces. By making the score so concrete, so inviolable, so recalcitrant to interpretation, the graphic composer obeys the demand for the dignity of the individual sound, an event that cannot be reduced to the facile code of the music engraver. Concreteness in sound properly leads to concreteness in the score that signifies it—or, more accurately, that fails to signify it, but manages to evoke it.

It fascinates me that Brown sought sanction for his method of writing music in the novels of Joyce:

> Like Proust's or Whitehead's or Einstein's world, Joyce's world is always changing as it is perceived by different observers and by them at different times. It is an organism made up of "events" which may be taken as infinitely inconclusive or infinitely small and each of which involves all of the others; and each of these events is unique.[27]

One modernist way of reading *Ulysses* is to insist on Joyce's supreme authorial control. But according to Brown's ultra-Bakhtinian reading strategy, Joyce's novels are the result of an indeterminate negotiation of myriad free agencies, as if each voice or word or grapheme in the text had an independent power of action. *Ulysses* or *Finnegans Wake*, then, feels like a concert of signs, exactly like the sort of concert produced by a gang of semicoordinated musicians, each of whom must puzzle out how to make a noise by staring at an opaque visual cue.

Perhaps the final movement of belletristic music can be found in a rejection of the alphabet letter and a fascination with the empty space on which a letter might be, but is not, figured. This is the musical equivalent of the blank page of Mallarmé, the prestige of the billboard in the absence of the sign. Cage's silent piece *4'33"* is one important document of this aesthetic, but later composers have improved on it. For example, Pauline Oliveros, Stuart Dempster, and Panaiotis experimented with improvisations inside a two-million-gallon water tank, a concrete underground cistern near Seattle built to withstand bombing. Its reverberation time is forty-five seconds. The reverberations are almost as loud as the original noise, so that any finite sound event is effortlessly absorbed into the overwhelm, the acoustic backwash. To speak of music in this situation is venturesome; in fact it is venturesome even to speak of sound, since every vibration is so thick-feathered with other vibrations. Cage considered each noise on earth as an equally precious, equally meaningless fact to be savored separately or in accidental combination. Oliveros and her allies consider that the ultimate acoustic fact is not the noise but the space in which the noise takes place. To listen to these improvisations, recorded under the title *Deep Listening*,[28] is more like listening to a waterfall than listening to music. Here music loses artificiality, recedes into the *natura* that no human act can ever truly mean. Here the sublime materializes itself in sound.

In his novel *A Passage to India* (1924), E. M. Forster describes a cave consisting of a circular chamber about twenty feet in diameter, connected to the outside world by a narrow shaft. Its echoes have a peculiar property. In fact, when a certain old woman, a pious Christian, enters the cave, she finds her religious faith undermined by the echoes:

> The echo . . . is entirely devoid of distinction. Whatever is said, the same monotonous noise replies, and quivers up and down the walls until it is absorbed into the roof. "Boum" is the sound as far as the human alphabet can express it, or "ou-boum,"—utterly dull. Hope, politeness, the blowing of a nose, the squeak of a boot, all produce "boum." . . . [The echo] had managed to murmur, "Pathos, piety, courage—they exist, but are identical, and so is filth. Everything exists, nothing has value." If one had spoken vileness in that place, or quoted lofty poetry, the comment would have been the same—"ou-boum." . . . Religion appeared, poor little talkative Christianity, and she knew that its divine words from "Let there be Light" to "It is finished" only amounted to "boum." . . . Visions are supposed to entail profundity, but—Wait till you get one, dear reader! The abyss also may be petty, the serpent of eternity made of maggots.[29]

If one can manage to read this passage without Forster's sense of revulsion, it anticipates certain postmodernist moods. Language has enormous prestige.

Indeed, the whole universe is a bundle of texts, but words have no prestige, since their reference vectors lead nowhere, simply bounce off walls until their force is spent and they recede into a wordless, worldless murmur of sound. American art has always been fascinated by large open spaces; but perhaps those large spaces are starting to turn into the closed space of a huge cave. Perhaps the object of veneration of art is becoming not poetry, not painting, not music, but the plangent void on which poetry, painting, and music might place themselves if they were so fortunate as to exist. Perhaps a whole book of such empty pages will be a gift that will allow each of us to write our own musics on it.

Part Two

Dance

Chapter Ten

Golden Calves

The Role of Dance in Opera

Imagine a performance of *Swan Lake* in which Odette waves her arms up and down and runs in circles while a puzzled Prince Siegfried looks on, scratching his head. Eventually the exasperated ballerina simply stops, turns to him, and says, "Don't you get it?—I'm supposed to be a swan!" Few rules in any art form are more stringent than the rule in classical ballet that dancers can't talk. Long ago I saw at Covent Garden a performance of Kenneth MacMillan's ballet *The Song of the Earth,* in which Anthony Dowell made a megaphone of his hands in front of his wide-open mouth, as if he were going to shout something. As it turned out it was only a mime of a scream, but the strong implication of taboo breaking made that one of the most memorable moments in the whole genre of ballet, comparable to the end of Balanchine's *Sonnambula,* when the woman picks up the man and carries him offstage.

But if speech and song are forbidden to dancers, dance is perfectly acceptable for operatic singers, even in the case of singers constitutionally unable to dance. A happy soprano surprised by an expensive present from her lover might skip with joy; a cunning mezzo might raise her skirt and clack her castanets; a dying basso in his dragon suit might even get a little choreography for his final spasms. Often in opera the dancing is quite unobtrusively integrated into the drama, as in the ballroom scenes in *La traviata* and *Eugene Onegin.* But what interests me here is the other kind of operatic ballet, in which there is a certain strain or even fracture about the copresence of dancing and singing; in which the conventions of opera and the conventions of ballet jostle uncomfortably; in which the composer may have been forced to provide a ballet against his will; in which there is little sense of *Gesamtkunstwerk* but a strong sense of *Zerstückelnkunstwerk* (shattered work of art).

The great master of the inconsequential ballet was of course Meyerbeer, who thought it a fine thing to provide, in *Le prophète* (1849), a little relief for the bloodthirsty, war-torn Anabaptists in the form of a delicious ballet in which provisions sellers on ice skates—simulated with those newfangled contrivances, roller skates—take a break from their capitalist enterprise by dancing. Wagner considered the typical Meyerbeer opera a series of effects without causes, "a

First published in *Opera Quarterly* 22, no. 1 (Winter 2006): 22–37.

monstrously piebald, historico-romantic, diabolico-religious, fanatico-voluptuous, frivolo-sacred, mysterio-jaunty, sentimento-knavish dramatic hodgepodge."[1] You might get the impression that Wagner disapproved. But you have only to hear Wagner's words to understand that Meyerbeer's time has come: no pithier description of the postmodern sensibility exists. Rauschenberg's goat plugged into an automobile tire, Serrano's *Piss Christ*, Schnittke's *Dr. Faustus*, the whole canon of Damien Hirst: what are these but more recent manifestations of the piebald, diabolico-religious, sacro-frivolous, mysterio-criminal? Maybe the patron saint of our age is Giacomo Meyerbeer.

We can take *Le prophète* as a sort of limit point of unrelatedness between a ballet and the opera in which it is included. At this degree of delamination there can be no critique of one medium by another: at one moment you're watching an opera, at the next a ballet, and you forget all about the first when watching the second. But few composers possessed Meyerbeer's godlike indifference to dramatic propriety. Typically some relation, however tenuous, can be found between opera and ballet, and in the relation there is often something disturbing, challenging—something that calls into question our usual ease at accepting the conventions of either ballet or opera.

I think I should try to categorize the sorts of relations a ballet might have to its surrounding opera. But before I do that, I have to speak a little on the general problem that results when one artistic medium is asked to support or to do the work of another artistic medium—one of the most important problems that a student of the comparative arts faces.

A work of art that plays at the boundaries of its medium may try to usurp another medium's content or technique. The first case is usually the less interesting. For example, Franz Liszt wrote a tone poem, *Hunnenschlacht* (1857), which depicts a large fresco, by Kaulbach, of the battle between the Huns and the Romans.

So this is a case of musical ekphrasis, in which the composer is trying to translate a painting into sound. But as far as I can tell, Liszt would have written exactly the same work if he'd been thinking, not about the painting of the battle, but about the battle itself. There's nothing pictorial in Liszt's handling of the usual noise trajectory of battle, familiar from so many instrumental pieces by Biber, Byrd, Kuhnau, Beethoven, and others. Liszt is more interesting when he fools around on the boundaries between speech and music, as in his piano piece *Il penseroso,* based on both a statue by Michelangelo—*La notte*—and the poem that Michelangelo wrote as the statue's inscription. Again, Liszt attempts some imitation of the content: the music is subdued, veiled, almost immobile, restless within extremely narrow limits. But here Liszt imitates not just the content of his model, but also the form. He exactly follows the prosody of Michelangelo's verse in rhythm and phrase shape. His music attempts to translate the very speechlikeness of speech, the inner lilt of the poem. To take another example, Stravinsky said that the subject of his ballet *Apollo* was versification. Indeed, the ballet can be heard as the apotheosis of the iambic foot.

It is possible to go still further in usurping the technical aspects of an alien medium. When Gloria Coates decided to write a symphonic piece presumably based on Vincent van Gogh's *A Still Life with Quinces*—the piece is called *The Quinces' Quandary, Homage to Van Gogh* (1993/94)—she faced a difficult problem in ekphrasis. The content resisted any ordinary strategy for musicalizing. Even Richard Strauss might have had trouble in writing a quince-flavored symphonic movement, as opposed to an apple- or pear-flavored one. The concept of a cornucopia or outspilling fruit might lend itself to translation into music, perhaps in some sort of ramifying structure such as those in Henri Dutilleux's *L'arbre des songes* and the chain pieces of Witold Lutosławski. But what Coates chose to imitate was not the notion of quince but the notion of impasto: the thick smears of pigment are imaged by overlapping glissandi. As Coates remarked:

> [*A Still Life with Quinces* is] not really a still life inasmuch as all the objects were in motion. Van Gogh painted it during the last year of his life. . . . I felt something of his own fears and disappointments. . . . And the quinces were beginning to move, one was already falling. . . . The form which I selected corresponded to the movement of my eye across the canvas from the upper left to the lower right with the falling fruit. The brushstrokes were like my own glissandi. . . . But in another medium, creating musical forms similar to those on the canvas.[2]

Everything I mention about the arts in relation to one another is perfectly familiar; but sometimes it's good to put obvious things clearly on the table.

Now, back to the case of dance versus opera. A ballet may have many sorts of relations to the opera in which it finds itself. The ballet can try to advance the opera's action; or the ballet can complement the opera's action; or the ballet can offer relief from the opera's action. In theory, the ballet could even resist the opera's action, but direct instances of this are hard to come by. One instance might be the ballet chanté *The Seven Deadly Sins,* by Kurt Weill and Bertolt Brecht, in which the dancer half of Anna continually rejects the "good" advice offered by the singer half of Anna. But here the ballet isn't so much contained within an opera as secreting an opera around itself. But perhaps in another sense *every* opera ballet resists, to some degree, its opera, though this will take some demonstrating.

First let's take the case of the obedient ballet—the ballet that wants to help its opera accomplish its mission. How can a dance hope to do the work of opera? According to the general model described above, a ballet could try to imitate an opera's content, or it could try to imitate its form or technique. A ballet can imitate an opera's *content* by becoming pantomime. Writing in 1719, Jean-Baptiste Dubos credited Jean-Baptiste Lully with introducing imitative dance into opera. In former times (he says) everyone, whether shepherdess or cyclops, danced the same steps as everyone else, but after Lully's innovations dances became specific in character and action. In fact, Dubos says that Lully had to choreograph a number of imitative dances himself:

Lulli... commença de composer pour les ballets de ces airs qu'on appelle des airs de vitesse. Comme les danseurs qui executoient les ballets composez sur ces airs, étoient obligez à se mouvoir avec plus de vitesse et plus d'action que les danseurs ne l'avoient fait jusqu'alors, bien des personnes dirent qu'on corrompoit le bon goût de la danse, et qu'on alloit en faire un baladinage. Les danseurs eux-mêmes n'entrerent qu'avec peine dans l'esprit des nouveaux airs, et souvent il arriva que Lulli fut obligé de composer lui-même les entrées qu'il vouloit faire danser sur les airs dont je parle.... Comme les compositeurs de ballet dont Lulli se servoit, ne se perfectionnoient pas aussi vîte que lui, il fut obligé souvent de composer encore lui-même le ballet des airs d'un caractere marqué. Lulli, six mois avant que de mourir fit lui-même le ballet de l'air sur lequel il vouloit faire danser les ciclopes de la suite de Poliphême.[3]

Lully... began to compose for his ballets airs that could be called *airs de vitesse*. Since the dancers who executed the steps devised for these airs were obliged to move more nimbly and busily than dancers had formerly done, many people said that dancing had become tasteless and clownish. The dancers themselves had difficulty entering into the spirit of these new airs, and it often happened that Lully was obliged to devise the steps that he desired to be danced.... As Lully's choreographers did not improve quickly enough, he was often obliged to choreograph himself the airs with a determined character. Six months before his death Lully himself made the ballet for the cyclopes in Polyphemus's retinue [in *Acis et Galatée*].

As Ken Pierce and Jennifer Thorp have shown,[4] many of Lully's "imitative" dances (wrestling matches, bestowals of gifts, forging metal on anvils) were combinations of ordinary dance steps and pantomime. But the movement toward action, plot advancement, by means of dance was clear.

It is clear from the abbé Dubos that the mimetic elements of dance offended some of Lully's spectators. Pantomime, of course, has a long if not too distinguished history of its own; Polyhymnia has generally been considered one of the weaker sisters among the Muses. Pantomime has a certain charadelike, effortful quality, tending to overcompensate for its muteness. In her remarkable book on the ballet during the time of *Giselle,* Marian Smith has described how certain Parisian dance performances tried every conceivable means to find surrogates for language: "Composers, choreographers, and designers at the Opéra introduced words into ballet performances in every way but actually having performers intone them."[5] These ways included on-stage placards and orchestral quotations of familiar tunes whose lyrics were relevant to the action. Still, it would seem that pantomime, with its pointed, specific action, ought to be the norm for operatic ballet, but in fact it is far from the norm. In many scenes in opera (such as the beginning of Act 3 of *Der Rosenkavalier*), singers perform pantomime, but in only a few scenes do dancers perform pantomime. Perhaps the Hecate pantomime that Verdi added to the 1865 Paris *Macbeth* is the most impressive example. I think I understand why. The ballet dancer generally has no role in the drama outside the ballet, so a dramatic ballet is likely to be at best a metadrama. This explains why Hecate works so well in a pantomime ballet: she belongs to a higher theatre than the one shown on stage. During her dumb show, Hecate announces the arrival of Macbeth and orders the witches to answer his questions; she instructs the spirits of the air to revive him if he faints; and she ordains that Macbeth's destruction shall happen immediately. In short, she predicts exactly what will occur and takes account of every contingency. Whereas the Macbeths can anticipate nothing properly, clairvoyant Hecate can anticipate everything properly; no thickened light befogs her eyesight. During this ballet we are lifted out of the world of opera into some controlling, string-pulling upper domain of foreordination.

There may be still another, more hidden reason for the scarcity of ballet-pantomime in opera: pantomime destroys musical continuity. Marian Smith cites a number of Parisian critics from the 1830s and 1840s:

> Ballet music has a particular character: it is more accented, more *parlante*, more expressive than opera music, because it is not destined only to accompany and enhance the words of the librettist, but to be itself the entire libretto. Generally, one does not ask for music from a ballet-pantomime composer, but for an orchestra that is the translation, the commentary of the text that one would not otherwise be able to understand.[6]

A ballet-pantomime score, then, isn't music: it's just a transposition of words and story into wordless sound. If a sylphide flaps her wings, the composer will oblige with a dainty flutter of thirty-second-notes.[7] The music's spine is broken as it's wrestled into the shape of the drama. Ballet-pantomime, then, by fighting against musical consequence, tends to resist placement in opera. This is the first of the forms of balletic resistance that we'll see today. Verdi tries to avoid discontinuity in the Hecate scene by writing a ballet that's a loose series of variations on a theme. But despite Verdi's superior skills, the ballet is a somewhat lurching affair, and Verdi wrote it out of contractual obligation.

So balletic imitation of an opera's content didn't prove especially productive. Can ballet succeed better by imitating an opera's technique? What indeed would it mean for a dance to imitate opera? Insofar as opera means virtuoso vocal display, a dance can provide a simulacrum by the simple means of virtuoso legwork. As a teenager in Chicago I first experienced music theater with a performance of *Prince Igor*, in which the recent defector Rudolf Nureyev danced the Polovetsian Dances. He leaped so high and bent his back so far that, at least in my unreliable memory, the back of his fingertips nearly touched his heels. This remains my only experience in which the quality of the dancing matched the quality of the singing (I mean, in a good way).

But insofar as opera means not show-off singing but the regulation and expression of human action by music, a ballet that tries to do the work of opera must attempt other strategies. If Gloria Coates attempted to imitate the thickness and spread of Van Gogh's paint, a ballet composer might attempt to embody the way in which music controls action—the sheer fatedness of plot by rhythm. In this sense the slave is the ideal subject for an opera ballet. Indeed, there are some fine slave dances in opera, such as the dance of the Persian slaves in Musorgsky's *Khovanshchina* and the slave dance in the fourth act of Berlioz's *Les Troyens*. At the end of the latter the Nubian women perform a tom-tom-like dance while the chorus sings wild nonsense syllables. Soon Ascanius, *semblable à Cupidon*, will take the wedding ring from Dido's finger to promote her love of Aeneas. The slave ballet, like the sex pantomime during the royal hunt and storm, enforces the notion that we are all slaves of Eros and that music incarnates the rhythm of our sexual lives.

Music is the preeminent art of time. It is true, as Gotthold Ephraim Lessing says in *Laokoon* (1766), that literature is also a species of *nacheinander*, sequential rather than spatial. But literary time is unpredictable and adventitious—Who knows how long it takes to read "Ode to a Nightingale," let alone *War and Peace?*—whereas musical time is usually determined, precise. A number of famous opera ballets take time itself as their subject matter, most notably the four seasons ballet in Verdi's *Les vêpres siciliennes* and the dance of the hours in Ponchielli's *La gioconda*. Ponchielli's music has an unforgettable off-kilter tick to it, as if an arrogant metronome had decided to assert its own will. The clock and the wobbling revolutions of the earth about the sun are in charge of things. Such time ballets are in effect obeisances to the force of destiny, illuminations of the time canvas on which all dramas, fictitious and real, are inscribed. Time's impasto is thrust forward by the dance.

So far we've seen two possible functions for ballet in opera: first, to provide relief from the stress of plot (the more meaningless or irrelevant, the greater the relief); second, to translate something of the experience of opera into the medium of dance. But there are others. A third function might be to complement opera, to complete the drama by doing things that opera cannot do.

Often this entails display of the body. The premise of opera is that nakedness is transposed from the skin to the larynx: vulnerability, modesty, wild abandon, are all reseated in throat; all sex is oral sex.[8] But from the beginning of the operatic genre it has been understood that an audience might enjoy seeing a copulation that was more vivid, less metaphorical, than two voices in parallel thirds. Monteverdi's *Orfeo* ends with a dance called a moresca, a Moorish dance. I've been unable to discover just how decorous or obscene an early seventeenth-century moresca might be, but if it's anything like the vocal moresche that Lassus was writing twenty-five years before, in 1581, it might be quite raunchy indeed:

Chi chi li chi? Cu cu ru cu!
 U scontienta, u beschina, u sprotunata, me Lucia. Non sienta Martina galla cantara?

Lassa canta possa clepare! Porca te picscia sia licata, Ia dormuta tu scitata. Ba condia, non bo più per namolata. Tutta note tu dormuta, Mai a me tu basciata.⁹

"Who's going cocorico?" "It's me, unhappy wretched me, Lucia! Don't you hear your cock Martino crowing?" "Ah, you know where you can shove your song, you pigful of shit! I was asleep and you woke me up! Go to hell, I don't love you any more, you slept all night and didn't fuck me once!"

This is jazz as the late sixteenth century understood it—in fact as I myself understand it. Not only *Orfeo* (1607) but Marco da Gagliano's *Dafne* (1608) and Jacopo Peri's *Euridice* (1600) end with dances of remarkable rhythmic intensity. The catchy final dance scene that Emilio de' Cavalieri wrote for the deluxe proto-opera *La pellegrina* (1589) became one of the hit tunes of the age. Nietzsche considered the pallid shepherds of early opera, intoning their blanched recitativi, to be sad thin caricatures of the Dionysiac actors of Greek tragedy. But I think that opera, like Greek tragedy itself, was born as a genre intimate with sex dance. As Wendy Heller has shown, by the time of Francesco Cavalli's opera *La Venere gelosa* (1643), the librettist Niccolò Bartolini was consciously basing the dramatic action on the dances of the old Dionysiac festivals—and Priapus was near at hand.¹⁰

In later opera, as in Jules Massenet's *Thaïs* and Camille Saint-Saëns's *Samson et Dalila*, a prostitute heroine would be surrounded by dancers who acted as her vicarious flesh. Sometimes, as in many performances of Strauss's *Salome*, a dancer would literally take the role of the soprano and teasingly unveil the body that Salome would have if she really were a sixteen-year-old girl. But is all this carnality a good idea? The trick of opera—the displacement of body into voice—is exposed as a trick whenever it has to compete with actual nakedness. There is a necessary moment of focal readjustment, unease, when the bacchanale or strip-tease stops and the opera resumes. Barbara Johnson wrote that "the linguistic 'noise' of the act of translating, in not being meant or intended, comes close to the pure linguisticness of language itself."¹¹ I sometimes feel that the operaticness of opera is felt most strongly at the moment just after the dance stops, and we suddenly have to reerect the whole corpus of convention on which opera depends. In *Salome*, Herod always feels slimy, but nowhere quite so goggling, panting, outlandish, inhumanly lewd, a drooling mouth and a rolling tongue standing in for a man, as when he sings his applause just after the Dance of the Seven Veils. Maybe we also feel the balleticity of ballet most strongly when dance interrupts opera. Aesthetic contortions of the body seem especially unnatural when we're accustomed to another sort of unnaturalness.

In a great many opera ballets the unnatural feel of dance in opera becomes a conscious theme. This is another sort of complementarity: insofar as the stage picture of the opera represents a norm, the ballet twists itself into the image of the abnormal, the distant, the eerie. Even Verdi, no great lover of ballet or of exoticism, provided for *Otello* a ballet that begins in full Orientalist fig with Turkish slaves who, as Verdi explains, "dance reluctantly and with bad grace because they are slaves. However . . . on hearing the Canzone Araba they liven up gradually and end by dancing wildly."[12] Verdi even asked Ricordi to send him furlanas, fandaroles, and Turkish and Greek-Cypriot melodies to stimulate his imagination. In operas that were already set in obtrusively unreal places, the desire for a still more exotic ballet could drive the scenarist to remarkable extremes. My favorite example is Massenet's *Hérodiade,* in which the search for something that would feel strange to a first-century community in Judea led the composer to write dances for Gauls and Babylonians.

Wagner thought that opera should be a *Gesamtkunstwerk,* a total art work, in which every element was perfectly integrated, cooperant to the dramatic telos. But in the operatic world that Wagner opposed, the world of Meyerbeerian grand opera, another kind of totalizing impulse was at work, though as far as I know it had no theorist to bring its principles to light. According to this countermodel, an opera could be an image of the whole experience of being human by piling up discrepant theatres in discrepant media, that is, by *refusing* to integrate ballet and opera, Meyerbeer and his cohort give extraordinarily full perspectives by yoking together heterogeneous and jarring theatrical modes. It is as if the opera plus the ballet plus the visual spectacle had to add up to the whole universe. At the beginning of the third act of *Les troyens,* Berlioz devised a pageant in which builders, sailors, and workmen come forth to celebrate peace in Carthage. Queen Dido pays homage to all the craftsmen that have created the city, just as Berlioz, in the course of his five acts, pays homage to every sort of theatrical representation that makes up grand opera, including the pantomime, the ballet, the march, the ghost apparition, the national anthem, the battle scene, the musical storm, the huge voice of an oracle, the harp-accompanied song recital, and some spectacles quite unusual in opera, such as the wrestling match. Even Wagner was not immune to the charms of this other sort of totalized artwork. In *Die Meistersinger* the apprentices dance amid a pageant of tailors bleating like goats, bakers battening in the lower registers—the whole trade-guild structure of Nuremburg. Drama critics often speak of World Theater, in capital letters—the theater of medieval morality plays and Goethe's *Faust,* the theater that spans the whole gamut of earth, heaven, and hell. Perhaps instead of grand opera we should speak of World Opera, the opera that throws in the kitchen sink.

We've been examining ballet as the complement to opera. The next step, taxonomically speaking—maybe the last step—is to think of ballet as opera's Other, an alien medium representing all that opera can never attain. This is a symbolist and modernist way of thinking about opera ballet: where opera leaves off, grows mute, perhaps the mute art of dance can speak. The earliest trace of this attitude that I can find occurs in 1843, if I try to put together two creative acts that were occurring in different corners of Europe, each unknown to the other. The first is a passage from Kierkegaard's *Either/Or:*

The Middle Ages had much to say about a mountain not found on any map, which is called the mountain of Venus. There the sensuous has its home, there it has its own wild pleasures, for it is a kingdom, a state. In this kingdom language has no place, nor sober-minded thought, nor the toilsome business of reflection. There sound only the voice of elemental passion, the play of appetites, the wild shouts of intoxication; it exists solely for pleasure in eternal tumult. The first-born of this kingdom is Don Juan. That it is the kingdom of sin is not yet affirmed, for we confine ourselves to the moment at which this kingdom appears in aesthetic indifference. Not until reflection enters does it appear as the kingdom of sin, but by that time Don Juan is slain, the music is silent.[13]

The second is the opera *Tannhäuser*, which Wagner was starting to compose as Kierkegaard published these words. The official ballet, of course, wasn't composed for some fifteen years, but in the 1845 version, the first act opens with wildly dancing bacchantes and a strange languid murmurous song of the nymphs, as if only music's echo can speak in words. According to Kierkegaard's critique of the unwritten opera, the Venusberg is intricately voluptuous but wholly innocent. It is sinful only insofar as Elisabeth, or her phantom in memory, steps forth to provide some ethical coordinate system according to which sexual license may be judged sinful. Maybe dance tends to constitute a sort of orthogonal to the plane of opera, innocent in that the moral norms of opera don't apply. Maybe any sort of wordless action tends to be an alterity in the overwhelmingly vocal world of opera. For Kierkegaard the Venusberg is where language has no place; the mons veneris looms above, before, or to the side of language. Dance is another domain where language has no place. The dancing body is what Mallarmé, writing in 1886, called a corporeal scripture, a hieroglyph intense, fraught with sensuous meaning, beyond speech or song:

> À savoir que la danseuse *n'est pas une femme qui danse,* pour ces motifs juxtaposes qu'elle *n'est pas une femme,* mais une métaphore résumant un des aspects élémentaires de notre forme, glaive, coupe, fleur, etc., *qu'elle ne danse pas,* suggérant, par le prodige de raccourcis ou d'élans, avec une écriture corporelle ce qu'il faudrait des paragraphes en prose dialoguée autant que descriptive, pour exprimer, dans la redaction: poème dégagé de tout appareil du scribe.[14]

That is to say that the dancing woman *is not a woman who dances*, on the related grounds that she *is not a woman* but a metaphor summing up one of the elementary aspects of our form, sword, cup, flower, etc., and *that she does not dance,* suggesting, through the wonder of contractions or leaps, with a corporeal scripture what one would need many paragraphs of dialogue as well as descriptive prose to express, in the wording: a poem disengaged from all the apparatus of writing.

Where there is no speech, no writing, there can be no moral judgment.

It is true that some operatic dances toy with vulgar tropes of sexual arousal: the castanets of Carmen's gypsy song and dance; the castanets and the buzzings of Spanish flies in Wagner's 1861 Venusberg ballet; the augmented-second scale in the *Samson et Dalila* bacchanale, probably suggestive of snake charming and belly dancing; and any number of slinky or sudden musical effects in the Dance of the Seven Veils, correlative to the desired visual effects. Strauss asked the Salome dancer to assume poses derived from specific illustrations of bacchantes, Japanese dancers, Egyptian women, bayadères, and even a certain girl on page 315 of *Le Paradis de Mahomet*.[15] Excessive refinement of gesture was evidently not a problem. Strauss imagined his Salome alternating between "passionate wooing" and tearing off her veils "violently." And yet it frequently happens that the dancing Salome seems quite self-involved, self-engrossed, indifferent to her effect on Herod, less like an Asiatic sexpot than like the Hérodiade of Mallarmé:

J'aime l'horreur d'être vierge et je veux	The horror of my virginity
Vivre parmi l'effroi que me font mes cheveux . . .	Delights me, and I would envelope me
Rare limpidité d'un coeur qui le songea,	In the terror of my tresses . . .
Je me crois seule en ma monotone patrie	So rare a crystal is my dreaming heart,
Et tout, autour de moi, vit dans l'idolâtrie	And all about me lives but in mine own
D'un miroir qui reflète en son calme dormant	Image, the idolatrous mirror of my pride,
Hérodiade au clair regard de diamant.[16]	Mirroring this Herodiade diamond-eyed.[17]

In fact the more Salome seems to dance only for self-delight, the closer she comes to the transcendental perversity of Wilde's original play. The dancing Carmen, too, seems to be playing a sort of abstract seduction game with Don José—a game that she knows will have fatal consequences, but a form of self-indulgence nonetheless. She maddens José, because he knows there are parts of her wholly beyond the reach of hand or phallus. She is a *oiseau rebelle* always flying beyond anyone's grasp. In Prosper Mérimée's novel, Carmen tells José that the surest way of guaranteeing that she'll do something is to tell her that she's not permitted to do it; she is taboo incarnate. As such she is most at home not in flexible operatic musical discourse, but in diegetic strophic song and in dance. She likes the more eccentric regions of the opera stage. The dancer tends to inhabit some other plane of being; all operatic dancing tends to be a dancing away. Normal categories of dramatis personae are suspended. In the act of dancing, Salome is at her most whorish and most virginal at the same time.

In certain modernist works this sense that dance is a portal into some other dimension, crystalline and spectral, is remarkably strong. Albert Roussel's *Padmâvatî* (1923), to a libretto by the distinguished scholar of Asian music Louis Laloy, is an opera ballet in two acts. In the first act the sultan of the Mogul army decides that he will spare the city of Tchitor only if the king of Tchitor will give him his wife, the spectacularly beautiful Padmâvatî. In the second act Padmâvatî stabs her husband to death for agreeing to this scheme and steps into a blazing pyre rather than break her vow of fidelity, even if it means the destruction of everyone she knows and loves. In the first act the dancing is about what you would expect in an exotic opera ballet: the slave women of the king of Tchitor perform routines that excite the sultan to the point where he insists on seeing unveiled the legendary Padmâvatî. But in the second act the dancers enact a supernatural pantomime in which the vampirish white daughters of Siva are drawn to the king's corpse, while the black daughters of Siva try to seize Padmâvatî. Eventually Padmâvatî, shuddering, performs a rite of exorcism as the priests sing the magic syllable *Om*, and the dancers transform themselves into kindly spirits who escort Padmâvatî into the flames. It is a dance about superseding all human desire, about entering nirvana.

The most striking piece in Roussel's opera is an aria in the first act that a Brahmin sings in praise of Padmâvatî:

Ses yeux sont les étoiles du ciel des immortels,
Elle glisse dans l'air comme un cygne sur l'eau immobile des lacs.
Les fleurs naissent de son sourire.
Padmâvatî est le rêve dont s'éveilla le créateur des mondes; son visage est
    l'aurore du néant bienheureux.[18]
Vers elle les désirs de l'univers s'élancent et meurent à sa vue.
Sa voix est le chant de l'oubli.

Her eyes are stars in the heaven of the gods,
She glides in the air like a swan on the still water of lakes.
Flowers are born from her smile.
Padmâvatî is the dream from which the creator of the worlds awoke; her countenance is the dawn of blessed nothingness.
Toward her the desires of the universe rush, and die at her sight.
Her voice is the song of oblivion.

Padmâvatî's voice may be oblivion's own voice, but it is dance that leads us into the pyre. By the end we have left almost all singing behind and entered a pure domain of wordless, worldless music and gesture. Roussel was an atheist and the only composer I know of who tried to embody an atheistic philosophy in music drama, most notably his ballet *The Spider's Feast* (1913), in which human life is imaged as a sober and delicate dance of ephemerae. The opera *Padmâvatî* is a self-superseding work in which drama leaves off at the threshold of apathy, aphasia, athambia, nothingness. A real Brahmin named Mohini Chatterjee once told Yeats that "we ourselves are nothing but a mirror and that deliverance consists in turning the mirror away [from the sensible world] so that it reflects nothing."[19] Few works of art provide this effect as strongly as *Padmâvatî*. The drama swivels away from representation, turning its gaze backward into its eye sockets.

Roussel finished composing this opera in 1918, and it may be read as a response to the Great War, which made earthly life especially worth forgetting. A few years later, in 1930, another composer with good reason for political disgust, Arnold Schoenberg, started work on an another opera that explores the metaphysics of speech, song, and dance: *Moses und Aron* (see chapter 6). It is a long meditation on the commandment against graven images. The hero, Moses, can (with one brief exception) only speak, not sing, for he feels that any compromise with the beautiful, the rapt, the charming, is a movement toward idolatry. Song is the province of the eloquent Aron, who simplifies and falsifies Mosaic truth in order to make it comprehensible to the crowd. The opera's authentic action lies in Moses' inarticulate communion with the one and only, eternal, almighty, all-present, invisible God. This is what is real. The whole plot concerning Aron and the other characters—the miracle of the serpent, the miracle of the leprous hand, the building of the Golden Calf, the presentation of the Tables of the Law—all these represent the low, the fallen, the temporal, in short the Other. The opera takes place in eternity, in the endless circumvolutions of the twelve-tone row, and stares downward at the sodden failure of the human race to know truth and embody right conduct.

In this reversed opera, where the transcendental is the norm and the ciscendental—our usual life—is the exotic, the whole semantics of opera is turned upside down. We begin with the Burning Bush, the voice of God, a delirious atonal interweave of speaking and singing. Schoenberg's God, like the Hebrew word *Elohim*, is a plural used as a singular. Out of this tohu-bohu there eventually precipitates a firmament of themes, the recognizable discourse of operatic drama. As we approach the great dance scene that takes up most of the second act—the orgy around the Golden Calf—the tone row starts to fragment. A piece of the sixth transposition of the basic series, containing blatant fourths and minor thirds, detaches itself and is obsessively repeated on the xylophone, as butchers cut up live oxen and the Hebrews eat the bleeding chunks. Soon the butchers start to dance to this and other parodically tonal chunks of the butchered tone row. Just before the main orgy begins, a tumult of sex, murder, and suicide, four naked virgins sing a slow, glassy hymn to the Golden Calf. They praise its cold chastity, its fruitlessness, and ask the priests to give them their first and final rapture. The priests fondle the virgins, and then, as the virgins hand them knives, stab them to death. The eeriness of this scene, and of the whole bacchanale, is both like and unlike the other sorts of symbolic dance scenes we've been studying here: like, in that exotic instrumentation, irregular rhythm, and representations of unusual sexual practice provide a frisson of excitement; unlike, in that the frisson seems to be God's shudder at seeing human depravity, rather than a normal audience's oo-la-la response. Where serialism is divine, the comfortable sound of triads becomes evil. Schoenberg inverts the normal structure of interpretation, as in Saint-Saëns's *Samson et Dalila,* in which virtue is diatonic and vice is chromatic. The dance tempts us to enter that bizarre place, ordinary Western life. The suggestions of jazz trumpet, unmistakable in the dance of the butchers, remind us all the more strongly that, to Schoenberg, Berlin, London, New York were all gigantic images of the Golden Calf. In his 1928 opera *Von heute auf morgen,* Schoenberg's characters dance in a living room to music from a radio, the ugliest, most garish caricature of popular music that Schoenberg could construct. In 1949 Schoenberg, distressed at recent tendencies to squash together low music and high, asked, "Why not play a boogie-woogie when Wotan walks across a rainbow to Valhalla?"[20] In a sense, the dances in *Moses und Aron* are boogie-woogies played as Moses tries to walk up the mountain to God—a sort of dances exactly opposite in tenor, yet curiously similar in function, to the dance that impels Padmâvatî across the threshold to nirvana.

But one twentieth-century opera is preeminent for its refusal to integrate ballet into the rest of the musical discourse: Benjamin Britten's *Death in Venice* (1973). I noted before that in the Paris in the 1840s, the music that accompanied pantomimes wasn't considered music but a series of disconnected, gestural spasms in sound. In Britten's opera, Tadzio (the boy who provokes intellectual rapture and disturbing sexual desire in the repressed artist-hero Aschenbach) is played by a dancer who dances to the weird sonority of the gamelan, the Javanese percussion band that is the antiself of the Western orchestra: little melody, little harmony, all rhythm. Aschenbach is himself an unusual sort of character. His musical voice is almost as speechlike as that of Schoenberg's Moses, for he often sings in a talky, piano-accompanied recitative, as if he were performing a voice-over to his own life. Frequently he sounds like the Male Prologue in Britten's *The Rape of Lucretia,* standing on the margin of the stage and offering sober moral analysis of the events on stage. Song is the province not of Aschenbach but of the tempters who conduct him toward Venice, toward forbidden desire, toward hell. Britten carefully parcels out the components of music theater into different, somewhat hostile areas of the drama.

In *The Artwork of the Future,* Wagner deplored the way in which Meyerbeerean opera had separated into three immiscible elements, Poetry, Music, and Dance: "opera becomes the mutual compact of the egoism of the three arts."[21] But Britten, like Schoenberg, uses this very separation to aesthetic advantage. In *Death in Venice,* ballet not only seems to resist the opera in which it finds itself, but also seems to resist the whole idea of opera. Tadzio exists on another plane of reality, taking little notice of that fact that he's surrounding by a bustle of singers. In Yeats's phrase, he is self-delighting, self-appeasing, self-affrighting.

Tadzio is less a lovely adolescent than the statue of a lovely adolescent, a Platonic form of beauty itself, arrested in a vibraphone's bronzy shimmer, as if shaped metal could speak. Tadzio is an idol, a living violation of the second commandment, a golden calf. The main musical figure that Britten uses to characterize Tadzio is an erratic descent through a major seventh, from G♯ to A, and it is sometimes accompanied by a chord consisting of G♯–A–C♯–D—that is, a chord consisting of a squash of the two semitonal areas (scale degrees $\hat{7}$–$\hat{1}$ and $\hat{3}$–$\hat{4}$) of the A-major scale, the greatest dissonances that the major scale can provide, the opposite or complement of a triad. Here is hieroglyph, this sonority outside the normal workings of the harmonic system, outside the usual semantic meaning of dissonance.

Describing the *Apocalypsis* oratorio by the imaginary composer Adrian Leverkühn at the end of chapter 34 of Thomas Mann's novel *Doktor Faustus* (1947), the narrator marvels that the meanings of consonance and dissonance are reversed. Hell is all parodically familiar consonance, whereas heaven is depicted by "a piece of cosmic music of the spheres, icy, clear, glass-transparent, acridly dissonant to be sure, and yet with a . . . charm of sound inaccessibly-extraterrestrial and strange, filling the heart with longing without hope."[22] This description seems pertinent both to certain features of Schoenberg's *Moses und Aron* and to Tadzio's celestial eeriness in Britten's *Death in Venice*. Tadzio's figure is a kind of music that excludes music as we know it, a kind of music that frustrates normal procedures of interpretation as human feeling, as if Britten provided Tadzio with a device inscribed in some lost or unknown musical language without a Rosetta stone. Mann hoped that Britten would write an operatic version of *Doktor Faustus*, but in a sense Britten's operatic version of *Death in Venice* does duty for *Doktor Faustus* as well. We may also remember that one of the first recordings (1941) of the young Britten was as a pianist in Colin McPhee's *Balinese Ceremonial Music*, a transcription for two pianos of gamelan music, the fruit of McPhee's extensive ethnomusicological research in Bali. It is impossible to exaggerate the Otherness of Tadzio's unconsciously seductive dance. It means nothing except remoteness, the remoteness of Bali, or of the planet Neptune, or of that domain of ideal forms to which, according to Plato, our backs are always turned. Like the dances in *Padmâvatî*, Tadzio's dance is a dance of annihilation, at once arousing desire and obliterating it.

I will end this brief tour of the ways in which opera and ballet resist one another by asking a question: Is there any opera so resistant to dance that a ballet would be completely impossible? One would look for such a thing first in the world of German opera, always uneasier about frivolous entertainment than French or Italian opera, and perhaps first at the operas of Wagner. Few Wagner operas have official dance scenes, but, as it happens, almost all of them could profit from the attention of a choreographer. Rhine maidens, Flower Maidens, Valkyries, charming masses of Norwegian girls; wedding festivities in Brabant or in the realm of the Gibichungs: all require patterned movement. An exception is *Tristan und Isolde,* which could take place on a black stage, so unimportant are visibly moving bodies. In *Tristan,* the trick of opera, the transposition of the corporeal—skittishness, flush, embrace, orgasm—into pure voice seems to have found its ultimate triumph.

And yet, the impossible thing—the *Tristan* ballet—does exist, though Wagner didn't write it. It is Emmanuel Chabrier's *Souvenirs de Munich: Quadrille sur les thèmes favoris de "Tristan et Isolde" de Richard Wagner.* Kurwenal's hearty tunes make perfect sense here, but to hear the melody of the *Liebestod* as a jaunty dance is disconcerting, sacrilegious even, in certain frames of mind. But this is part of the potential of the Leitmotiv, and Chabrier was right to realize it. Just out of the range of the ecstasy of voice, the orchestra convulsing in black fire, lies a homely scene of spiffy young folks and spry old folks dancing a quadrille. This quadrille has no business on the operatic stage, but it is a reminder that every opera somewhere contains the dance that resists it—that every opera, no matter how solemn, is, and ought to be, a monstrously piebald, historico-romantic, diabolico-religious, fanatico-voluptuous, frivolo-sacred, mysterio-jaunty, sentimento-knavish dramatic hodgepodge.

Chapter Eleven

Elephant Swan Space Grace

What is the origin of dance? According to one distinguished authority, dance precedes speech, precedes thinking, precedes feeling itself. Dance is the very first art of being human. The distinguished authority I have in mind is Ludwig van Beethoven, who described the beginning of his ballet *The Creatures of Prometheus* as follows:

> The two [statues] move slowly across the stage from the background.—P[rometheus] . . . is pleased when he sees that his plan is such a success; he is inexpressibly delighted, stands up and beckons to the children to stop—They turn slowly towards him in an expressionless manner. . . . He explains to them that they are his work, that they belong to him, that they must be thankful to him, kisses and caresses them.—However, still in an emotionless manner, they sometimes merely shake their heads, are completely indifferent, and stand there, groping in all directions.[1]

Prometheus has shaped clay into a man and a woman, and animated them with the fire that he stole from heaven; but he is disappointed that they are just zombies, brainless creatures capable only of blank, uncertain movement. The music that Beethoven wrote to accompany their coming to life is startling: first we hear a vague, rhythmless prelude, then Prometheus' temporary pleasure in his new creation. How are these half-baked gingerbread figures to be turned into a man and a woman capable of reason and affection? Prometheus ponders the problem and decides to take them to Parnassus, where Apollo and the Muses will instruct them how to be human by means of music and dance. As the scenario puts it:

> Euterpe, assisted by Amphion, starts to play music, and at the sound of their harmonies the two young people start to show signs of understanding, of the power of reflection, of an appreciation of the beauties of nature and of human feeling.[2]

The intelligent and moving scenario was devised by the great choreographer Salvatore Viganò, who commissioned the music from Beethoven and danced the role of the male Urmensch. By means of various dances from Terpsichore, the Graces, and Bacchus, the new man and woman learn the arts of pleasure and the arts of war.

Figure 11.1. Beethoven: Piano Variations, Op. 35, beginning, from Ludwig van Beethoven, *Variations for Piano* (New York: Dover, 1986), 144.

So far the ballet seems to have little drama, little conflict; but Beethoven and Viganò have a surprise for us. Melpomene, the Muse of tragedy, takes a dagger and mimes the act of dying. Overcome by her own art, she denounces Prometheus for having created a new race born only to die—and she kills Prometheus with her dagger. But the ballet will end happily: Pan and his fauns perform a grotesque dance that brings the dead Titan back to life. At the beginning Prometheus gives life to the human race; at the end the life-giver is himself in need of resurrection. Beethoven described the resurrection with a theme that came to obsess him: the theme we know from the final of the Third Symphony, the *Eroica* (1804, three years after *The Creatures of Prometheus*). Beethoven also used this theme in a contradanse and in a set of piano variations from 1802 (figure 11.1). The piano piece begins with the theme's naked bass line, then slowly outfits it first with its true melody, and then with countermelodies. The drama is like that of a statue that gradually comes to life, as if the variations were a miniature version of the preceding year's ballet.

In the Third Symphony, the theme appears after a funeral march, another suggestion of resurrection. The simple melody seems to represent for Beethoven some cosmic vivacity, some primal dance that catches up trees and rocks and men in its irresistible toils of grace. The theme begins delicately, but soon moves toward three heavy clonks. In the *Eroica* finale, these clonks undergo a remarkable development that could be called the apotheosis of the stomp.

One of the minor characters in *The Creatures of Prometheus* is Amphion, who sang the city of Thebes into being through the sheer force of music. Amphion might be called the patron saint of ballet décor, since every set designer and stage carpenter must hope to be a proper instrument through which music and dance can summon up a proper environment. On the other hand, dancers have little need of décor, since they *are* the space in which they move—and now I arrive at my main theme. A dance is a kind of art in which the performer's physical presence constitutes the surround in which the dance takes place. As Yeats put it, "How can we know the dancer from the dance?"[3]

The action of Beethoven's ballet opens with two statues—"Prometheus comes running through the wood towards his statues of clay, to whose hearts he hastily draws the divine torch," as the scenario puts it.[4] Statues are aspects of décor; but once they come to life they are actors inside the décor. This equivocation between character and place, person and thing, is quite typical of ballet. Indeed, ballet is founded on this equivocation. On one hand, dance is humane, intensely expressive, a leaping for joy or a drooping with sorrow; on the other hand, dance is soulless, virtuosic, a mobile made up of pendula in the form of arms and legs, naked movement for movement's sake, prior to all thinking and feeling. From one point of view, a ballerina is a woman in a state of perfect emotional volatility; from another she's simply a marionette tugged and jerked by someone else's obsession—by Coppélius's, by the fairground charlatan's, by the demon Rothbart's.

The statue that moves is a kind of totem, not just for ballet, but for all experiments at the boundaries between one artistic medium and another—what might be called *Zwischenkunst*, or interart. Jean-Philippe Rameau's first experiment in what he called an *acte de ballet* was the wildly successful *Pygmalion* (1748), in which musical gesture is quite specific. In the overture the hammering of Pygmalion's chisel is clearly heard, and the statue comes to life in a wonderfully spare, hesitant, unsure manner. In 1770, Jean-Jacques Rousseau, no admirer of Rameau, wrote a kind of riposte in the form of another *Pygmalion*, devised in a completely original form, the melodrama: a spoken text interrupted by or glossed with music. English-speakers can experience something of the wonder of Rousseau's melodrama from a piece of incidental music that William Boyce composed in 1756 for a version of Shakespeare's *Winter's Tale* called *Florizel and Perdita*. Recall the scene: Leontes, a jealous, raging king, believes that his wife Hermione has been dead for sixteen years, but in fact she has been in hiding. She reveals herself by pretending to be a statue that thaws into human flesh as music plays—just as in Rameau's ballet, there is a moving tentativeness to the music as the statue gropes toward life.

A statue that feels, speaks, and dances dwells in a threshold state between life and death—between the arts of space and the arts of time. The Greek word *mousikē*, though it is the source of the word *music* in all Western languages, does not mean "music"; it means anything pertaining to the Muses. The breathing statue is as close to an entity of pure, uninflected *mousikē* as can be imagined. The formal study of the comparative arts begins, to some extent, with Gotthold Lessing's 1766 book *Laokoon*—a study that begins with a meditation on the problem of the too-expressive statue.

Of course the Beethoven-Viganò *Creatures of Prometheus* isn't, and can never be, part of the standard repertoire; too little of its choreography survives. But by 1801 we are not far from the artistic milieu of *La sylphide* (1832) and *Giselle* (1841). In both these early favorites, dance at its highest pitch seems to belong in some domain beyond human life: in *La sylphide* in the ether of discarnate, winged beings who seem to learn emotion from contact with men; in *Giselle* in the world of the dead, who inflict human beings with the compulsion to dance as a sort of infernal punishment. The large rhythm of the romantic ballet of Taglioni, de Bournonville, Gautier, Adam is the large rhythm of *The Creatures of Prometheus* or *Pygmalion:* a descent from inexpressive, superhuman dancing to a sort of dancing fevered and fretted with passion. The sylph first learns to mime human tears by putting her index fingers to her eyes and tracing down her cheek the outline of a fall, and finally learns spasms of human pain when the poisoned scarf is placed on her shoulders. The Wilis first dance with cool spectral aplomb, then grow excited by Hilarion's agony as he dances himself to death. The romantic ballet is a ghost's dream of human life, a statue's fantasy of frenzy.

This curriculum for romantic ballet was anticipated by Heinrich von Kleist, whose 1810 essay on the marionette theater argues that no human dancer can approach the grace of a certain kind of dancing puppet:

> I wanted to know how it is possible, without having a maze of strings attached to one's fingers, to move the separate limbs and extremities in the rhythm of the dance. His answer was that I must not imagine each limb as being individually positioned and moved by the operator in the various phases of the dance. Each movement, he told me, has its centre of gravity; it is enough to control this within the puppet. The limbs, which are only pendulums, then follow mechanically of their own accord, without further help.... Often shaken in a purely haphazard way, the puppet falls into a kind of rhythmic movement which resembles dance....
>
> "And what is the advantage your puppets would have over living dancers?"
>
> "The advantage? First of all a negative one, my friend: it would never be guilty of affectation. For affectation is seen, as you know, when the soul, or moving force, appears at some point other than the centre of gravity of the movement. Because the operator controls with his wire or thread only this centre, the attached limbs are just what they should be ... lifeless, pure pendulums, governed only by the law of gravity. This is an excellent quality. You'll look for it in

vain in most of our dancers. . . . take that young fellow who dances Paris when he's standing among the three goddesses and offering the apple to Venus. His soul is in fact located (and it's a frightful thing to see) in his elbow. . . . Grace appears most purely in that human form which either has no consciousness or an infinite consciousness. That is, in the puppet or in the god."[5]

The enhaloed puppet, the puppet as god, would have a considerable role to play in the theater of the future: both Gordon Craig and Antonin Artaud tried to devise a theater in which human actors aspired to the devastating impassivity of dolls. But ballet was the venue in which Kleist's piecemeal statues would triumph.

In *Coppélia* (1870)—based on E. T. A. Hoffmann's *Der Sandmann*—the human dancer Swanhilde competes with Coppélia, a life-size, wind-up toy, for the love of the male lead, Franz. In the original production, Franz was played by a woman, further perplexing the erotics of the dance, its travesties between the quick and the dead. As an object of sexual desire, the puppet seems more a figure of robot fun that a serious Kleistian investigation of the dead force of grace. Yet it is only by pretending to be Coppélia that Swanhilde can win Franz's love. But what is most remarkable is the fact that once you admit a puppet as protagonist in a ballet, the puppet starts to take over; the whole stage, the whole action, is puppetized. The puppet's status as décor as well as actor asserts itself: Dr. Coppélius's workshop comes to life, and the corps de ballet can't refuse to join the spectacle. Swanhilde and her friends all start to dance puppetwise, usually with little smirks and jerks. Puppetness is hard to confine to the body of the dancer; it infects the whole theatre with its clockwork elegance. In Manuel de Falla's *El retablo de Maese Pedro* (1923), a little puppet show depicting an adventure of Charlemagne's knight Roland is watched by an audience of life-size puppets, including Don Quixote. He becomes so grieved at the spectacle of a toy damsel in distress that he upsets the little theater in order to rescue her. Let loose in the theater, puppets seem able to charm the audience into becoming puppets as well.

By the time we reach the stage dances of twentieth century, the statue and the puppet are more eager to assert their status as gods. When we think of modern dance, as opposed to ballet, we probably first think of the hyperexpressivity of Martha Graham—poses of hysteria, ecstasy, dismemberment, the whole repertoire of Dionysus. But early modern dance had a strong classicizing component. Isadora Duncan based her work on the postures of Greek statues. Ted Shawn liked to play the role of Adonis. There are film clips of Shawn, powdered white, naked except for a discreet loincloth, going through a series of postures, somewhat in the manner of a bodybuilder showing off his noble musculature. I like to think that the opening of *The Creatures of Prometheus* might have looked something like Shawn's Adonis. Here we have the primary act of dance, inert matter heaving itself into motion by means of music. But most of the living statues of twentieth-century dance turned out to be not Greek but Asiatic. Ted Shawn can still be seen, in other old movies, dancing the role of Shiva. Shawn's wife, Ruth St. Denis, confessed that her career was inspired by an advertisement she saw in Buffalo, New York, for Egyptian Deities cigarettes. The advertisement made her want to become Isis. The gestures of the modern dancer are sometimes hotly expressionistic, sometimes hieratic, simple, cold, Egyptian—or Greek in the Winckelmannesque sense of the general and serene.

An idol is not the same as a statue, and a dancer who tries to become an idol is assuming a certain burden of fetish. An idol is not just the image of a god, but a god itself, saturated with a sort of phlogiston of godhead. Ezra Pound wrote in 1928, "The best Egyptian sculpture is magnificent plastic; but its force comes from a non-plastic idea, i.e. the god is inside the statue."[6] In a number of modernist works, an idol has a powerful deific effect. In D. H. Lawrence's *The Plumed Serpent* (1926), the hero and heroine stand before the black, crouching statue of an Aztec god and feel themselves turning into Huitzilopochtli and Malintzi. In the world of dance, the idol can sometimes steal the show, as perhaps in the case of the Golden Idol that Nikolai Zubkhovsky added to *La Bayadère* in 1948. Interestingly, Zubkhovsky's poses closely resemble those of Ted Shawn's Shiva from many years before; orientalist routines quickly became standardized. But Zubkhovsky's idol may lack seriousnesss of purpose compared with Shawn's. Shawn and St. Denis visited India and made a study of Indian dance, but no spectator of *La Bayadère* would imagine that the god is actually inside the dancer. Even the characters in the ballet don't seem much moved by the idol's shenanigans.

But other modern-dance idols have a more powerful effect: for example, the confrontation with the savage god in José Limón's 1956 dance version of *Emperor Jones*. Today I think that we watch this with a mixture of embarrassment and awe: embarrassment at the blackface makeup, the Zulu-kitsch mask designs, the oogabooga shaking; awe at a certain evocation of a terror god with many heads and a thousand arms, a spider god made up of dancers' bodies. Just as the puppet tries to fill the whole stage with puppetry in the case of *Coppélia*, so the idol tries to fill the whole stage with the god's presence, as the dance company agglomerates into an eerie, compound being.

So far we have studied the problem of places that turn into people, and people that turn into places, by means of statues and idols. But the strange reciprocity of dancers and décor manifests itself in other ways as well. The intimacy of ballet and architecture has always been clear. In Taglioni's 1832 *La sylphide*, the minor sylphs form themselves into a sort of gated gazebo into which the main sylph enters, as contemporary drawings show. In Balanchine's *The Prodigal Son* (1929), the tempters actually turn into a merry-go-round. Indeed, the prodigal is about to be taken for a ride, as the bad men fleece him out of everything he has. The vehicular form of this section of the ballet is that of a centrifuge, a mad whirl that goes nowhere.

If dancers can shape themselves into bizarre stage constructs, it is also true that stage constructs can dance. Sometimes a stage prop will discreetly partner a lead dancer. In the movie *Royal Wedding* (1951), a hatrack obliges Fred Astaire with the favor of her company, and in *The Red Shoes* (1948) Moira Shearer discovers a newspaper that transfigures into a real man, a suave dance partner. As we know from Michael Powell and Emeric Pressburger's 1978 novelization of their film script, this scene represents the heroine's lust for fame; she seems to be enjoying a little pressburger of her own.

In fact, one can dispense with the human dancers entirely, and simply let the props do the work. The locus classicus of this theme is Giacomo Balla's 1917 futurist ballet *Fireworks*, based on Stravinsky's four-minute orchestral razzle (figure 11.2):

Figure 11.2. Balla: set design for *Fireworks*. © Scala/Art Resource, NY.

This was a ballet without dancers, in fact a ballet without movement except insofar as clever variations in the lighting exposed new angles in the odd assemblage of star-shaped and tent-shaped contraptions that occupied the stage. Balla programmed forty-nine different lighting moves, with some of the lights hidden inside small, translucent stage objects in the fashion of Chinese lanterns.

But ultimately the architecture of dance depends not on the ingenuity of set designers, or even on the ingenuity of choreographers, but on the architecture of the human body itself. In a kind of manifesto written for a dance-architecture workshop at the Isadora and Raymond Duncan Centre for Dance in 2003, the choreographer Carol Brown wrote:

> Dance and Architecture have much in common. Both are concerned with practices of space. For a dancer the act of choreography as a writing of place occurs through the unfolding of spatial dimensions through gesture and embodied movement. For the architect space is the medium through which form emerges and habitation is constructed. For both, the first space we experience is the space of the body. . . . We became space through stillness. In tracking the interior shifts of attention and awareness and inhibiting a desire to move we could feel the voids and solids, cavities and densities of our corporeal selves.[7]

Brown goes on to speak of the "dancer's kinesphere or personal envelope of space." I find the notion of a kinesphere (the term is Laban's) illuminating. Like everybody else, I have a certain sense that my body space isn't strictly delimited by my skin, but extends in an irregular manner on all sides, and I feel uncomfortable when my territorial limit is invaded. As W. H. Auden put it:

> Some thirty inches from my nose
> The frontier of my Person goes,
> And all the untilled air between
> Is private *pagus* or demesne.
> Stranger, unless with bedroom eyes
> I beckon you to fraternize,
> Beware of rudely crossing it:
> I have no gun, but I can spit.[8]

I think of my kinesphere as extending to every point that I can reach with my arms or legs. Since I'm not a very limber person, there's a sort of ozone hole in my kinesphere, somewhere between my shoulder blades. But for the spry, the kinesphere is more or less the sphere traced by a full rotation of the circle in which Leonardo inscribed Vitruvian Man. A dancer's kinesphere, of course, is much larger than this—in fact, enormous. In a solo dance we sense not only the dancer's actual movement, but the modulations of the kinesphere in which the dancer is enveloped. At full run the kinesphere thins out in front, with gusty tatters trailing behind the body in a sort of wake of air (figure 11.3).

I have no reason to think that the famous futurist sculpture by Umberto Boccioni pertains to dance, but it seems a good representation of the quivering tunnels in the atmosphere that a dancer's body creates.

Figure 11.3. Boccioni: *Unique Forms of Continuity in Space* (1913), bronze. © Mattioli Collection, Milan/The Bridgeman Art Library.

ELEPHANT SWAN SPACE GRACE 187

Figure 11.4. Schlemmer: Figurines for *Das triadische Ballett* (1919). Wuerttembergisches Landesmuseum, Stuttgart, Germany. Photo credit: Erich Lessing/Art Resource, NY.

A great many aspects of ballet costume and stage movement pay homage to the kinesphere. For example, tutus come in many shapes and sizes, but the standard tutu is pretty close to the circumference of the circle that represents the full extension of a ballerina's hip swivel; a tutu is a way of visualizing one aspect of the kinesphere. Certain Modernist costume experiments go far in visualizing other aspects of the kinesphere. Consider the costumes that Oskar Schlemmer created for his *Triadic Ballet* (1921) (figure 11.4).

Note the figure on the left panel, second from the bottom: her knob of a head represents, more or less, the kinecylinder that a dancer's head makes when she jumps straight up. The balls at the ends of her arms represent the lesser kinespheres that her hands would make if rotated in every direction (it's not clear from the picture, but she wore spheres covering her hands, attached at the wrists). To her right, we see costumes that represent different forms of twirls and swirls, sometimes eccentric, sometimes perfectly centered. The motion trace of the dance is imprinted on the costumes themselves. Even as static architectural elements in a picture, the costumes prescribe choreography. The costumes constitute a stage set but are nevertheless icons of rotation and gesture, icons of pure dance; the line between dance and décor has rarely been so thoroughly erased. The music for the *Triadic Ballet* was written by Paul Hindemith for mechanical organ. Nothing of it survives except a few minutes' worth of recordings, which go nicely with the puppetoid costumes of Schlemmer, with their suggestions of sproing and whomp and the huffing of bellows.

So we see that costume can be a means for elucidating the kinesphere. But choreographers have found other means as well. Streamers tied to the wrists or cloths dangled in air are potent markers of the slipstream of the dancer's body. In *La sylphide*, for example, a witch tricks James into giving the sylph a poisoned scarf, the object of much waving about. Similar comet tails can be found in *La bayadère* and many other old ballets.

The expansion of the radius of the kinesphere by means of fans and fabric became one of the projects of early modern dance. Isadora Duncan liked scarves. As everyone knows, she died when her long, iridescent silk scarf got tangled in the tire of an automobile. But the most important experiments with lengths of cloth were performed by Loïe Fuller, who inspired more symbolist painting and poetry that any other native of Chicago, Illinois. Figure 11.5 shows her as Kolomon Moser saw her:

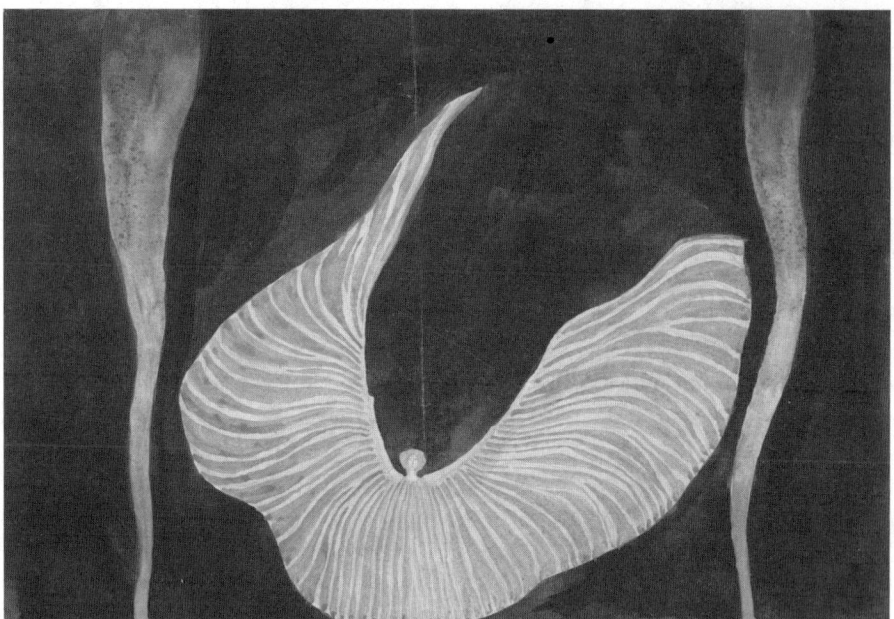

Figure 11.5. Moser: *The Dancer Loïe Fuller*. Used by permission of the Albertina, Vienna.

Figure 11.6 shows her as Toulouse-Lautrec saw her:

Figure 11.6. Toulouse-Lautrec: *Miss Loïe Fuller*. Scala/Art Resource, NY.

Fuller used sticks to manipulate fabric, continuously reshaping her kinesphere into various cloud forms—a giant butterfly in Moser's painting. Or as Isadora Duncan wrote:

> Before our very eyes she turned to many coloured, shining orchids, to a wavering, flowing sea flower, and at length to a spiral-like lily. . . . She became fluid; she became light; she became every colour and flame, and finally she resolved into miraculous spirals of flames wafted toward the Infinite.[9]

Fuller occupied so much of the stage that she became, more than a dancer, a sort of weather. Duncan was the least of the poets preoccupied with Fuller's genius. W. B. Yeats wrote:

> When Loie Fuller's Chinese dancers enwound
> A shining web, a floating ribbon of cloth,
> It seemed that a dragon of air
> Had fallen among dancers, had whirled them round
> Or hurried them off on its own furious path;
> So the Platonic Year
> Whirls out new right and wrong,
> Whirls in the old instead;
> All men are dancers and their tread
> Goes to the barbarous clangour of a gong.[10]

Stéphane Mallarmé went still further. He called Loïe Fuller "an inexhaustible fountain of herself," and spoke of her "vertigo of soul," "her quick nuances sloughing off their limelight phantasmagoria of twilight and grotto, such speed of passion, delight, grief, anger."[11] But of primary interest for our purposes today is Mallarmé's meditation from 1893 on the relation of dance to décor:

> This transition from sonority to pieces of cloth . . . is, uniquely, the spell that Loie Fuller puts into effect, instinctively, with a thrusting-forward or a withdrawing of a skirt or a wing, constituting a place. The enchantress makes the ambiance, pulling it out of herself and drawing it back into herself, through a silence pulsating with crêpes de Chine. Instantly there vanishes an imbecility: the traditional planting of permanent or stable décor, as opposed to the mobile choreography. . . . The pure result is a free stage . . . exhaled in the play of a veil, with poses and gestures.[12]

A dancer that constitutes a place: this is the ideal fusion that we've been tracing throughout this essay. Those skeptical that this is truly possible should watch a 1903 film, not of Loïe Fuller herself, but of an imitator named Ameta. Ameta describes a kinesphere at least twelve feet in diameter, but perhaps most impressive of all is the tornado of cloth she creates at the end.

Around 1914, Wyndham Lewis and Ezra Pound created an artistic movement called vorticism. As Pound wrote,

> The image is not an idea. It is a radiant node or cluster; it is what I can, and must perforce, call a VORTEX, from which, and through which, and into which, ideas are constantly rushing. In decency one can only call it a VORTEX.[13]

Ten years before vorticism came into being, Ameta's dance clearly shows how a storm of movement can focus itself into a burning tip of energy. In the fixed stage sets of the old ballet—the décor that Mallarmé deplores—the painted perspective lines lead the spectator's eye to some vanishing point of no particular interest. But in Ameta's dance the role of the perspective lines is taken by the two sticks she manipulates, and their line of sight leads us directly to the dancer herself. The stage set is in the dancer's hands and swells, deflates, spins, and erects itself in exact response to the music.

The search for larger and larger kinespheres eventually led to truly vast dance objects. In 1942 Balanchine choreographed a polka for circus elephants and commissioned Stravinsky to write the music. These were not the first elephants to attract a choreographer's attention. In 1877, at the première of Petipa's *La bayadère*, a live elephant appeared on the Mariinsky stage. Modern productions rarely include actual elephants, but Nureyev's staging made do with a fine elephant simulation. The apotheosis of the dance elephant occurred in Walt Disney's *Fantasia* (1940), where Ponchielli's *Dance of the Hours* is choreographed for ostriches, hippos, elephants, and crocodiles. In a cartoon ballet, the dance and the décor really are one, since there are no static elements at all. The décor transmogrifies as effortlessly as the personages. Indeed ever since the early days of Steamboat Willie, a certain orphic panpsychism was part of Disney's stock in trade, as buildings lifted their foundations, trees lifted their roots, and danced. In *Fantasia*, the kinesphere attains a visible presence at once ponderous and ethereal, as an elephant floats off in a bubble. The Doric columns of Disney's stage architecture remind us, once again, that behind even this absurd dance fantasy lies some dream of classical Greece.

At the end of the sequence, the pachyderm thump becomes too great, and the stage itself collapses. There were precedents for this general crash of the theater. Disney's animators may have been thinking of the Marx Brothers' *Night at the Opera* (1935), but long before that there was Saint-Saëns's *Samson et Dalila* (1877), at the end of which Samson pulls down the pillars of the Temple of Dagon and exterminates the Philistines, along with himself. Through the centuries, many clerics have used this story from the book of Judges as a metaphor for the inherent corruption of the theater itself. For example, in Ben Jonson's *Bartholomew Fair* (1614), a Puritan named Zeal-of-the-land Busy gets into a shouting match with a puppet at a puppet show, and finally becomes so angry that he shouts "Downe with Dagon . . . I will remoue . . . that heathenish Idoll."[14]

Gentle lovers of the ballet, let that be a lesson to you: the theater is a venue of sin and ruin. But I'd like to propose a different sort of allegorical reading. Disney's *Dance of the Hours* is an ideal specimen of that dance theater advocated by Mallarmé and Loïe Fuller. And if the stage set crashes down on the heads of the very large dancers, it is a sign that external décor is unnecessary. The dancers themselves have to constitute the place in which they dance. There is a line of Balanchine's used in advertising a video documentary of Balanchine's career: "It's like a fish goes through the water. The music is the aquarium and the dancer is a fish." But sometimes, you might say, the dancer is the aquarium and the music is the fish.

Strange inversions of actor and environment are a striking aspect of recent stage productions. Richard Strauss's opera *Salome* is a puzzle for stage directors: it's often difficult or impossible to find a soprano—a sixteen-year-old with an Isolde voice, Strauss called her—who can sing the role and dance a convincingly seductive Dance of the Seven Veils. Since the opera's première in 1905, a dancer double has often taken over the choreographic chores. But in an imaginative 1989 version from Barcelona, the director employed Montserrat Caballé—then an obese, rather elderly woman with an almost ideal voice for the part—as a human stage set. Caballe is perched on top of a pedestal, with much of the stage concealed by a curtain that dangles down from her. Soon a dancing Salome emerges from the vast skirt of the singing Salome; Caballé's womb seems to give birth to the entire production. In Samuel Beckett's *Happy Days*, the lead character is a woman buried in a great mound of earth, first up to her waist, then up to her neck; place and person are eerily confused. In the Barcelona *Salome*, the singer is the aquarium and the dance and the music and the drama are all fish. Indeed, in one scene, the dancers seem in danger of drowning in the crests and troughs of the stage-filling skirt.

I'll conclude by discussing another aspect of décor. Dancers glide across a stage that may be adorned with a painted backdrop and various sorts of props; but they also glide across a stage that may be filled, in some sense, with words, mute words. The nineteenth-century ballet grew out of the pantomime spectacle. As Marian Smith has shown, the Parisian pantomime tried every conceivable means to find surrogates for language: "Composers, choreographers, and designers at the Opéra introduced words into ballet performances in every way but actually having performers intone them."[15] These ways included on-stage placards and orchestral quotations of familiar tunes whose lyrics were relevant to the action. We've looked at some of the elisions between dance and visual décor; but there are elisions between dance and language décor as well.

In ballet as we know it, there are pantomime scenes full of encoded words: I [pointing to self] you [pointing to someone else] love [hands over heart]. *Coppélia* is more easily understood by an audience that knows that the word for *doll* in terpsichorese consists of outlining an hourglass shape with your hands, followed by sharp up-and-down gestures with rigidly crooked elbows. (I can't guess what the dance word for a male doll would be.) But these incarnations of language in gesture are considered slightly subballetic. No ballerina ever became a *danseuse-étoile* on the basis of her elegant pantomime. Is it possible to find a language in the grand solos and duets that make up the highlight reel of ballet—a language with words more specific than *sad* and *glad*?

One way to approach this problem is through the study of choreographic notation. Dance and dance notation have always been twins, but in 1928, when Rudolf Laban published his book on kinetography, dance notation attained a new precision. It might be interesting to record in labanotation a speech in American Sign Language. The notation could give an exact description of every aspect of the performance except what it means. The spectator of a ballet sees all sorts of emphatic diagonals and thrusts and flingings out, but these vectors rarely terminate in paraphrasable meanings. Ballet, with its eternal array of outstretched limbs in a ecstasy of pointing—pointing with arms, with elbows, with index fingers, with index toes—is a perfect demonstration of the poststructuralist linguistics in which every signifier points to another signifier without ever quite become a sign.

In this sense, a book of labanotation is a text just as meaningful or unmeaningful as the text of *David Copperfield*. I suspect that there has been a certain tendency in recent dance to construct ballets that deliberately resemble labanotation, as if ballet's status as an art form could be heightened by making it approximate the look of a text. For example, we might take note of Edouard Lock's suite of dances for a 2003 production of Rameau's *Les boréades*. Lock's dance company goes by the whimsical name of La La La Human Steps, but the dancers step less in the manner of human beings than of letters in an alphabet of arms and legs. There are many old demonstrations that dancers can shape themselves into the letters of the Latin alphabet, for example a finely salacious alphabet from 1534 devised by Peter Flötner (figure 11.7).

I think I see quick glimpses of N, M, and X in some of the dances by La La La Human Steps, but the arms and legs seem more like mad semaphore flags emancipated from any particular code. The dancers seem to dwell in a paroxysm of communicative fury, without communicating anything in particular—perhaps appropriately, since they're dancing (in one scene) in celebration of a wedding that the bride hopes will not take place. In his meditation on Loïe Fuller, Mallarmé remarked, "The theatre always alters its component arts according to a special or literary point of view.... In Ballet one could not recognize the name of Dance; it is, if you wish, hieroglyph."[16] In Lock's dances, the hieroglyphs whirl past with incredible speed, like an instantaneous scan of the whole Egyptian Book of the Dead.

Could dance attain a language of such urgency and precision that it could step out of the theater and become a mode of discourse? A possible answer to this question can be found in one of the world's remote places.

Figure 11.7. Flötner: anthropomorphic alphabet.

In the summer of 2006 I spent some time in the Yunnan province in southwestern China. Yunnan is marketed by the Chinese authorities as Shangri-La, because the dreamy refuge of James Hilton's 1933 novel *Lost Horizon* is located in a place that pretty well coincides with the northern tip of Yunnan. Now, Yunnan is no paradise, but it is a startling and eerie land, with a culture that challenges many of our assumptions; it is almost an antiworld. It is a shivery thing to see alpine lakes set in whole forests of rhododendrons, and I found it strange to talk with my guide, Li Qiong, a woman of the Naxi minority, about the cultural predilection of her people. The Naxi are matriarchal. The women plough the fields and control money and land. In one particular Naxi tribe called the Mosuo, a woman will take several husbands, all of whom continue to live with their mothers while visiting their wife at night. But I mention the Naxi not for the sake of their agriculture or their sex lives, but for the sake of their alphabet.

The Naxi speak a Tibeto-Burman dialect, and their script is the only pictographic language in use today—although it may be not in use much longer, since the number of fluent Naxi readers is estimated to be between ten and two hundred. Figure 11.8 shows an example.

Happy birthday! Birth is represented by an obvious picture of a woman giving birth; day is the sun; and happy is a couple singing and dancing. Note the little streamer proceeding from the singer's mouth, a symbol of vocal emission. As in

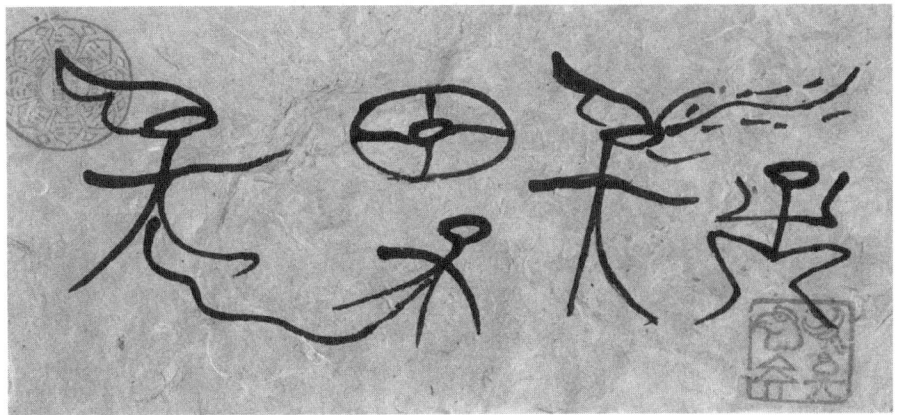

Figure 11.8. Naxi Happy Birthday.

Chinese, there is no clear boundary between noun, verb, and adjective; even Naxi nouns often imply a great deal of motion.

The Naxi script is also said to constitute the earliest form of dance notation known anywhere in the world. The script is, of course, a sacred language. The Naxi always used a much simplified script for daily use and now write to each other in Mandarin. The sacred books of their shamanistic religion contain exact prescriptions for dance rites. These notations differ from labanotation in that they are true sentences. You can read a Naxi dance out loud, just as you can read any sentence. And, as you can see from the Naxi happy birthday signs, many ordinary Naxi sentences read like gestural inscription—dance notation. I'm charmed by the notion of speaking dance, as if dance isn't reserved for special theatrical occasions, but might be a regular feature of our conversation. I talk not only with my larynx, but with my hands, with my whole body. I want to learn how to speak dance, how to speak music.

Notes

Chapter One

1. It was Donald Francis Tovey who misattributed this remark to Liszt, according to Michael Steinberg. See Steinberg, *The Concerto: A Listener's Guide* (Oxford: Oxford University Press, 1998), 69.
2. E. M. Forster, "Word-Making and Sound-Taking," in *Abinger Harvest* (New York: Harcourt, Brace and Company, 1936), 105.
3. Jean Jacques Rousseau, *On the Origin of Language*, trans. John Moran (New York: Frederick Unger Publishing, 1966), 49.
4. George J. Buelow, "Rhetoric," *New Grove Dictionary of Music and Musicians*, ed. Stanley Sadie (Oxford: Oxford University Press, 1980), 15:800.
5. Carolyn Abbate, *Unsung Voices: Opera and Musical Narrative in the Nineteenth Century* (Princeton, NJ: Princeton University Press, 1991), 29.
6. Jean-Jacques Nattiez, *Music and Discourse: Toward a Semiology of Music*, trans. Carolyn Abbate (Princeton, NJ: Princeton University Press, 1990), 128.
7. Benedetto Marcello, *Il teatro alla moda*, trans. R. G. Pouly, in *Source Readings in Music History*, rev. ed., ed. Oliver Strunk and Leo Treitler (New York: W. W. Norton, 1998), 522–23, 526–27.
8. Jorge Luis Borges, "Tlön, Uqbar, Orbis Tertius," trans. James E. Irby in *Labyrinths: Selected Stories and Other Writings*, ed. Donald A. Yates and James E. Irby (New York: New Directions, 1964), 8.
9. Igor Stravinsky, *An Autobiography* (New York: W. W. Norton, 1962), 53.
10. Ludwig Wittgenstein, *Philosophical Investigations*, trans. G. E. M Anscombe (New York: Macmillan, 1958), §527.
11. Paul de Man, *Allegories of Reading: Figural Language in Rousseau, Nietzsche, Rilke, and Proust* (New Haven: Yale University Press, 1979), 269–70.

Chapter Two

1. All quotations of Heine's poetry in this chapter are from Emily Ezust, *The Lied and Art Song Texts Page*, http://www.recmusic.org/lieder.
2. Susan Youens, *Heine and the Lied* (Cambridge: Cambridge University Press, 2008), 11.

3. Michael Nyman, booklet accompanying *The Man Who Mistook His Wife for a Hat*, Michael Nyman Band, CBS CD MK 44669 (1987), 111.
4. Ibid., 11–12.
5. Ibid., 135.
6. Ibid., 137.
7. William Wordsworth, "On the Power of Sound," 1828.
8. Oliver Sacks, booklet accompanying *The Man Who Mistook His Wife for a Hat*, 16.
9. A slight misquotation from Roland Barthes, "Rasch," in *The Responsibility of Forms: Critical Essays on Music, Arts, and Representation*, trans. Richard Howard (New York: Hill and Wang, 1985), 299, in the notes to *The Man Who Mistook His Wife for a Hat*, 13.
10. Jules Laforgue, "Complainte de l'organiste de Notre-Dame-de-Nice," in *An Anthology of French Poetry from Nerval to Valéry*, ed. Augel Flores (New York: Anchor Books, 1958), 383.
11. Guy Ropartz, *Si j'étais Roi*, Vincent le Textier, baritone and Philippe Biros, piano, Audivis Valois CD V 4701 (1995).
12. Ibid., 25.

Chapter Three

1. Heinrich Heine, *Aus den Memoiren des Herrn von Schnabelewopski*, http://www.digbib.org/Heinrich_Heine_1797/Aus_den_Memoiren_des_Herren_von_Schnabelewopski.
2. Translated from ibid.
3. Translated from ibid.
4. As cited by Thomas Grey in *Richard Wagner: Der fliegende Holländer* (Cambridge: Cambridge University Press, 2000), 181.
5. Ibid., 181–82.
6. Ibid., 65.
7. Heinrich Marschner's, *Der Vampyr*, Romantische Oper in zwei Akten, Dichtung von Wilhelm August Wohlbrück, neu eingerichtet von Hans Pfitzner, Klavierauszug (Berlin: Adolf Fürstner, 1925), 175.
8. According to a pamphlet of 1602, Ahasuerus met a Bishop Paulus in 1542 and told him that he had seen Christ carrying the cross and mocked him by saying, "Go on quickly." Christ replied, "I go, but thou wait till I return." For further discussion, see http://en.ikipedia.org/wiki/Wandering_Jew.
9. Carolyn Abbate, *In Search of Opera* (Princeton, NJ: Princeton University Press, 2001), 108.
10. Friedrich Nietzsche, *The Case of Wagner*, chapter 2.
11. Ibid., chapter 9.
12. Grey, *Richard Wagner*, 200.

13. Ibid., 48.
14. Ibid., 65.
15. Ibid., 18.
16. Ibid., 191.
17. Thomas Percy, *Reliques of Ancient English Poetry* (London: J. Dodsley, 1765).
18. As cited by Annika Stawe, booklet accompanying *Carl Loewe, Lieder & Balladen*, cpo CD 999 417-2 (1998), 13.
19. Ezust, *The Lied and Art Song Texts Page*.
20. Ibid.
21. Grey, *Richard Wagner*, 187.
22. Ibid., 18.
23. Richard Strauss, *Feuersnot*, Opus 50, Ein Singgedicht in einem Akt von Ernst von Wolzogen, Klavierauszug von Otto Singer (Berlin: Adolf Fürstner, n.d.), 156.
24. Michael Tippett, "The Flying Dutchman," from *Songs for Dov*, for Tenor and Orchestra (London: Schott, 1970), 33.

Chapter Four

1. Translated from Louis de Jaucourt, "Opéra," in Denis Diderot and Jean le Rond d'Alembert, *Encyclopédie*, http://artfl.uchicago.edu/cgi-bin/philologix31/getobject.pl?c.83:319.encyclopedie1108.
2. Translated from Théophile Gautier "Carmen," http://www.florilege.free.fr/florilege/gautier/carmen.htm.
3. Jaucourt, "Opéra."
4. Translated from Richard Wagner, "Die Oper und das Wesen der Musik," in *Oper und Drama* (Leipzig: Weber, 1852; repr. Stuttgart: Philipp Reclam, 1984), 100.
5. Christoph Willibald von Gluck, "Preface to *Alceste*," in *The Lives of the Great Composers*, ed. Harold C. Schonberg (New York: W. W. Norton, 1997), 75.
6. See Julian Rushton, "Berlioz' Roots in 18th Century French Opera," *Berlioz Society Bulletin* 50 (April 1965): 3–10.
7. Hector Berlioz to Princess Caroline Sayn-Wittgenstein, 12 August 1856, in *Briefe von Hector Berlioz an die Fürstin Carolyne Sayn-Wittgenstein*, ed. La Mara [Marie Lipsius] (Leipzig: Breitkopf & Härtel, 1903), cited by Hugh Macdonald in "Berlioz's Self-Borrowings," *Proceedings of the Royal Musical Association*, 92nd sess. (1967–68).
8. Virgil, *Aeneid*, trans. John Dryden, ed. Frederick M. Keener (New York: Penguin, 1997), 2.1038–44.
9. Berlioz to Hans von Bülow, 20 January 1858. See Artur Holte, "A Little-Known Letter by Berlioz and Unpublished Letters by Cherubini, Leoncavallo, and Hugo Wolf," *Musical Quarterly* 37, no. 3 (July 1931), 340.

10. William Shakespeare, *The Merchant of Venice*, in *The Riverside Shakespeare*, ed. G. Blakemore Evans (Boston: Houghton Mifflin, 1974), 5.1.1–6.

11. Hector Berlioz, *Les Troyens*, Grand Opéra en cinq actes, Partition chant et piano orientée à l'original de la Nouvelle Édition Berlioz d'Eike Wernhard (Kassel: Bärenreiter, ca. 2003), 422–23.

12. William Shakespeare, *Troilus and Cressida*, in *The Riverside Shakespeare*, 4.2.99–101.

13. William Shakespeare, *Caesar and Cleopatra*, in *The Riverside Shakespeare*, 5.2.216–21.

14. William Shakespeare, *The Merchant of Venice*, 5.1.9–12.

15. Berlioz to Sayn-Wittgenstein, 12 August 1856, in *Briefe von Hector Berlioz an die Fürstin Carolyne Sayn-Wittgenstein*, 30–31, cited by Macdonald in "Berlioz's Self-Borrowings," 43–44.

Chapter Five

1. Adelaide Anne Procter, "The Lost Chord," *English Woman's Journal* (1858); music by Arthur Sullivan (1877).

2. Francis Toye, *Giuseppe Verdi: His Life and Works* (New York: Vintage, 1959), 5.

3. E. T. A. Hoffman, "Kreisleriana," in *E. T. A. Hoffmann's Musical Writings*, ed. David Charlton, trans. Martyn Clarke, 105 (Cambridge: Cambridge University Press, 1989).

4. Ibid., 124.

5. Ibid., 161.

6. Edgar Allan Poe, "The Fall of the House of Usher," http://www.bartleby.com/195/10.html.

7. Samuel Beckett, "First Love," in *First Love and Other Shorts* (New York: Grove, 1974), 32–33.

8. Booklet accompanying *Gustav Holst Songs*, Collins CD 15322 (1998), 26.

9. Antony Beaumont, *Zemlinsky* (Ithaca, NY: Cornell University Press, 2000), 144.

10. Alexander Zemlinsky, *Der Traumgörge*, Oper in zwei Akten und einem Nachspiel, Text von Leo Feld, Klavierauszug (Milan: Ricordi, ca. 1991).

11. Beaumont, *Zemlinsky*, 66.

12. Ibid., 44.

13. Thomas Mann, "Enttäuschung," in *Sämtliche Erzählungen in zwei Bänden* (Frankfurt am Main: S. Fischer Verlag, 1967), 1:99.

14. Francis Picabia, "Jésus-Christ Rastaquouère," in *Écrits*, vol. 1, *1913–1920*, ed. Olivier Revault d'Allonnes (Paris: P. Belfond, 1975–78), 252.

15. Johannes Brahms, *Rinaldo*, http://www.recmusic.org/lieder/get_text.html?TextId=41398.

16. Beaumont, *Zemlinsky*, 391.
17. Franz Kafka, "Der Bau," in *Sämtliche Erzählungen* (Frankfurt am Main: Fischer Taschenbuch, 1990), 383.

Chapter Six

1. To see a picture of Kiselewski's Moses, and to read more about the furor at Syracuse, see http://www.moseshand.com/studies/moses.htm.
2. Elliott Gyger, personal communication.
3. Gyger, personal communication.
4. Alex Rehding, personal communication
5. Arnold Schoenberg, *Theory of Harmony*, trans. Roy E. Carter (Berkeley and Los Angeles: University of California Press, 1983), 313.
6. Schoenberg, *Texte* [1926], trans. Michael Graubart, cited by Regina Busch in "On the Horizontal and Vertical Presentation of Musical Ideas and on Musical Space (I)," *Tempo* 154 (September 1985).
7. From the booklet accompanying Arnold Schoenberg, *Die Jakobsleiter*, Sony CD 48462 (1993), 25.

Chapter Seven

1. Richard, "Music's Duel," 1646, a translation of a 1617 Latin poem by Famianus Strada)
2. Elliott Carter, "A Further Step," in *The Writings of Elliott Carter*, ed. Else Stone and Kurt Stone (Bloomington: Indiana University Press, 1977), 188.
3. Allen Edwards, *Flawed Words and Stubborn Sounds: A Conversation with Elliott Carter* (New York: Norton, 1971), 37.
4. Ibid., 213.
5. Ibid., 213.
6. Elizabeth Bishop, "Sandpiper," in *The Complete Poems, 1927–1979* (New York: Farrar, Straus, and Giroux, 1983), 131.
7. William Blake, "Mock on Mock on Voltaire Rousseau."
8. As quoted in Brett C. Millier, *Elizabeth Bishop: Life and the Memory of It* (Berkeley and Los Angeles: University of California Press, 1995), 517.
9. Bishop, "View of the Capitol from the Library of Congress," in *The Complete Poems, 1927–1979*, 69.
10. Elliott Carter, in *The Writings of Elliott Carter*, 147.
11. Anne Shreffler, "'Give the Music Room': Elliott Carter's 'View of the Capitol from the Library of Congress' aus *A Mirror on which to Dwell*," in *Quellenstudien II: Zwölf Kompositionen des 20. Jahrhunderts*, ed. Felix Meyer (Basel: Amadeus, 1993), 275.

12. Bishop, "O Breath," in *The Complete Poems, 1927–1979*, 79.
13. Robert Lowell, "Across the Yard: La Ignota," in *Collected Poems*, ed. Frank Bidart and David Gewanter, with an introduction by Frank Bidart (New York: Farrar, Straus, and Giroux, 2007), 563.
14. Elliott Carter, *A Mirror on which to Dwell: Six Poems of Elizabeth Bishop, for Soprano and Chamber Orchestra* (New York: Associated Music Publishers, ca. 1977).
15. John Ashbery, "Syringa," as quoted in Elliott Carter, *Syringa for Mezzo-Soprano, Bass, and Guitar, with 10 Instruments* (New York: Associated Music Publishers, ca. 1980).
16. Robert Morgan, "Secret Languages: The Roots of Musical Modernism," *Critical Inquiry* 10, no. 3 (March 1984): 447.
17. Elliott Carter, *Syringa for Mezzo-Soprano, Bass, and Guitar, with 10 Instruments*, 48.
18. Lawrence Kramer, "Syringa," in *Beyond Amazement: New Essays on John Ashbery* (Ithaca, NY: Cornell University Press, 1980), 255–71.
19. David Schiff, *The Music of Elliott Carter* (London: Eulenberg Books, 1983), 302.
20. As translated by Richard Abram, in booklet accompanying *Vanitas vanitatum*, Teldec CD 4509–98410–2 (1995), 25–26.
21. William Carlos Williams, "Lear," in *The Collected Later Poems* (New York: New Directions, 1967), 237.
22. William Shakespeare, *The Tempest*, in *The Riverside Shakespeare*, ed. G. Blakemore Evans (Boston: Houghton Mifflin, 1974), 4.1.152–56.
23. Elliott Carter, composer's notes to *Partita*, http://www.boosey.com/pages/cr/catalogue/cat_deail.asp?musicid=7364.

Chapter Eight

1. Aristophanes, *The Frogs*, ed. and trans. Matthew Dillon, from *Perseus Project*, http://perseus.mpiwg-berlin.mpg.de/cgi-bin/ptext?doc=Perseus%3Atext%3A1999.01.0032 (accessed 9 March 2009), lines 837–39, 827–29.
2. Aristophanes, *The Frogs*, lines 841–42.
3. Michael Ewans, *Opera from the Greek* (Burlington: Ashgate, 2007).
4. Sophocles, *Antigone*, ed. and trans. Richard Jebb, from the *Perseus Project*, http://www.perseus.tufts.edu (accessed 9 March 2009), lines 100–25.
5. Giovanna Ferrara, "Pity, Terror, and the Eternal Light of Reason," in booklet accompanying *Traetta: Antigona*, Decca CD 460 204–2 (2000), 12.
6. Eduard Devrient, *Meine Erinnerungen an Felix Mendelssohn-Bartholdy und seine Briefe an mich* (Leipzig: J. J. Weber, 1869), 218–19. Cited and translated by Jason Geary in "Reinventing the Past: Mendelssohn's *Antigone* and the Creation of an Ancient Greek Musical Language," *Journal of Musicology* 23, no. 2 (Spring 2006): 190.

7. Sophocles, *Oedipus at Colonnus*, ed. and trans. Richard Jebb, from the *Perseus Project*, http://www.perseus.tufts.edu (accessed 9 March 2009), lines 1568–78.

8. William Butler Yeats, *Sophocles' Oedipus at Colonus, The Variorum Edition of the Plays of W. B. Yeats*, ed. Russell K. Alspach (New York: Macmillan, 1966), lines 1446–51.

9. Arthur Honegger, *Antigone: tragédie musicale en 3 actes*, paroles de Jean Cocteau, adaptation libre d'après Sophocle (Paris: Éditions Salabert, ca. 1927), 16.

10. Arthur Honegger, booklet accompanying recording of the Fifth Symphony, Erato CD 2292–045208–2 (1984).

11. Igor Stravinsky and Robert Craft, *Dialogues* (Berkeley and Los Angeles: University of California Press, 1982), 23–24.

12. Ibid., 25.

13. Cocteau, as quoted in booklet accompanying *Igor Stravinsky: Oedipus Rex*, Disques Montaignes CD TCE 8760 (n.d.), 23.

14. Stravinsky and Craft, *Dialogues*, 28.

15. Ibid., 28.

16. Stravinsky used the letter *k* in Latin (rather than the letter *c*) to help singers with pronunciation.

17. Stravinsky and Craft, *Dialogues*, 27.

18. Leonard Bernstein, *The Unanswered Question* (Cambridge: Harvard University Press, 1976), 399.

19. Igor Stravinsky, *Oedipus Rex*, Opéra-Oratorio en deux actes d'après Sophocle par Igor Stravinsky et Jean Cocteau, Nouvelle révision 1948, Réduction pour chant et piano par L'auteur (New York: Boosey & Hawkes, 1949), 79.

20. Stravinsky and Craft, *Dialogues*, 30.

21. Ibid., 29.

22. Translated from Theodor Adorno, *Philosophie der neuen Musik* (Frankfurt: Europäische Verlagsanstalt, 1966), 159.

23. Quoted in Daniel Albright, *Modernism and Music* (Chicago: University of Chicago Press, 2004), 332–33.

Chapter Nine

1. Clement Greenberg, *The Collected Essays and Criticism*, ed. John O'Brien (Chicago: University of Chicago Press, 1986), 1:26.

2. Translated from Theodor Adorno, *Philosophie der neuen Musik*, 176, 180, respectively.

3. Linda Whitesitt, *The Life and Music of George Antheil, 1900–1959* (Ann Arbor: UMI Research Press, 1983), 105–6.

4. Morton Feldman, in *Essays*, ed. Walter Zimmermann (Kerpen: Beginner Press, 1985), 136–37.

5. Bohumír Štědroň, *Leoš Janáček: Letters and Reminiscences,* trans. Geraldine Thomsen (Prague: Artia, 1955), 90. Cited in *Composers on Music,* ed. Josiah Fisk (Boston: Northeastern University Press, 1997), 175–76.

6. Jacques Derrida, "Signature, Event, Context," in *A Derrida Reader: Between the Blinds,* ed. Peggy Kamuf, trans. Alan Bass (New York: Columbia University Press, 1991), 94.

7. Translated from Alois Hába, *Mein Weg zur Viertel- and Sechsteltonmusik* (Düsseldorf: Im Verlag der Gesellschaft zur Förderung der systematischen Musikwissenschaft, 1971), 12, 14.

8. Translated from Arnold Schoenberg, Foreword to *Pierrot lunaire* (Vienna: Universal Edition, 1914).

9. As given in Ellen Rosand, "Operatic Madness," in *Music and Text: Critical Inquiries,* ed. Steven Paul Sher (Cambridge: Cambridge University Press, 2006), 244.

10. As given in Philip Blackburn, *Enclosure 3: Harry Partch* (St. Paul: American Composer's Forum, 1997), 31.

11. William Butler Yeats to Harry Partch. From Partch's project report to the Carnegie Foundation, in Philip Blackburn, *Enclosure 3: Harry Partch* (St. Paul: American Composer's Forum, 1997), 28.

12. Harry Partch, *Genesis of a Music* (Madison: University of Wisconsin Press, 1949), 32–33.

13. Barthes, "Rasch," 299.

14. Partch, *Genesis,* 53–54.

15. Samuel Beckett, *Disjecta,* ed. Ruby Cohn (New York: Grove, 1984), 27. Beckett quotes James Joyce, *Finnegans Wake* (New York: Viking, 1966), 462.

16. Joyce, *Finnegans Wake,* 104.

17. John Cage, interview with Klaus Schöning, in booklet accompanying *Roaratorio: An Irish Circus on Finnegans Wake,* Mode CD 28/29 (1992), 36.

18. Cage, *Roaratorio* booklet, 6.

19. Ibid., 38.

20. Ibid., 50.

21. Ibid., 41.

22. Ibid., 39.

23. Igor Stravinsky and Robert Craft, *Conversations with Igor Stravinsky* (Berkeley and Los Angeles: University of California Press, 1980), 17–18.

24. As translated in booklet accompanying *Persepolis,* Fractal CD (n.d.).

25. As translated in booklet accompanying *Wolfgang Rihm: Gejagte Form, Verborgene Formen, Chiffre I, Silence to be beaten,* Kairos CD 0012072KAI (2000), 16–17.

26. Earle Brown, quoted by Franck Mallet in booklet accompanying *New York School 2,* hat Art CD 6146 (1993), 7.

27. Earle Brown, in booklet accompanying *Earle Brown: Collected Early Works,* CRI CD 851 (2000), 10.

28. Pauline Oliveros, Stuart Dempster, and Panaiotis, *Deep Listening*, New Albion CD NA 022 (1989).
29. E. M. Forster, *A Passage to India* (New York: Harvest, 1952), 147, 149–59, 208.

Chapter Ten

1. "Ein ungeheuer buntscheckiges, historisch-romantisches, teuflisch-religiöses, bigott-wollüstiges, frivol-heiliges, geheimnisvoll-freches, sentimental-gaunerisches, dramatisches Allerlei," from Wagner, "Die Oper und das Wesen der Musik," in *Oper und Drama*, 100.
2. Gloria Coates, quoted by Detlef Gojowy in booklet accompanying *Time Frozen*, CPO CD 999 590–2 (1995), 9–10.
3. Jean-Baptiste Dubos, *Réflexions critiques sur la poésie et la peinture* (Paris: Mariette, 1719, 1733), 3:169–71.
4. Ken Pierce and Jennifer Thorp, "The Dances in Lully's *Persée*," *Journal of Seventeenth-Century Music* 10, no. 1 (2004), http://sscm-jscm.press.uiuc.edu/v10/n01/pierce.html (accessed 17 December 2008).
5. Marian Smith, *Ballet and Opera in the Age of Giselle* (Princeton: Princeton University Press, 2000), 97.
6. Ibid., 5–6.
7. Ibid., 8.
8. Wayne Koestenbaum addresses this theme in *The Queen's Throat: Opera, Homosexuality, and the Mystery of Desire* (New York: Da Capo Press, 2001).
9. Anonymous, "Chi chi li chi?" in *Chi Chi Li Chi*, ed. Bernard Thomas (Brighton, England: London Pro Musica, 1995), 2–3.
10. Wendy Heller, "Dancing Desire on the Venetian Stage," *Cambridge Opera Journal* 15, no. 3 (2003): 284.
11. Barbara Johnson, *Mother Tongues: Sexuality, Trials, Motherhood, Translation* (Cambridge, MA: Harvard University Press, 2003), 61.
12. Quoted in Julian Budden, *The Operas of Verdi* (New York: Oxford University Press, 1981), 3:401.
13. Søren Kierkegaard, *Either/Or*, trans. David F. Swenson and Lillian Marvin Swenson (Princeton, NJ: Princeton University Press, 1971), 88–89.
14. Stéphane Mallarmé, "Ballets" in *Oeuvres complètes* (Paris: Gallimard, 2003), 2:171.
15. Derrick Puffett, *Richard Strauss: Salome* (Cambridge: Cambridge University Press, 1989), 166.
16. Mallarmé, "Hérodiade," in *Oeuvres complètes*, ed. and annoted by Henri Mondor and G. Jean-Aubry (Paris: Éditions Gallimard, 1945), 47–48.
17. Mallarmé, "Hérodiade," trans. Arthur Symons, in *The Symbolist Movement in Literature*, rev. and enl. ed. (New York: E. P. Dutton and Company, 1919), 370.

18. Albert Roussel, *Padmâvatî*, Partition pour Chant et Piano par l'auteur (Paris: Durand, no date).
19. William Butler Yeats to T. Sturge Moore, 3 February 1926, in *W. B. Yeats and T. Sturge Moore: Their Correspondence 1901–37*, ed. Ursula Bridge (New York: Oxford University Press, 1953), 68.
20. Arnold Schoenberg, "This Is My Fault," in *Style and Idea: Selected Writings of Arnold Schoenberg*, ed. Leonard Stein, trans. Leo Black (Berkeley and Los Angeles: University of California, 1984), 146.
21. Translated from "So wird die Oper zum gemeinsamen Vertrage des Egoismus der drei Künste," in Wagner, *Dichtungen und Schriften; Jubiläumsausgabe in zehn Bänden*, ed. Dieter Borchmeyer (Frankfurt am Main: Insel Verlag, 1983), 95.
22. Translated from Thomas Mann, *Doktor Faustus* (Frankfurt: Fischer-Taschenbuch, 1973), 378.

Chapter Eleven

1. Beethoven's holograph of choreographic notes for the scenario for no. 1, from the Berlin "Landsberg 7" sketchbook, as cited in Rainer Cadenbach's essay, trans. Alfred Clayton, in booklet accompanying *Beethoven: Die Geschöpfe des Prometheus*, Teldec CD 4509–90876–2 (1995), 4.
2. Quoted in ibid., 7.
3. William Butler Yeats, "Among School Children," in *W. B. Yeats: The Poems*, ed. Daniel Albright (London: J. M. Dent, 1994), 263.
4. Quoted in Cadenbach, *Die Geschöpfe*, 7.
5. Heinrich von Kleist, "On the Marionette Theatre," trans. Idris Parry, http://www.southerncrossreview.org/9/kleist.htm.
6. Ezra Pound, "Cavalcanti," in *Literary Essays of Ezra Pound* (New York: New Directions, 1935), 152.
7. Carol Brown, "dance architecture workshop," Her Topia: A Dance Architecture Event, Isadora and Raymond Duncan Centre for Dance, Athens, Greece, 29 September–5 October 2003, http://www.carolbrowndances.com/writings_pubs.html (accessed 18 December 2008).
8. W. H. Auden, "'Thanksgiving for a Habitat': Prologue: The Birth of Architecture," in *Collected Poems* (New York: Random House, 1976), 519.
9. Isadora Duncan, *My Life* (New York: Liveright Publishing, 1996), 71.
10. William Butler Yeats, "Nineteen Hundred and Nineteen," in *W. B. Yeats: The Poems*, ed. Daniel Albright (London: J. M. Dent, 1994), 254.
11. Stéphane Mallarmé, "Mimiques" and "Les fonds dans le ballet," in *Oeuvres complètes* (Paris: Éditions Gallimard, 1945), 311, 308 respectively.
12. Ibid., 308–9.

13. Ezra Pound, "Vorticism," in *Ezra Pound and the Visual Arts,* ed. Harriet Zinnes (New York: New Directions, 1980), 207.
14. Ben Jonson, *Bartholomew Fair,* Act 5, scene 5.
15. Smith, *Ballet and Opera in the Age of Giselle,* 97.
16. Mallarmé, "Les fonds dans le ballet," 312.

Selected Bibliography

Abbate, Carolyn. *In Search of Opera*. Princeton, NJ: Princeton University Press, 2001.
———. *Unsung Voices: Opera and Musical Narrative in the Nineteenth Century*. Princeton, NJ: Princeton University Press, 1991.
Adorno, Theodor. *Philosophie der neuen Musik*. Frankfurt: Europäische Verlagsanstalt, 1966.
Albright, Daniel. *Modernism and Music*. Chicago: University of Chicago Press, 2004.
Auden, W. H. "'Thanksgiving for a Habitat': Prologue: The Birth of Architecture." In *Collected Poems*. New York: Random House, 1976.
Beaumont, Antony. *Zemlinsky*. Ithaca, NY: Cornell University Press, 2000.
Berlioz, Hector. *Briefe von Hector Berlioz an die Fürstin Carolyne Sayn-Wittgenstein*. Edited by La Mara [Marie Lipsius]. Leipzig: Breitkopf & Härtel, 1903.
Barthes, Roland. *The Responsibility of Forms: Critical Essays on Music, Arts, and Representation*. Translated by Richard Howard. New York: Hill and Wang, 1985.
Beckett, Samuel. *Disjecta*. Edited by Ruby Cohn. New York: Grove, 1984.
———. "First Love." In *First Love and Other Shorts*. New York: Grove, 1974.
Bernstein, Leonard. *The Unanswered Question*. Cambridge: Harvard University Press, 1976.
Bishop, Elizabeth. "O Breath." In *The Complete Poems, 1927–1979*. New York: Farrar, Straus, and Giroux, 1983.
———. "Sandpiper." In *The Complete Poems, 1927–1979*. New York: Farrar, Straus, and Giroux, 1983.
———. "View of the Capitol from the Library of Congress." In *The Complete Poems, 1927–1979*. New York: Farrar, Straus, and Giroux, 1983.
Blackburn, Philip. *Enclosure 3: Harry Partch*. St. Paul: American Composer's Forum, 1997.
Borges, Jorge Luis. *Labyrinths: Selected Stories and Other Writings*. Edited by Donald A. Yates and James E. Irby. New York: New Directions, 1964.
Bridge, Ursula, ed. *W. B. Yeats and T. Sturge Moore: Their Correspondence 1901–37*. New York: Oxford University Press, 1953.
Budden, Julian. *The Operas of Verdi*. New York: Oxford University Press, 1981.
Busch, Regina. "On the Horizontal and Vertical Presentation of Musical Ideas and on Musical Space (I)." *Tempo* 154 (September 1985).
Carter, Elliott. "A Further Step." In *The Writings of Elliott Carter*, edited by Else Stone and Kurt Stone. Bloomington: Indiana University Press, 1977.
de Man, Paul. *Allegories of Reading: Figural Language in Rousseau, Nietzsche, Rilke, and Proust*. New Haven: Yale University Press, 1979.
Derrida, Jacques. "Signature, Event, Context." In *A Derrida Reader: Between the Blinds*, edited by Peggy Kamuf, translated by Alan Bass. New York: Columbia University Press, 1991.

Devrient, Eduard. *Meine Erinnerungen an Felix Mendelssohn-Bartholdy und seine Briefe an mich.* Leipzig: J. J. Weber, 1869.

Dubos, Jean-Baptiste. *Réflexions critiques sur la poésie et la peinture.* Paris: Mariette, 1719, 1733.

Duncan, Isadora. *My Life.* New York: Liveright Publishing, 1996.

Edwards, Allen. *Flawed Words and Stubborn Sounds: A Conversation with Elliott Carter.* New York: Norton, 1971.

Ewans, Michael. *Opera from the Greek.* Burlington: Ashgate, 2007.

Feldman, Morton. *Essays.* Edited by Walter Zimmermann. Kerpen: Beginner Press, 1985.

Fisk, Josiah, ed. *Composers on Music.* Boston: Northeastern University Press, 1997.

Forster, E. M. *A Passage to India.* New York: Harvest, 1952.

———. "Word-Making and Sound-Taking." In *Abinger Harvest.* New York: Harcourt, Brace and Company, 1936.

Geary, Jason. "Reinventing the Past: Mendelssohn's *Antigone* and the Creation of an Ancient Greek Musical Language." *Journal of Musicology* 23, no. 2 (Spring 2006).

Gluck, Christoph Willibald von. "Preface to *Alceste.*" In *The Lives of the Great Composers,* edited by Harold C. Schonberg. New York: W. W. Norton, 1997.

Greenberg, Clement. *The Collected Essays and Criticism.* Edited by John O'Brien. Chicago: University of Chicago Press, 1986.

Grey, Thomas. *Richard Wagner: Der fliegende Holländer.* Cambridge: Cambridge University Press, 2000.

Hába, Alois. *Mein Weg zur Viertel- und Sechsteltonmusik.* Düsseldorf: Im Verlag der Gesellschaft zur Förderung der systematischen Musikwissenschaft, 1971.

Heller, Wendy. "Dancing Desire on the Venetian Stage." *Cambridge Opera Journal* 15, no. 3 (2003).

Hoffman, E. T. A. "Kreisleriana." In *E. T. A. Hoffmann's Musical Writings,* edited by David Charlton, translated by Martyn Clarke. Cambridge: Cambridge University Press, 1989.

Holte, Artur. "A Little-Known Letter by Berlioz and Unpublished Letters by Cherubini, Leoncavallo, and Hugo Wolf." *Musical Quarterly* 37, no. 3 (July 1931).

Johnson, Barbara. *Mother Tongues: Sexuality, Trials, Motherhood, Translation* Cambridge, MA: Harvard University Press, 2003.

Joyce, James. *Finnegans Wake.* New York: Viking, 1966.

Kafka, Franz. "Der Bau." In *Sämtliche Erzählungen.* Frankfurt am Main: Fischer Taschenbuch, 1990.

Kierkegaard, Søren. *Either/Or.* Translated by David F. Swenson and Lillian Marvin Swenson. Princeton, NJ: Princeton University Press, 1971.

Koestenbaum, Wayne. *The Queen's Throat: Opera, Homosexuality, and the Mystery of Desire.* New York: Da Capo Press, 2001.

Kramer, Lawrence. "Syringa." In *Beyond Amazement: New Essays on John Ashbery,* 255–71. Ithaca, NY: Cornell University Press, 1980.

Laforgue, Jules. "Complainte de l'organiste de Notre-Dame-de-Nice." In *An Anthology of French Poetry from Nerval to Valéry,* edited by Augel Flores. New York: Anchor Books, 1958.

Lowell, Robert. "Across the Yard: La Ignota." In *Collected Poems,* edited by Frank Bidart and David Gewanter, with an introduction by Frank Bidart. New York: Farrar, Straus, and Giroux, 2007.
Macdonald, Hugh. "Berlioz's Self-Borrowings." *Proceedings of the Royal Musical Association,* 92nd sess. (1967–68).
Mallarmé, Stéphane. *Oeuvres completes.* Paris: Éditions Gallimard, 1945.
Mann, Thomas. *Doktor Faustus.* Frankfurt: Fischer-Taschenbuch, 1973.
———. "Enttäuschung." In *Sämtliche Erzählungen in zwei Bänden.* Frankfurt am Main: S. Fischer Verlag, 1967.
Marcello, Benedetto. *Il teatro alla moda.* Translated by R. G. Pouly. In *Source Readings in Music History,* rev. ed., edited by Oliver Strunk and Leo Treitler. New York: W. W. Norton, 1998.
Millier, Brett C. *Elizabeth Bishop: Life and the Memory of It.* Berkeley and Los Angeles: University of California Press, 1995.
Morgan, Robert. "Secret Languages: The Roots of Musical Modernism." *Critical Inquiry* 10, no. 3 (March 1984).
Nattiez, Jean-Jacques. *Music and Discourse: Toward a Semiology of Music.* Translated by Carolyn Abbate. Princeton, NJ: Princeton University Press, 1990.
Partch, Harry. *Genesis of a Music.* Madison: University of Wisconsin Press, 1949.
Percy, Thomas. *Reliques of Ancient English Poetry.* London: J. Dodsley, 1765.
Picabia, Francis. "Jésus-Christ Rastaquouère." In *Écrits.* Vol. 1, *1913–1920,* edited by Olivier Revault d'Allonnes. Paris: P. Belfond, 1975–78.
Pierce, Ken and Jennifer Thorp. "The Dances in Lully's *Persée.*" *Journal of Seventeenth-Century Music* 10, no. 1 (2004).
Pound, Ezra. "Cavalcanti." In *Literary Essays of Ezra Pound.* New York: New Directions, 1935.
———. "Vorticism." In *Ezra Pound and the Visual Arts,* edited by Harriet Zinnes. New York: New Directions, 1980.
Puffett, Derrick. *Richard Strauss: Salome.* Cambridge: Cambridge University Press, 1989.
Rosand, Ellen. "Operatic Madness." In *Music and Text: Critical Inquiries,* edited by Steven Paul Sher. Cambridge: Cambridge University Press, 2006.
Rousseau, Jean Jacques. *On the Origin of Language.* Translated by John Moran. New York: Frederick Unger Publishing, 1966.
Rushton, Julian. "Berlioz' Roots in 18th Century French Opera." *Berlioz Society Bulletin* 50 (April 1965): 3–10.
Schiff, David. *The Music of Elliott Carter.* London: Eulenberg Books, 1983.
Schoenberg, Arnold. *Style and Idea: Selected Writings of Arnold Schoenberg.* Edited by Leonard Stein, translated by Leo Black. Berkeley and Los Angeles: University of California, 1984.
———. *Theory of Harmony.* Translated by Roy E. Carter. Berkeley and Los Angeles: University of California Press, 1983.
Shakespeare, William. *The Merchant of Venice.* In *The Riverside Shakespeare.* Ed. G. Blakemore Evans. Boston: Houghton Mifflin, 1974.
———. *The Tempest.* In *The Riverside Shakespeare.* Ed. G. Blakemore Evans. Boston: Houghton Mifflin, 1974.

———. *Troilus and Cressida.* In *The Riverside Shakespeare.* Ed. G. Blakemore Evans. Boston: Houghton Mifflin, 1974.

———. *Caesar and Cleopatra.* In *The Riverside Shakespeare.* Ed. G. Blakemore Evans. Boston: Houghton Mifflin, 1974.

Shreffler, Anne. "'Give the Music Room': Elliott Carter's 'View of the Capitol from the Library of Congress' aus *A Mirror on which to Dwell.*" In *Quellenstudien II: Zwölf Kompositionen des 20. Jahrhunderts,* edited by Felix Meyer. Basel: Amadeus, 1993.

Smith, Marian. *Ballet and Opera in the Age of Giselle.* Princeton: Princeton University Press, 2000.

Steinberg, Michael. *The Concerto: A Listener's Guide.* Oxford: Oxford University Press, 1998.

Štědroň, Bohumír. *Leoš Janáček: Letters and Reminiscences.* Translated by Geraldine Thomsen. Prague: Artia, 1955.

Stravinsky, Igor. *An Autobiography.* New York: W. W. Norton, 1962.

Stravinsky, Igor and Robert Craft. *Conversations with Igor Stravinsky.* Berkeley and Los Angeles: University of California Press, 1980.

Symons, Arthur. *The Symbolist Movement in Literature.* Rev. and enl. ed. New York: E. P. Dutton and Company, 1919.

———. *Dialogues.* Berkeley and Los Angeles: University of California Press, 1982.

Toye, Francis. *Giuseppe Verdi: His Life and Works.* New York: Vintage, 1959.

Virgil. *Aeneid.* Translated by John Dryden. Edited by Frederick M. Keener. New York: Penguin, 1997.

Wagner, Richard. "Die Oper und das Wesen der Musik." In *Oper und Drama.* Leipzig: Weber, 1852. Reprint, Stuttgart: Philipp Reclam, 1984.

———. "So wird die Oper zum gemeinsamen Vertrage des Egoismus der drei Künste." In *Dichtungen und Schriften; Jubiläumsausgabe in zehn Bänden,* edited by Dieter Borchmeyer. Frankfurt am Main: Insel Verlag, 1983.

Whitesitt, Linda. *The Life and Music of George Antheil, 1900–1959.* Ann Arbor: UMI Research Press, 1983.

Williams, William Carlos. "Lear." In *The Collected Later Poems.* New York: New Directions, 1967.

Wittgenstein, Ludwig. *Philosophical Investigations.* Translated by G. E. M Anscombe. New York: Macmillan, 1958.

Yeats, William Butler. "Among School Children." In *W. B. Yeats: The Poems,* edited by Daniel Albright. London: J. M. Dent, 1994.

———. "Nineteen Hundred and Nineteen." In *W. B. Yeats: The Poems,* edited by Daniel Albright. London: J. M. Dent, 1994.

———. *Sophocles' Oedipus at Colonus, The Variorum Edition of the Plays of W. B. Yeats.* Edited by Russell K. Alspach. New York: Macmillan, 1966.

Youens, Susan. *Heine and the Lied.* Cambridge: Cambridge University Press, 2008.

Index

Abbate, Carolyn, 11, 46, 197, 199, 209
Adam, Adolphe, 181
Adorno, Theodor, 3, 143, 145
Aeschylus, 122–24
Alexander the Great, 46
Ameta, 190–91
Antheil, George, 13, 145
Apelles, 13
Ariosto, Ludovico, 69
Aristotle, 125, 132, 135
Artaud, Antonin, 182
Ashbery, John, 106, 115–19
Astaire, Fred, 184
Auden, W. H., 185
Augustus Caesar, 69

Bach, Carl Philipp Emanuel, 20, 94; *Die Israeliten in der Wüste,* 94
Bach, Johann Sebastian, 16, 36, 152
Bakhtin, Mikhail, 106, 158
Bakker, Tammy Faye, 47
Balanchine, George, 163, 183, 191–92
Balla, Giacomo, 184
Barber, Samuel, 153
Barthes, Roland, 31–32, 151, 198
Bartók, Béla, 77, 148
Baudelaire, Charles, 74
Beaumont, Antony, 85–87, 89–90, 92
Beckett, Samuel, 75, 152, 154, 156. 192
Beethoven, Ludwig, 5–6, 16, 96–97, 99, 101, 105, 123, 152, 157, 164, 178–81, 206; *Die Geschöpfe des Prometheus,* 178–81
Benjamin, Walter, 92
Berio, Luciano, 153–54; *Thema (Omaggio a Joyce),* 153–54
Berlioz, Hector, 58–71, 168, 170, 199; *Les troyens,* 58–71, 170
Bernstein, Leonard, 139
Biber, Heinrich von, 164
Bishop, Elizabeth, 106–12
Bizet, Georges, 58–59
Blake, William, 108
Boccioni, Umberto, 186
Borges, Jorge Luis, 12
Borodin, Alexander, 167
Bournonville, August, 181
Boyce, William, 180
Brahms, Johannes, 13, 91–92; *Rinaldo,* 91–92
Braunfels, Walter, 54; *Die Vögel,* 54
Brecht, Bertolt, 39, 95–96, 165
Brema, Marie, 5
Britten, Benjamin, 8–9, 29, 175–76; *Death in Venice,* 175–76; *Six Metamorphoses after Ovid,* 8–9
Brown, Carol, 185
Brown, Earle, 157–58
Bruch, Max, 94; *Moses,* 94
Buelow, George J., 10
Bülow, Hans von, 62
Busch, Regina, 102
Byrd, William, 164

Caballé, Montserrat, 192
Caccini, Giulio, 126, 146, 150
Cage, John, 13–14, 130, 133, 153–57, 159; *Roaratorio,* 153–56
Calder, Alexander, 13
Carissimi, Giacomo, 91, 119
Carter, Elliott, 105–21; *In Sleep, in Thunder,* 106, 113–15; *A Mirror on which to Dwell,* 106–9; *Syringa,* 106, 115–19
Cavalieri, Emilio de', 119, 169
Cavalli, Francesco, 60, 169
Chabrier, Emmanuel, 177
Charpentier, Marc-Antoine, 9; *Les Plaisirs de Versailles,* 9

214 • INDEX

Chatterjee, Mohini, 174
Chirico, Giorgio de, 142–43
Churchill, Winston, 7
Coates, Gloria, 165, 168; *The Quinces' Quandary*, 165, 168
Cocteau, Jean, 128–30, 132–35, 138–41
Coltellini, Marco, 125
Corelli, Arcangelo, 21
Craig, Gordon, 182
Crashaw, Richard, 106, 119, 121

D'Alembert, Jean le Rond, 58
Dante Alighieri, 75
de Man, Paul, 14
Debussy, Claude, 76, 111
Delacroix, Eugène, 68
Dempster, Stuart, 159
Derrida, Jacques, 14, 106, 147
Devrient, Eduard, 126
Diaghilev, Serge, 143
Diderot, Denis, 58
Dietrich, Marlene, 133
Disney, Walt, 133, 191–92
Donizetti, Gaetano, 64
Donner, Johann Jakob, 127
Dowell, Anthony, 164
Dryden, John, 130
Dubos, Jean-Baptiste, 165–66
Duncan, Isadora, 182, 185, 188, 190
Duncan, Raymond, 185
Dutilleux, Henri, 165

Einstein, Albert, 158
Eliot, T. S., 111
Enesco, Georges, 124
Euripides, 60, 122–23, 151
Ewans, Michael, 124

Feldman, Morton, 146, 157
Fichte, Johann Gottlieb, 46
Flaubert, Gustave, 47
Flötner, Peter, 194
Forster, E. M., 5, 159
Franz, Robert, 36–37; "Ja, bist du elend," 36–37
Friedrich Wilhelm IV, 126
Frost, Robert, 116

Fuller, Loïe, 188–93

Gagliano, Marco da, 122, 169
Galilei, Vicenzo, 126
Gautier, Théophile, 58–59, 181
Geary, Jason, 126–27
Gershwin, George, 56
Gide, André, 89
Giraud, Albert, 149
Giusti, Giambattista, 127
Glass, Philip, 46, 84
Gluck, Christoph Willibald, 5, 59–61, 64, 67, 70–71, 118, 123–25, 140; *Alceste*, 59–60; *Armide*, 70–71; *Orfeo ed Euridice*, 5, 60, 118, 124–25, 140
Godowsky, Leopold, 16
Goethe, Johann Wolfgang von, 18, 51, 56, 79, 91, 170
Gouvy, Théodore, 124
Graham, Martha, 182
Greenberg, Clement, 145–46
Grey, Thomas, 49
Guston, Philip, 146
Gyger, Elliott, 96–97

Hába, Alois, 148
Handel, George Frideric, 123, 143, 140
Hannibal, 64
Hanslick, Eduard, 13
Haydn, Franz Joseph, 105
Heine, Heinrich, 15–38, 40–41, 44, 47–48, 54, 56
Heller, Wendy, 169
Henry, Pierre, 154
Hermann, Oliver, 36
Hindemith, Paul, 55–56, 188; *Ouvertüre zum "Fliegenden Holländer" fur Streichquartett, wie sie eine schlechte Kurkapelle morgens um 7 am Brunnen vom Blatt spielt*, 55–56
Hoffmann, E. T. A., 74–75, 116, 182
Hölderlin, Friedrich, 18, 129–31
Holst, Gustav, 79–80; *The Planets: Neptune*, 79–80
Honegger, Arthur, 128–30, 133; *Antigone*, 128–30, 133
Hopkins, Lightnin,' 56

Horace, 18
Humperdinck, Engelbert, 95

Iamblichus, 81
Ives, Charles, 7, 110–11; *Second String Quartet,* 7

Janáček, Leoš, 76, 81, 147–48, 150; *Káťa Kabanová,* 76; *Výlet pana Broučka do měsíce* (*Mr. Brouček's Excursion to the Moon*), 81; *Zápisník zmizelého* (*The Diary of One who Vanished*), 76
Jaucourt, Louis de, 58–60, 70
Johns, Jasper, 149
Johnson, Barbara, 169
Jonson, Ben, 191
Joyce, James, 111, 152–55, 158

Kafka, Franz, 32, 92–93, 156
Kandinsky, Vassily, 74, 149
Kaulbach, Wilhelm von, 164
Keats, John, 22, 111
Kierkegaard, Søren, 170–71
Kircher, Athanasius, 6, 26
Kiselewski, Joseph, 95
Kleist, Heinrich von, 103, 181–82
Klimt, Gustav, 88
Klopstock, Friedrich Gottlieb, 94
Koestenbaum, Wayne, 205
Kramer, Lawrence, 118
Krenek, Ernst, 143–44
Kuhnau, Johann, 164
Kupfer, Harry, 47

Laban, Rudolf, 185, 193, 195
Laforgue, Jules, 35–36
Lasso, Orlando di, 168–69; *Chi chi li chi,* 168–69
Lawrence, D. H., 152, 183
Leonardo da Vinci, 185
Lessing, Gotthold Ephraim, 181
Lewis, Wyndham, 191
Li Po, 150
Li Qiong, 194
Limón, José, 183
Lincoln, Abraham, 133

Liszt, Franz, 16, 99, 101, 123, 164, 197; *Eine Faust-Symphonie,* 99; *Hunnenschlacht,* 164; *Il penseroso,* 164
Lock, Édouard, 193
Loewe, Carl, 50–51; *Der Erlkönig,* 51; *Edward,* 50–51
Lorentz, Alfred, 130
Lowell, Robert, 106, 112–15
Lully, Jean-Baptiste, 58, 70–71, 123, 165–66; *Acis et Galatée,* 166; *Armide,* 70–71
Lutosławski, Witold, 165

Macdonald, Hugh, 199–200
MacMillan, Kenneth, 163
Magritte, René, 146
Mahler, Gustav, 6, 46, 90
Mallarmé, Stéphane, 159, 171–72, 190–93
Malvezzi, Cristofano, 122
Mandelbrot, Benoît, 133
Manet, Édouard, 11
Mann, Thomas, 91, 176
Marcello, Benedetto, 12
Marenzio, Luca, 123
Marschner, Heinrich, 42–43
Marx brothers, 191
Marx, Harpo, 3
Mascagni, Pietro, 58
Massenet, Jules, 169–70
Mattheson, Johann, 6, 9–10, 26
Mauke, Wilhelm, 9
McPhee, Colin, 176
Mendelssohn, Felix, 126–29; *Antigone,* 126–29
Mérimée, Prosper, 58, 172
Metastasio, Pietro, 61
Meyerbeer, Giacomo, 59, 163–64, 170, 175; *Le prophète,* 163–64
Michelangelo Buonarroti, 95, 164
Milhaud, Darius, 124
Mondrian, Piet, 146
Monteverdi, Claudio, 122, 149–50, 106, 118, 122–23, 130, 168–69; *Il combattimento di Tancredi e Clorinda,* 118; *Orfeo,* 122–23, 168–69
Moore, T. Sturge, 206

Morgan, Robert, 116
Morley, Thomas, 106
Morris, Robert, 98
Moser, Kolomon, 188, 190
Mozart, Wolfgang Amadeus, 14, 90–91, 127; *Die Zauberflöte,* 91, 127
Musorgsky, Modest, 150, 168

Napoleon Bonaparte, 67
Nattiez, Jean-Jacques, 11
Nielsen, Carl, 97
Nietzsche, Friedrich, 47, 96, 123, 130, 169
Nureyev, Rudolf, 167, 191
Nyman, Michael, 28–32; *The Man Who Mistook His Wife for a Hat,* 28–32

Oliveros, Pauline, 159; *Deep Listening,* 159
Orff, Carl, 124, 129–132; *Antigonae,* 129–32
Ovid, 8–9, 122–25

Panaiotis, 159
Parmenides, 102
Partch, Harry, 150–54; *Two Settings from Joyce's Finnegans Wake,* 152–53
Percy, Thomas, 199
Peri, Jacopo, 122, 150, 169
Petipa, Marius, 191
Picabia, Francis, 91
Piccinni, Niccolò, 60
Pierce, Ken, 166
Plato, 81, 116, 152, 176, 190
Poe, Edgar Allan, 75–76, 141
Poliziano, Angelo, 122
Pollock, Jackson, 13, 146, 156
Ponchielli, Amilcare, 168, 191–92; *La gioconda,* 168, 191–92
Pound, Ezra, 145, 183, 191
Powell, Michael, 184
Pressburger, Emeric, 184
Procter, Adelaide Anne, 73–74
Proust, Marcel, 158
Puccini, Giacomo, 58
Puffett, Derrick, 205
Purcell, Henry, 46, 60

Pythagoras, 12–13, 73, 81

Quinault, Philippe, 70

Rameau, Jean-Philippe, 58, 123, 180, 193; *Pygmalion,* 180; *Les boréades,* 193
Rauschenberg, Robert, 146, 164
Ravel, Maurice, 88, 115
Rawlence, Christopher, 28
Rehding, Alexander, 101
Reich, Steve, 153
Rempe, Burkhard, 82
Ricordi, Giulio, 170
Rihm, Wolfgang, 156; *Chiffre* I, 156
Rimsky-Korsakov, Nikolay, 4–5, 16; *Sheherazade,* 4–5
Rinuccini, Ottavio, 122
Ropartz, Guy, 36–37; "Depuis que nul rayon," 36–37
Rossetti, Dante Gabriel, 35
Rossini, Gioachino, 94–95, 127–28; *Edipo a Colono,* 127–28; *Mosè in Egitto,* 94
Rothko, Mark, 146
Rousseau, Jean-Jacques, 8, 108, 147, 180; *Pygmalion,* 180
Roussel, Albert, 173–74; *Padmâvatî,* 173–74

Sacchini, Antonio, 124
Sachs, Hans, 54
Sacks, Oliver, 28–29, 31
Saint-Saëns, Camille, 169, 175, 191; *Samson et Dalila,* 169, 175, 191
Sappho, 116
Satie, Erik, 13, 146; *Musique d'ameublement,* 13
Saussure, Ferdinand de, 14
Sayn-Wittgenstein, Carolyne, 61, 67
Schaeffer, Pierre, 154
Schäfer, Christine, 28, 37
Schenker, Heinrich, 73
Schiebeler, Daniel, 94
Schiller, Friedrich, 47
Schlemmer, Oskar, 187–88; *Das triadische Ballett,* 187–88
Schnittke, Alfred, 7, 90, 164; *Dr. Faustus,* 90, 164

Schoeck, Othmar, 22
Schoenberg, Arnold, 73–74, 91, 94–104, 106, 115, 119, 143, 148–50, 174–76; *Moses und Aron*, 74, 94–104, 149, 174–76; *Pierrot lunaire*, 95, 103, 148–49
Schopenhauer, Arthur, 46, 105
Schreker, Franz, 72, 76–81, 85, 88; *Der ferne Klang*, 76–81, 85
Schubert, Franz, 15–23, 26, 36, 51; "Der Atlas," 18–20, 22; "Der Doppelgänger," 15–20, 22, 36; "Die Stadt," 20–22
Schumann, Robert, 16, 22–38, 51–53, 151; "Der arme Peter," 23–25; *Des Sängers Fluch*, 51–53; "Die alten, bösen Lieder," 33–35; "Es treibt mich hin," 22–23; "Ich grolle nicht," 24, 26–29, 31–32
Schütz, Heinrich, 6
Schwitters, Kurt, 139
Scriabin, Alexander, 73–74
Sechter, Simon, 73
Serrano, Andres, 164
Shakespeare, William, 56, 64, 66, 91, 105–6, 180
Shawn, Ted, 182–83
Shearer, Moira, 184
Shostakovich, Dmitri, 106
Shreffler, Anne, 110
Smetana, Bedřich, 75–76, 84, 93, 96; *First String Quartet*, 75–76, 93; *Vltava (The Moldau)*, 84; *Z Českých Luhů a Hájů (From Bohemia's Woods and Fields)*, 84
Smith, Marian, 166–67, 192
Socrates, 96
Sophocles, 122–44, 150
Spears, Britney, 14
Spenser, Edmund, 69–70
St. Denis, Ruth, 183
Steinberg, Michael, 197
Strada, Famianus, 201
Strauss, Johann, 55
Strauss, Richard, 7, 9–11, 14, 38, 47, 54, 88–91, 98, 101, 124, 135–36, 165, 169, 172–73, 192; *Ein Heldenleben*, 7, 9; *Elektra*, 98, 124, 135–36; *Feuersnot*, 54; *Salome*, 90, 169, 172–73, 192; *Till Eulenspiegels lustige Streiche*, 9–11, 14

Stravinsky, Igor, 13, 118, 132–44, 145, 155, 157, 164, 184, 191; *Apollo*, 164; *Circus Polka*, 191; *Fireworks*, 184; *Oedipus Rex*, 132–44; *Orpheus*, 118; *Renard*, 13
Striggio, Alessandro, 149
Sullivan, Arthur, 72–73; "The Lost Chord," 72–73
Symons, Arthur, 205

Taglioni, Marie, 181, 183
Taneyev, Sergei, 123
Tasso, Torquato, 70, 91
Tchaikovsky, Piotr Ilyich, 163
Thorp, Jennifer, 166
Tieck, Ludwig, 116
Tintoretto, Jacopo, 95
Tippett, Michael, 56–57; *Songs for Dov*, 56–57
Toulouse-Lautrec, Henri de, 189
Tovey, Donald, 197
Toye, Francis, 73
Traetta, Tommaso, 124–26; *Antigona*, 124–26

Uhland, Ludwig, 51, 53

van Gogh, Vincent, 165, 168
Varèse, Edgard, 146
Ventris, Michael, 157
Verdi, Giuseppe, 58, 73, 101, 143, 163, 166–70; *Macbeth*, 166–67; *Otello*, 101, 170
Viganò, Salvatore, 178–79, 181
Virgil, 60–61, 64, 68–69, 71
Vivaldi, Antonio, 20

Wagner, Richard, 13, 15, 35, 37, 39–56, 59, 66–67, 69, 73, 82–84, 90, 101, 112–15, 124, 132, 138–139, 145, 163–64, 170–72, 175–77; *Der fliegende Holländer*, 15, 39–56; *Der Ring des Nibelungen*, 35, 41, 54, 82–84, 90, 101, 112–115, 124, 138; *Die Meistersinger*, 13, 54, 90, 132, 170; *Parsifal*, 37, 45–46, 70–71; *Tannhäuser*, 41, 53, 170–72; *Tristan und Isolde*, 73, 177

Walter von der Vogelweide, 54
Warminsky, Andrzeij, 14
Weill, Kurt, 39–40, 50, 165; *Die Dreigroschenoper,* 39–40, 50; *Die sieben Todsünden,* 165
Whitehead, Alfred North, 158
Wilde, Oscar, 85, 88, 90, 172
Williams, William Carlos, 120
Winckelmann, Johann Joachim, 127, 130, 183
Wittgenstein, Ludwig, 14
Wolfe, Humbert, 80
Wolfe, Thomas, 152
Wolff, Christian, 157–58; *Edges,* 157–58
Wolfram von Eschenbach, 38, 53

Wordsworth, William, 31

Xenakis, Iannis, 124, 155–56; *Persepolis,* 155–56

Yeats, William Butler, 16, 22, 74, 128, 150, 174–75, 180, 190

Zemlinsky, Alexander von, 72, 81–93; *Der König Kandaules,* 88–92; *Der Traumgörge,* 81–85, 90; *Der Zwerg,* 85–88, 92
Zeno of Elea, 103
Zimerman, Krystian, 5
Zubkhovsky, Nikolai, 183

Eastman Studies in Music

Ralph P. Locke, Senior Editor
Eastman School of Music

Additional Titles on Song Opera, and Dance

The Poetic Debussy: A Collection of His Song Texts and Selected Letters (Revised Second Edition)
Edited by Margaret G. Cobb

Concert Music, Rock, and Jazz since 1945: Essays and Analytical Studies
Edited by Elizabeth West Marvin and Richard Hermann

Music and the Occult: French Musical Philosophies, 1750–1950
Joscelyn Godwin

"Wanderjahre of a Revolutionist" and Other Essays on American Music
Arthur Farwell, edited by Thomas Stoner

French Organ Music from the Revolution to Franck and Widor
Edited by Lawrence Archbold and William J. Peterson

Musical Creativity in Twentieth-Century China: Abing, His Music, and Its Changing Meanings
(includes CD)
Jonathan P. J. Stock

Elliott Carter: Collected Essays and Lectures, 1937–1995
Edited by Jonathan W. Bernard

Music Theory in Concept and Practice
Edited by James M. Baker, David W. Beach, and Jonathan W. Bernard

Music and Musicians in the Escorial Liturgy under the Habsburgs, 1563–1700
Michael J. Noone

Analyzing Wagner's Operas: Alfred Lorenz and German Nationalist Ideology
Stephen McClatchie

The Gardano Music Printing Firms, 1569–1611
Richard J. Agee

"The Broadway Sound": The Autobiography and Selected Essays of Robert Russell Bennett
Edited by George J. Ferencz

Theories of Fugue from the Age of Josquin to the Age of Bach
Paul Mark Walker

The Chansons of Orlando di Lasso and Their Protestant Listeners: Music, Piety, and Print in Sixteenth-Century France
Richard Freedman

Berlioz's Semi-Operas: Roméo et Juliette *and* La damnation de Faust
Daniel Albright

The Gamelan Digul and the Prison-Camp Musician Who Built It: An Australian Link with the Indonesian Revolution
(includes CD)
Margaret J. Kartomi

*"The Music of American Folk Song"
and Selected Other Writings on
American Folk Music*
Ruth Crawford Seeger, edited by
Larry Polansky and Judith Tick

Portrait of Percy Grainger
Edited by Malcolm Gillies
and David Pear

Berlioz: Past, Present, Future
Edited by Peter Bloom

*The Musical Madhouse
(Les Grotesques de la musique)*
Hector Berlioz
Translated and edited by Alastair Bruce
Introduction by Hugh Macdonald

The Music of Luigi Dallapiccola
Raymond Fearn

*Music's Modern Muse: A Life of
Winnaretta Singer, Princesse de Polignac*
Sylvia Kahan

The Sea on Fire: Jean Barraqué
Paul Griffiths

*"Claude Debussy As I Knew Him" and
Other Writings of Arthur Hartmann*
Edited by Samuel Hsu,
Sidney Grolnic, and Mark Peters
Foreword by David Grayson

*Schumann's Piano Cycles and the
Novels of Jean Paul*
Erika Reiman

*Bach and the Pedal Clavichord:
An Organist's Guide*
Joel Speerstra

*Historical Musicology: Sources,
Methods, Interpretations*
Edited by Stephen A. Crist and
Roberta Montemorra Marvin

*The Pleasure of Modernist Music:
Listening, Meaning, Intention, Ideology*
Edited by Arved Ashby

*Debussy's Letters to Inghelbrecht:
The Story of a Musical Friendship*
Annotated by Margaret G. Cobb

*Explaining Tonality:
Schenkerian Theory and Beyond*
Matthew Brown

*The Substance of Things Heard:
Writings about Music*
Paul Griffiths

*Musical Encounters at the
1889 Paris World's Fair*
Annegret Fauser

*Aspects of Unity in J. S. Bach's
Partitas and Suites: An Analytical Study*
David W. Beach

Letters I Never Mailed: Clues to a Life
Alec Wilder
Annotated by David Demsey
Foreword by Marian McPartland

*Wagner and Wagnerism in Nineteenth-
Century Sweden, Finland, and the
Baltic Provinces:
Reception, Enthusiasm, Cult*
Hannu Salmi

*Bach's Changing World:
Voices in the Community*
Edited by Carol K. Baron

*CageTalk: Dialogues with and about
John Cage*
Edited by Peter Dickinson

*European Music and Musicians
in New York City, 1840–1900*
Edited by John Graziano

*Schubert in the European Imagination,
Volume 1: The Romantic and Victorian Eras*
Scott Messing

*Opera and Ideology in Prague:
Polemics and Practice at the National
Theater, 1900–1938*
Brian S. Locke

Ruth Crawford Seeger's Worlds: Innovation and Tradition in Twentieth-Century American Music
Edited by Ray Allen and Ellie M. Hisama

Schubert in the European Imagination, Volume 2: Fin-de-Siècle Vienna
Scott Messing

Mendelssohn, Goethe, and the Walpurgis Night: The Heathen Muse in European Culture, 1700–1850
John Michael Cooper

Dieterich Buxtehude: Organist in Lübeck
(includes CD)
Kerala J. Snyder

Musicking Shakespeare: A Conflict of Theatres
Daniel Albright

Pentatonicism from the Eighteenth Century to Debussy
Jeremy Day-O'Connell

Maurice Duruflé: The Man and His Music
James E. Frazier

Representing Non-Western Music in Nineteenth-Century Britain
Bennett Zon

The Music of the Moravian Church in America
Edited by Nola Reed Knouse

Music Theory and Mathematics: Chords, Collections, and Transformations
Edited by Jack Douthett, Martha M. Hyde, and Charles J. Smith

The Rosary Cantoral: Ritual and Social Design in a Chantbook from Early Renaissance Toledo
Lorenzo Candelaria

Berlioz: Scenes from the Life and Work
Edited by Peter Bloom

Beyond The Art of Finger Dexterity*: Reassessing Carl Czerny*
Edited by David Gramit

French Music, Culture, and National Identity, 1870–1939
Edited by Barbara L. Kelly

The Art of Musical Phrasing in the Eighteenth Century: Punctuating the Classical "Period"
Stephanie D. Vial

Beethoven's Century: Essays on Composers and Themes
Hugh Macdonald

Composing for Japanese Instruments
(includes 2 CDs)
Minoru Miki
Translated by Marty Regan
Edited by Philip Flavin

Variations on the Canon: Essays on Music from Bach to Boulez in Honor of Charles Rosen on His Eightieth Birthday
Edited by Robert Curry, David Gable, and Robert L. Marshall

Wagner and Venice
John W. Barker

Analyzing Atonal Music: Pitch-Class Set Theory and Its Contexts
Michiel Schuijer

Dane Rudhyar: His Music, Thought, and Art
Deniz Ertan

Music in German Immigrant Theater: New York City, 1840–1940
(includes CD)
John Koegel

In Search of New Scales: Prince Edmond de Polignac, Octatonic Explorer
Sylvia Kahan

The Ballet Collaborations of Richard Strauss
Wayne Heisler Jr.

Othmar Schoeck: Life and Works
Chris Walton

Irony and Sound:
The Music of Maurice Ravel
Stephen Zank

György Kurtág:
Three Interviews and Ligeti Homages
Bálint András Varga

August Halm:
A Critical and Creative Life in Music
Lee Rothfarb

Music Speaks:
On the Language of Opera, Dance, and Song
Daniel Albright

From Daniel Albright, the author of *Musicking Shakespeare* and *Berlioz's Semi-Operas,* comes a collection of recent essays on music and on dance. The volume's central themes probe the problems of articulating the meaning or meanings of music; the larger question of how music and language interact; how, in the world of Lieder, text-setting highlights certain areas of meter, or theme, or ironic undertone, and leaves others in darkness; how a musical composition can behave as a critique of a previous composition; and how one might rehabilitate certain underappreciated or much-scorned figures, such as Meyerbeer, by showing that the very terms of invective used against them can be seen, from another angle, as an indication of what is exciting in their work.

In these essays, Albright strives to show that music history has an aesthetic of its own, and how music history interacts with intellectual history (from Rousseau and the Encyclopédistes to Paul de Man). The method of these essays is juxtapositive: by abutting music against literature and painting, and by abutting the musics of different centuries, Albright tries to frame a particular work, to isolate what is arresting and important in it.

The essays range widely, from Schubert Lieder to Loïe Fuller to Xenakis and Elliott Carter; but they rarely stray far from opera, for the opera house is the venue where the performances speak the most intricate and significant language invented by our culture-a language that speaks in music, and words, and pictures, and light.

Daniel Albright teaches courses in the English, Comparative Literature, and Music departments at Harvard University.

"The key phrase comes toward the end of this zestful and stimulating collection: 'I think of music, of all music, as a teasing of the linguistic areas of the brain.' Much of Albright's writing springs from, around, out of, into, behind, and beyond this beautiful and illuminating thought, which he carries with him through encounters with works by Berlioz, Wagner, Schoenberg, Stravinsky, Carter, and others. And 'teasing'—in the senses of gently mocking, of pulling out, and indeed of titillating—is also his modus operandi."

—Paul Griffiths, noted music critic, author of *The Sea on Fire: Jean Barraqué* and *The Substance of Things Heard: Writings about Music* (University of Rochester Press)

"Criticism so relentlessly intelligent is rarely so buoyant, so ready to charm while it challenges. In staging this genial confabulation between the music of language and the language of music, Daniel Albright once again matches childlike openness with seasoned irony, humor with highmindedness, experience with poetry."

—Scott Burnham, professor of music,
Princeton University, and author of
Beethoven Hero